Lord Sugar is the owner of Amshold Group Ltd and the popular star of the award-winning BBC series *The Apprentice*, and the more recent *Junior Apprentice*. He has two honorary Doctor of Science degrees, one awarded by the City of London University in 1988, and the other from Brunel University in 2005. He was knighted in 2000. In 2008 he was appointed to the Government Business Council by PM Gordon Brown, and in 2009 he led the government's Apprenticeship advertising campaign and roadshow seminars. In the same year, the PM appointed him Enterprise Champion to advise the government on small business and enterprise, and he was also awarded a life peerage, becoming Baron Sugar of Clapton in the London Borough of Hackney.

Follow Alan Sugar on:

twitter.com/Lord_Sugar

facebook.com/LordSugar

youtube.com/amshold

Also by Alan Sugar

What You See Is What You Get:

My Autobiography

ALAN SUGAR

The Way I See It

RANTS, REVELATIONS AND RULES FOR LIFE

PAN BOOKS

First published 2011 by Macmillan

First published in paperback 2012 by Pan Books
an imprint of Pan Macmillan, a division of Macmillan Publishers Limited
Pan Macmillan, 20 New Wharf Road, London N1 9RR
Basingstoke and Oxford
Associated companies throughout the world
www.panmacmillan.com

ISBN 978-1-4472-0539-5

5 7 9 8 6

A CIP catalogue record for this book is available from
the British Library.

Typeset by Ellipsis Digital Limited, Glasgow
Printed by CPI Group (UK) Ltd, Croydon, CR0 4YY

Visit www.panmacmillan.com to read more about all our books
and to buy them. You will also find features, author interviews and
news of any author events, and you can sign up for e-newsletters
so that you're always first to hear about our new releases.

Contents

Warning:
This Book May Cause Offence

I've always been regarded as someone who speaks his mind. You probably know that already. Hopefully it's why you bought this book – because you like my straight talking. If someone bought it for you as a present and you're thinking, 'Who *is* this Sugar fellow?', then I should explain that this book contains opinions that may cause offence – especially to certain members of the press, the government and *The Only Way Is Essex*. Also restaurateurs, advertisers, flying bores, footballers and maybe Piers Morgan, although, knowing him, he'll see it as complimentary.

I don't know where this need to speak my mind comes from – my parents weren't the same way – but basically I cannot stand listening to people talking a load of rubbish. I can't resist butting in and saying, 'That's complete and utter nonsense.'

On the other hand, there are times when maturity has taught me to think, 'Keep your mouth shut, Alan. Yes, they *are* talking a load of bollocks, but can you be bothered to correct them?' I find this particularly to be the case when someone says something completely and utterly factually wrong. I kind of switch off; I think to myself, 'Who cares? Let them get on with it.' The problem is that if I adopt this silence when someone is spouting off wrong information about me or anything I'm involved in, the person spouting it will think that he or she is correct and will go on to dine out on it, repeating it several times as a fact cast in concrete.

It does make me laugh when you hear people with no actual inside information give their personal opinion – say, on a news story or famous person – telling you what's really going on. They come up with their own crazy ideas and theories, and when they get into wacky world, that's normally when I jump in. I've got some friends who insist that Princess Diana is still alive; it was all a plot to get her out of the limelight. Depending on how much they've had to drink, they might change their story to: 'Okay, she may not be alive, but she was *definitely* murdered by the Queen and Prince Philip, no question about it.' And these people are always so intent on their belief.

These same people, whose names I won't mention, said, following the announcement of the death of Bin Laden, '*He's* not dead. It's all a PR stunt by the Americans. He's still alive,' and all that kind of stuff. With their imaginations, these people would be very good at writing detective stories and thrillers.

Speaking my mind has got me into hot water on occasion, and I've upset people. My wife and some of my work colleagues are still amazed when I get involved in some controversy or other. We'll be in a conversation and I'll interrupt, telling someone they're talking a lot of rubbish. Ann will ask me later, 'Why do you bother? Why can't you resist it? Why can't you just shut up and let it go by?'

I really don't know the answer to that, other than to say that I don't care what other people think about me. I only concern myself with my immediate family, friends and work colleagues, and what *they* care about. I'm not particularly interested in portraying a goody-goody image – a Mr Nice Guy who says the right thing at the right time just to get people on his side; to get them to admire him; to say they like him. Frankly, I find that pathetic, and I've seen so many examples of it over the years. These people actually make me cringe when I see them grovelling, trying to put on this nicey-nicey persona. People have to take me as they find me because, as I've often said, what's on my lung is on my tongue.

The only thing I would say is that the first time people meet me, they do tend to have a preconceived idea of what I'm like from what they've read about me or from having seen me on TV. When I was chairman of Tottenham Hotspur, the sports media was negative and full of lies. Similarly, on *The Apprentice*, the production company cuts the film in a certain way to make me look aggressive, as it suits their agenda. I've often heard people say once they've got to know me, that they understand what makes me tick. But in general I have no desire to suck up to anyone or seek their friendship or support. This has not just been in recent years – since I've become more well known – I've always been the same. I just can't bear having to be false – talking to someone just to get something out of it, financially or socially. If you want new friends and associates, they should be just that – genuine friends and associates.

Straight talking, that's me, and I like people who are also straight talking. I like people who, if they don't know something, will say, 'I don't know – I'll go and find out and get back to you.' There's nothing worse than hearing some bullshitter trying to waffle his or her way around a situation when all you've done is ask them a simple question. I can see through it immediately and can tell that they haven't got a bloody clue what they're talking about. So why do these people do it? I suppose it's all to do with ego and them wanting to give the impression they know everything.

In fact, because I've got such a good memory, I sometimes wrongly assume that people I employ or deal with remember things in the same level of detail as I do. I used to get quite frustrated when I'd ask them a question about something and they didn't know what I was referring to. Now, as I've mellowed a little, I'll put my question in a different way. I'll say to them, 'You'll find some information in the such and such file about this or that transaction – can you let me know the exact number of items we shipped and get back to me?' So you see, I've learnt to become a little more tolerant. That said, if someone asked me a question like that, I'd most probably be able to rattle off the number straight away, or have a bloody good guess at it.

Another thing that annoys me is what I call the 'Basil Fawlty effect', when people schmooze and act politely to someone like me (maybe because there's an angle in it for them or they want something from the boss), and then you observe them with a less senior employee and they're talking to them as if they're a piece of rubbish. We all remember how Basil used to do that when he thought he had an influential guest arriving at his hotel – he would suddenly go into his over-polite, grovelling mode, then as soon as the person went away and one of his workers spoke to him, he'd go back to his normal arsehole self. Well, there are people in real life like that and I detest them, particularly the sort who try to affiliate themselves with me. They'll say, 'Of course, Alan, people like you and I understand these things, but as for the others – don't expect them to grasp it.'

Those people come close to getting a whack from me – they really wind me up. I normally say to them, 'Actually, you're nothing like me,' and it shuts them down pretty quickly. Put simply, I can't stand snobs who think they're a cut above other people and look down on them.

I'm amazed at how many so-called old 'friends' and 'acquaintances' I have. Ann always smiles when someone I know says to me, 'I met an old mate of yours the other day. He told me to send his regards.'

Now, I don't know what it is, but I have this kind of sixth sense that the next thing coming out of this person's mouth is going to be a name I've never heard before.

'Oh yes?' I say. 'Who is that then?'

'Charlie Saunders. He says you'll know him. He used to be the market manager down Ridley Road and Kingsland Waste, where you had a stall in your early days. He says he still remembers having a chat with you about getting a better pitch for your stall, and all those aerials and that electrical stuff you used to sell there. Do you remember Charlie? [Long pause] Why are you both smiling?'

'We're both smiling because: a) I've never heard of Charlie Saunders, b) I never had a stall in Ridley Road market, c) I never had a stall in Kingsland Waste market, and d) I never sold electrical goods off a stall.

'But don't worry, mate, you've just been speaking to one of those people who dine out on stories they make up about knowing me. They take snippets of information that they've seen in the press or on telly – or, who knows, maybe they even read it in my autobiography – then they just make up some pure fantasy. Anyway, trust me when I tell you it's all bollocks.

'What fascinates me is that when you told Charlie that *you* know me, he should have thought better of spinning you that load of crap, because he must have known it was absolute rubbish and that eventually you'd come back to him and tell him that I *don't* know him!'

I still don't know why people do this and, as hard as it may be for you to understand, this happens all the time! Sometimes I even get into arguments with people who swear they know me. 'I'm sorry, I *don't* know you, and I never sold phones to Tesco in the seventies.' In some cases, when I close the story down, it's like shattering a dream for these people; a dream they have lived on for ages.

I might be sounding like a bit of an arsehole here, but I simply can't resist it when I hear people spout off such rubbish, particularly if they're the loud, flash sort. However, there are also situations when some doting old-timer says something like that to me, such as how I went to school with their son, or that their daughter's first date was with me. It's all nonsense, but they are nice old people, so I never shatter their dream. I just say, 'Oh yes, give them my regards.'

Sometimes wealth can bring about snobbery, and I have seen examples of this with people I knew from my younger days; people who came from the same place I came from and elevated themselves financially in the business world. That's all fine, but they've forgotten their roots. When they speak to people now, it's as if they're royalty. I won't name them, but they do annoy me tremendously. I have always tried to keep my feet on the ground and talk to everybody the same way, regardless of their status, because I remember where I came from. It's just a shame that some of these other people don't.

There's another kind of snobbery I often encounter. Because I came from a working-class environment in Hackney, there are the snobs who wouldn't dream of talking to or mixing with me, despite me being a success and making a lot of money – in a way they may consider crude or vulgar. Heaven knows who these people think they are. Now, I can possibly understand an *actual* member of the royal family acting in this manner, perhaps, but these people take it to the extreme.

There are also those who wouldn't have given me the time of day in the past, but who changed their attitude when I became well known, whether it be in the commercial world as the darling of the City back in the eighties, or as the presenter of *The Apprentice* now. Suddenly they're interested in talking to me. Fortunately, because of my good memory, I can remember the people who ignored me, passed me by and looked down on me as if I were nothing. When they try to strike up a conversation, I take great delight in saying, for example, 'You've seen me around for the past thirty years and you've always walked past me like we're two ships in the night. Why is it that now you want to talk to me?'

I love rubbing it in. They get the point and normally we never speak again.

Anyway, that's that little lot off my chest, and it may give you an insight into my nature. And a few hints on what not to say if you meet me!

Reading on, you will find me expressing quite a lot of my opinions. You might agree with much of what I say, but I'm sure you will not agree with everything. Some of it might even anger you a bit, but that's the way I see it.

1

Has the World Gone Mad?

Getting angry about the health and safety police and today's compensation culture, and a revolutionary idea for solving our care-home crisis.

One of the biggest changes over the last forty years has been the creation of a politically correct health and safety culture, which seems to have been imposed upon us by the powers that be in Brussels. I'm sure the words 'Has the world gone mad?' must roll off your tongue when you hear about some of the latest goody-goody things one has to comply with.

But I have another angle. I'm convinced that these new rules and regulations are there to create more employment, to slow things down. In other words, if things take longer to get done, then less gets done within a set time frame. The result is that you have to employ more people to meet targets you could have achieved with fewer staff before all this stuff came in.

Certainly many of these laws impose heavy burdens on small companies. Once, twenty people were able to get on and do the work of the company; now they need to employ a further five just to make sure they are compliant with all the rules and regulations.

I often ask myself, in regard to health and safety, what was so bad that these regulations needed to be brought in? I've run offices and factories for the past forty years and I can honestly say that I don't recall one single occasion where there was a serious accident, a fire or any other disaster. Maybe I've just been lucky.

I am also active in the real-estate market, and from time to time we have to get involved in the complete refurbishment of buildings. It winds me up no end that, in some cases, at least 10 per cent of the total cost of the job is for what's called the 'preliminaries', the preparation – making sure all the workers have the necessary facilities, including separate toilets and washrooms, first-aid kits, safety scaffolding, protective headwear, protective footwear, hi-vis jackets, fluorescent armbands, fire extinguishers, the works. All this to do what we used to call in the old days 'a lick-of-paint job'.

We owned an old warehouse once, which had a hole in the roof. In the old days, a fellow would climb up a ladder, get on the roof and patch it up. Two hundred quid – job done. You can imagine my amazement when I was told that we'd have to erect scaffolding at a cost of £5,000 – in compliance with health and safety rules – so that somebody could climb up there simply to put a bit of asphalt over the hole. Unbelievable.

We now find a host of rules and regs in the workplace and, to put it bluntly (and be repetitive), it really *does* sometimes feel like the world's gone mad.

Now, I appreciate that these regulations were designed to reduce accidents in the workplace, which in turn would prevent loss of work hours and save costs to organisations like the NHS. However, I think we've gone into complete and utter overkill. What's worse, it has spawned these new industries and services which have popped up to exploit the vulnerabilities that exist in companies, large and small, which have no choice but to be compliant.

Let's look at the so-called experts – the health and safety consultants. Now, you might be surprised to hear that there are no mandatory qualifications required to call oneself a health and safety consultant. In fact, *you* could set yourself up as one. In many cases, the advice given is no more than plain common sense. All you need to do is go on the web – there are loads of government websites that dish out all the checklists and guidelines on how to be compliant. Nevertheless, some of these consultants come in, full of self-importance, and try to intimidate small businesses into using their alleged expertise. The easiest way of frightening somebody is to tell them that they may be exposing themselves to possible financial claims. Eventually it gets to the stage where, if you're running a small business and trying to comply, the cost of indemnity insurance and extra staff starts to make the business unviable.

So the small businessman not only has to worry about running his business, he also has to deal with all these other obstacles. He has to handle the day-to-day aggravation of trying to be competitive with his products or services while considering the possibility of claims, which, in some cases, could bankrupt or seriously damage the business. This *has* to be putting a load of people off.

I'm sure most of you will have come across a new breed of colleague or employee at work – the person who's in charge of making sure all the health and safety stuff is complied with. You know this person – they enjoy brandishing the new power bestowed upon them; they absolutely love it. They're just like little dictators. They can even go round telling the boss what they need to do and how they can shut the company down if this, that or the other is not done.

This brings me on to another subject: compensation culture. Doesn't it wind you up to see those TV adverts for so-called claim management companies who imply that they can get their clients substantial amounts of money for injuries they may have sustained? These distasteful people purport to be lawyers when in fact, they're not lawyers at all. They're backed by insurance companies and sell the claims on to a nucleus of lawyers around the country. It's all a money game.

The legal system in this country was once something we could be proud of, compared to the 'ambulance chasers' you see in America. However, since 1999, it's now possible for lawyers to work on what's known as a conditional fee basis – in other words, offering 'no win, no fee' contracts to their clients.

Now, this might sound like a good idea for some deserving causes, but when a new law comes in, regrettably, the good don't benefit. Instead, opportunists jump in and abuse and exploit the situation to its fullest extent. You can imagine how this situation breeds a certain type of employee who gets the seed of an idea planted in their head by those awful TV adverts and decides to dream up some derisory claim. I'm sure many of us have seen it happen – it's sickening.

And while all this is going on, the current government are talking about doing away with legal aid and access to free legal representation, which, up to now, has been a fundamental principle of civilised and modern society. We're talking about, for example, the battered wife who would no longer be able to protect herself against a violent partner; the divorcing father who could lose all access to his kids. Should they be silenced in court just because they cannot afford it?

These ambulance chasers wouldn't be interested in those sorts of claims – they're too complicated. They're interested in dreaming up false claims, knowing that the companies they're attacking on behalf of their clients will end up giving in and paying some money to avoid the hassle of going to court.

Most claims end up being settled by negotiation. Even though the company knows the claim is derisory, to defend it fully would cost a fortune and there is no way you could recover costs if you decided to pursue it, because the person who's bringing the claim is a 'man of straw', so it's a no-win situation.

The new breed of vulture-type lawyers know this only too well, as do most of the insurance companies. It is almost a licence to print money if you can convince a member of the public to make a claim. I've even heard of people being paid a modest fee of, say, five hundred quid upfront, just for agreeing to become a claimant or a plaintiff.

Something has to be done about these rogues. I'm sure that if the Advertising Standards Authority had some *real* authority, they could stop them making these misleading adverts and luring people into dreaming up claims that don't really exist.

Human nature being what it is, frivolous claims aren't new though. I vaguely remember one incident, about twenty-five years ago, when we had a factory in Southend. For some reason or other, a manhole cover in the factory's driveway had to be lifted for some maintenance, and somebody put a large, heavy wooden pallet over the top of the manhole so that people wouldn't fall into it accidentally. What transpired afterwards was a real joke. A van driver spotted the pallet, lifted it up and saw there was a hole. The next thing we heard was him screaming that he'd fallen down the hole. He duly rushed off to a solicitor to make some kind of claim.

Now, me being the type of person I am – I need to know everything that's going on in my company (I've often said that I know where every nut and bolt is) – my factory manager, Harold, rang me and told me about this incident and a letter he'd received from the bloke's solicitor. Harold told me that this fellow was a real Jack the Lad and that there was no way this was a genuine accident – he'd made it up and really milked it at the time, demanding an ambulance and all that stuff – so this wound me up even more.

To cut a long story, we were not going to give in to this derisory claim and I spent a fortune on a lawyer to fight this fellow, only to discover that he'd done this about four or five times previously! On one occasion, he'd walked into a warehouse and deliberately shaken some of the racking so that the cartons fell on him. Taking him on cost us a lot of money, but this chancer got nothing.

Actually, it has to be said that I'm a rare breed – I'd rather do the non-commercial thing than be held to ransom. Most employers would just give in to this blackmail.

But the story didn't end there. To add insult to injury, the geezer, from what I understand, later died from some natural cause, and his wife tried to bring a claim against us on the grounds that he'd died because of the trauma of me fighting him through the courts. Needless to say, she was also sent away on her bike.

I have one other example of how the compensation culture syndrome is out of control. In a new company I started a few years ago, we employed a woman in a managerial role but when things didn't work out, she decided that she would make a claim against the company. At the same time, she tendered her resignation, saying that she had been traumatised by the manner in which she had been treated and spoken to.

Now, cop this: throughout the course of her employment, I had never had a single conversation with this woman. She may have passed by me on the office floor and, at best, I might have nodded or said hello.

I remember she attended one meeting in the boardroom where I addressed the group overall, but I did not direct any of my questions to her personally. So you get the picture – I never spoke to the dame. But in her claim, she cited me as one of the people who had traumatised her – it was ridiculous.

This was all happening around the same time that I was appointed to the House of Lords, so when the formalities of officially becoming a lord were going through the system, I warned my senior management that this matter had to be dealt with correctly through our lawyers, as I could see that this person was going to go down the 'unfair dismissal' route – she'd be seen as the poor woman who had been suppressed by the male senior management. One of my senior managers suggested to me that he talk to her and come to some settlement, but I insisted that he should *not* talk to her, as it could possibly put us in an awkward legal position. My manager pointed out to me that it would cost a fortune to mount a defence if we went down the legal route.

I engaged our lawyers and, as you would expect, they gave us the full Rolls-Royce treatment: 'Don't do this, don't say that. Whatever you do, don't write to her, don't speak to her, don't look at her, don't talk about her to anyone else . . .'

You can imagine my frustration over all this, when, as far as I was concerned, we had done absolutely nothing wrong. By now I was pulling my hair out, getting angrier and angrier. I said to my lawyers, 'How can this be? Tell her to piss off!'

'No, Sir Alan [as I was at the time], I'm afraid to say that this will end up in a tribunal.'

'A tribunal? Why? Surely it should go in front of a judge?'

'No, I'm afraid not. It's actually a tribunal made up of two laymen and a solicitor. One of the laymen will no doubt be from some kind of trade union organisation and the other layman will be an independent person. The solicitor will just be there to advise on the finer points of law.'

'So you mean to tell me that if we ever end up in front of this tribunal and simply tell them that I've never spoken to this woman – not one word – the whole case wouldn't just get thrown out?'

'Well, maybe,' was the answer, 'but a lot of water has to go under the bridge before that.'

The woman had employed some lawyers who seemed to me to be a right bunch of ambulance chasers, but they were making my lawyers rack up huge bills dealing with them – which may have been their tactic.

Imagine my shock and dismay when the *Sunday Times* called to enquire about an alleged situation where I, the nasty Lord Sugar, had traumatised someone.

Our PR company gave them some standard words to the effect that we were not prepared to comment on this situation, save to say that Lord Sugar had never spoken to this woman in his life. Can you believe that my lawyers said, 'What are you doing? You mustn't comment to the media.'

I told them, 'I'm sick and tired of all this pussyfooting around and I'm going to do what I damn well want to do.'

My lawyers called me up to tell me that I had to calm down and leave the matter in their capable hands. Bloody capable hands – £220,000 later, we were getting nowhere. Barristers, lawyers, pre-trial hearings, court hearings, pre-tribunal hearings – all that crap.

My lawyers were soon back on the phone to me. 'Lord Sugar, do you really want to go in front of a tribunal and wash all this dirty laundry in public? The media will love it – to them it'll be like winning the lottery.' I told him that that's exactly what these people were banking on.

Furthermore, I told them that they should know me better than to imagine I was going to allow anybody to walk all over me, and that, if I had to go to a tribunal, I would go, and I would have my say.

And not only would I have my say, I would also ask the tribunal why it is that people can bring such claims and defendants have no recourse to recover costs from them if the claim fails?

Eventually, this woman caved in and the whole thing went away. I say the whole thing went away; I found out later that we ended up paying £17,000 to this bloody woman and her lawyers. I went ballistic. My manager tried to calm me down by explaining to me that this new, small company of ours could ill afford to continue to pay these ridiculous legal costs, so he'd made a managerial decision to knock it on the head.

How sick is all of that? And this is what the legal system in this country allows to happen. Other side effects of this little outing emerged. During the process of my appointment to the House of Lords, a certain big-mouthed peer, Lord Oakeshott – whom I've since found out has a son, Luke, who once dressed up in Nazi uniform for a fancy-dress party – decided to get on his high horse and object to my appointment on the basis that I wasn't a fit and proper person to be a lord if I abused employees. He then went on to allege that I didn't pay corporation tax.

Can you see how all of this escalates? Can you see the game plan of these nasty types of people who have signed on to try to make a fast buck through derisory compensation claims? Needless to say, I gave this Lord Oakeshott a bit of stick and threatened to sue him. He finally wrote to me and apologised, though his apology was a little bit guarded in respect of his accusations of my not paying taxes in this country because one of my property companies happens to be registered in Guernsey, which is another load of bollocks. It was registered in Guernsey for good and proper reasons, and we've always paid our tax in the UK.

There seems to be a recurring story in the media, but especially the *Daily Mail*, about a woman who brings a claim to a tribunal. It's funny, because in the pictures all these women look similar. Dressed in the same black business suit, they all seem to be complaining that their colleagues – usually in the financial services sector – have treated them badly, and therefore they seek compensation for hundreds of thousands of pounds. The system is being abused. Just one landmark case, where someone walked off with half a million quid, was enough to start an avalanche. And, of course, the *Daily Mail* is delighted to report it.

This leads me to another subject. A few years ago, a couple of female journalists from the *Daily Telegraph* came to visit me on the basis of interviewing me about youth and enterprise in general and how to encourage young people. This was all on the back of *The Apprentice*. During the course of the interview, they touched upon the subject of the employment of women in companies, and I happened to say that I felt the current laws preventing me from discussing an interviewee's matrimonial situation or whether or not she had children were counter-productive.

Well, you would have thought they had just got the scoop of the century. Their eyes lit up and they suddenly re-jigged their agenda to discuss this subject. Despite the fact that they had set out to talk about enterprise, no more questions were asked about that – it was all about women's rights and employment and all that stuff. And, me being me, I said it as I saw it.

This resulted in a completely out-of-context article being printed in the *Telegraph*, followed closely by criticism from every other commentator in the country. That nasally congested hag Janet Street-Porter, for example, only has to hear a bloke mention the word 'women' and she starts ranting like a foghorn, without listening to any of the facts or taking any context on board. 'That bloody Sugar should get back into his cave. He's a dinosaur,' was her response. And *she* wasn't even present at the meeting.

The point I had tried to make to these two journalists was one of a positive nature as far as women are concerned. I was saying that I felt the current laws are not helping women.

One has to understand that the employer interviewing someone has their hands tied by not being able to ask a woman how she has her life organised – whether she has any children or if indeed she is pregnant. Not allowed to ask, you see? So what transpires is a sort of psychological charade. The interviewer just pays the woman a bit of lip service and, unfortunately, she doesn't get the job because, in the interviewer's mind, this woman – who has not volunteered any information regarding children or childcare – *might* be intending to take lots of time off work, with big gaps for maternity leave, while the employer is looking to hire someone who's going to be a reliable part of the company machine, a significant cog in the wheel.

So my advice to women would be: pre-empt this bullshit, go in there with all guns blazing and say, for example, 'I've got two kids.

One is seven, the other's five and they're both settled at school. I've got a carer who picks them up, so I have no problems in that direction. I just need to get back to work. Of course, if there were ever a problem, health-wise, with one of my kids, they would always have to come first, but I'm sure you, Mr or Mrs Interviewer, will fully understand that.'

I tell you what, if someone spoke to me like that, I would have the utmost respect for them. But no – employers are not allowed to ask, and so women don't always get the job. It's as simple as that.

I have the greatest respect for women in business. Some of the best people I've ever employed have been women. The woman who ran my business in France was unbelievable, as indeed was the woman who ran my Hong Kong office. She was so good that I seconded her to the UK to run my manufacturing-procurement operation worldwide. It's well known that Margaret Mountford has been my lawyer for more than twenty-five years and has sat on the board of my companies, and there are a host of other women who have served me very well in business. I find them very focused; I find that they're not there simply to build their egos. I find them very straightforward. They get on with the job in hand. And, of course, in the seven years since The Apprentice started, three women have won, and deservedly so.

On the other hand, is it fair that a woman accepts a job knowing that she's two months pregnant but without disclosing it to her employer, in order to be able to take maternity leave for up to nine months or a year? Dropping a bombshell like that must be crippling for a small company.

Let's get down to brass tacks here. You don't employ someone just to make up the numbers. In small companies they're part of a well-oiled machine, and if one of the components of the machine is taken away, the whole machine comes to a standstill. There's nothing wrong with working women becoming pregnant and having maternity leave – I've lost count of the number of people who have worked for me and who've quite rightly used this facility in the proper way. I've been delighted for them and, in all cases, they've come back to work. But the ones who really annoy me are those who deliberately go out of their way to get free pay for no work. And, if that's not bad enough, there are changes afoot so that men too will be able to take months off for paternity leave. What is going on in this world? It's unbelievable. Who has allowed all this nonsense? It's got to be the government – or is it the old story of things being forced on them by the European Union?

What next? Wedding leave? Bar Mitzvah leave? Painting the house leave? A total bloody joke. And you wonder why small companies are now reluctant to employ full-time staff. Instead, they're using outside contractors or the new wave of foreign employees from recent EU countries such as Poland and Romania. These people have a completely different work ethic. Dare I say, they are grateful and happy to have a job. They've not been poisoned by the benefits mentality, not yet anyway. Though, from what I hear, they're picking it up pretty quickly!

We've seen the building industry completely dominated by Polish workers, thankful for their jobs. By contrast, so many British workers can't be bothered, because someone actually asks them to do some work – shame about that.

The biggest thing that has happened in the industrial world over the period in which I've been active in business is the change in manufacturing territory; in fact, the total decline in manufacturing in Britain and the USA. I recall the days when television sets and stereos were made in the UK, with famous brand names like Ferguson, Bush and Murphy. I remember when pride was taken in our porcelain and china products, which came from the Potteries, when great names such as Royal Doulton or Wedgwood led the way. Look around us now and everything we buy is made in China – from TV sets to door knobs. Building materials, baths, toilet bowls, clothing, carpets, knives and forks – you name it, it's all made in China, and it's all now available at a fraction of the price we used to pay.

What caused this shift? Again, I say work ethic. With my own eyes I saw Taiwan and South Korea rise to become the greatest force in electronics over a period spanning thirty years. They were eager to learn, they worked hard and were relentless; they never gave up. If they wanted to be in a certain sector, they did it, and they did it well.

Now we have the Chinese doing the same. When you look at the size of the country, you realise that it has only just scraped the surface in becoming a commercial power. The Chinese started in the provinces near Hong Kong, like Shenzhen and Canton, and now they are slowly expanding northwards to places like Shanghai and Beijing, utilising the mass of labour available with their 1.3 billion population.

In Taiwan and South Korea the factory workers wanted to better themselves and wanted a more commercial, Westernised way of life, and so the manual work has migrated to China. The average Taiwanese or Korean person now has a good standard of living, and it won't be long before the Chinese population will want the same. The difference, however, is that the country is so large that regions of prosperity will spring up while other regions start to grow and copy. How long will that take? I would say another thirty years. Make no mistake, you are looking at the greatest economic force in the world – China will take over from the USA. Consumer demand alone in China will outstrip that of every Western economy. There are already more millionaires in China than there are in the UK, and I'm sure that one day the number will overtake the USA's. Big brands such as Louis Vuitton, Chanel, Prada, Burberry and Cartier are doing a bomb of business there. The irony is that although a lot of their lower-priced stuff is made in China, the affluent Chinese consumers want to buy the stuff that's made in Italy and France.

How forward thinking are the Chinese? Look at the investment they are making in Africa. They are slowly nibbling away at the edges, building facilities in places that no Westerners ever went. Why? Well, perhaps they want to take over another large continent and labour force in anticipation of theirs becoming too affluent to do menial work.

Here is a message for the kids of today – learn to speak Chinese. I can tell you, they are going to take over the world economically, and a new generation of Westerners who speak Chinese will do well in this massive business opportunity. Be warned – you'd better learn to speak Chinese quicker than their kids learn to speak English, or you will miss a great opportunity.

But back to the Polish and Romanian workers – all I've ever heard from employers is how great they are, diligent and hard-working. On the other hand, the culture that has grown in our country is one of a load of lazy people who have become experts in knowing what they're entitled to as far as benefits, freebies and other bits and pieces are concerned.

Part of this culture is 'throwing a sickie'. I have calculated that you don't have to work for more than 150 days per year. The annual amount of days that a person *should* be at work is roughly 210 (if you take into account thirty days' holiday, weekends and bank holidays). However, if you play the game right, you can say you are sick on Friday and Monday (on your own say-so, without having to get a doctor's certificate) and pull that one at least five times a year. Then there's the time you *do* get a week off for flu *with* a doctor's certificate.

Then, of course, you might have 'stress'. You can go to the doctor, who, if you're lucky, will actually look up at you while signing you off for another two weeks. And if you go back and tell them you're *still* stressed, they'll sign you off for another week. I mean, if you say that you're stressed, no thermometer or stetho-scope can prove otherwise.

Then you hear there's a bit of snow coming – you rush home quickly and say that you can't get a bus or a train for two days. Now, if you graft at this, you can end up with an extra fifty days off per year. The thing is, there are serial offenders who do this year in, year out. They're normally buried in large companies or government offices, where there is no real boss to clock what's going on.

How many times have I heard people say, 'It's not worth working forty hours a week – I'd get twenty quid less than I get on benefits.'

This is particularly true of parents with large families, who can clock up quite a bit of money that way. We've all seen the stories about people living in large houses – sometimes in very affluent areas, where these properties would normally cost a couple of million pounds – free of charge, at the expense of the taxpayer, with no intention of supporting themselves! They've done a simple calculation: I've got five or six kids; I've worked out how much money I can get. I've got nowhere to live and so the government should provide a home for me. Oh, and by the way, I can't find a job that will pay me anywhere near the amount of money I need to finance this lifestyle, so I'll be claiming unemployment benefit as well. Have we gone mad or what? Only in Britain does this seem to happen.

This is an extreme example, but it shows how the system can be abused by people who think it's okay to take from society and not give anything back in return. I've raised this point for many years, but obviously no one is listening. *I* say that no one should be able to get their benefits unless they do some work (unless, of course, they're *genuinely* unable to). And if they claim they can't get any work, then the person behind the counter dishing out the benefits should give them a broom and tell them to go down to the local council's street-cleaning department, sign up there and start sweeping the streets or cleaning some of the graffiti off the walls in public places. Then come back on Friday with a signed piece of paper from the foreman and we'll give you your money. That would soon sort a few people out, I can tell you. But, of course, that's impossible – we're too far gone. My vision would break every single European human rights law.

There are families, particularly in the north of England, where young children are growing up watching their fathers and their grandfathers sitting at home on the couch all day long and end up thinking that what you do is go to some place once a week where you get money to buy food and then go to the football. They don't know what it is to work.

Of course, I can't tar everybody with the same brush. There are still a lot of people around who think like me; who would hate the thought of losing their jobs and resorting to benefits, and who do everything they can to find work when that happens. And of course there are some very genuine cases of people who are ill or have become disabled and literally cannot find work. These are the people for whom the benefit system was designed but, as always, once you introduce something beneficial, it gets abused by those who see a chance to get paid for doing nothing. And heaven forbid you say something out of place about these people – political correctness does not allow it. The laws are set in stone, but our government has not got the guts to tell Brussels that we've had enough of their PC nonsense.

You may ask, why is it that we're inundated with immigrants? Well, it's very simple. What I've just described must sound, to outsiders, like Disneyland, with a giant, free cashpoint. It's not a question of colour – it's not racism – it's just common sense.

Of course, as we have seen over the years, immigration has really helped boost the British economy, with people who come here prepared to work hard, but we cannot sustain this unrestricted open-door policy. We should at least make sure that anyone coming here can speak English to a basic standard and can support themselves financially. They need to be able to prove they are here to work and not simply to abuse our benefits system. The USA and Australia don't stand for it, so why do we? Why is it we let people in who are guilty of violent or drug-related crimes, simply because they are dependants of British citizens? In the United States, they're not even allowed to visit, let alone emigrate there. Why can't there be some regulation here that says that immigrants can't receive any social security benefits for at least twenty-four months?

And then there are the so-called 'asylum seekers', who pass through countless European countries on their way here from wherever – what was wrong with stopping in Germany or France? Why Britain? Why us? To be fair, I have heard some noises that the new coalition government is going to do something about this, but I won't be convinced until I see it.

Talking of political correctness, I'm sick and tired of seeing these crazy situations such as councils abolishing the singing of Christmas carols or the putting up of Christmas trees in case it offends minority faiths. Bloody hell, this is Britain – Christmas is Christmas!

We've also heard about people being told to stop strawberry-picking. Why? Because EU inspectors reckon that the fields are too uneven and it could lead to injury. Unbelievable! Strawberry-picking has gone on for centuries without a single problem.

How long have we got to put up with this nonsense, local authorities in the UK banning nativity displays on council premises and kids' nursery rhymes like 'Baa Baa Black Sheep' from being sung in schools because it may offend some minorities? This is supposed to be a country with freedom of speech, yet this sort of stuff is banned. On the other hand, fundamentalist hate speeches can be shouted out in the streets and it's freely allowed! I say that any immigrant who preaches hatred or incites violence against any religion or ethnic minority should be deported. If they're screaming hatred against Britain, then let the countries they praise so highly look after them.

I recall doing an interview with Gordon Brown where I put some of these things to him. His answers were quite guarded as, of course, he could not be seen to agree. Instead, he just laughed at my cheeky, probing questions, one of which was to address the ridiculous situation of the Muslim women who demand the right to cover their faces in inappropriate situations.

Now, let me go on record here and say that I have nothing against people who wear certain clothing in observance of their religion. Indeed, if you look at the male Hasidic Jews you see in Stamford Hill, north London, one has to admit they do look a little strange. But the difference here is that I don't think there has ever been a court case or claim made by one of these people demanding to wear their kit in places where it's not appropriate. They are happy to accept that they are in the minority and, as long as they are left alone and allowed to walk the streets freely, they don't make waves or any demands.

However, under human rights laws, women dressed in burqas, with their faces covered, are able to teach young schoolkids. Common sense says that a five-year-old child from a non-Muslim background would be frightened by this dress code. Fully veiled Muslim women also demand the right to hold jobs such as being a receptionist, the primary interface between a company and the general public.

I put it to Gordon: 'Can you imagine Katie Price, in her Jordan persona, being allowed to sit at the front desk at the offices of some corporation in any of the countries these women originated from?'

What was Gordon's reaction? Again, a burst of laughter as he ducked the question. 'Oh, Alan, you are so funny.'

'It's not bloody funny; it's true.'

If I owned a bank and didn't allow motorbike riders to enter the premises wearing their helmets, then I should be able to say that *anyone* who covers their face, for any reason, is not allowed in.

Fair enough, everyone should be able do as they want in the public streets and their own homes, but on my premises I should be able to make the rules – not the bloody human rights idiots in Strasbourg.

As for human rights in our schools, that's a whole new ball game. A teacher can't hug a kid anymore, to comfort them. You can no longer take a camera into school to film little Johnny in the school play or on sports day – people think you're a paedo. And talking of sports day, schools don't even announce the winners of events any more, because to do so might upset the poor little dears who *didn't* win. Instead, everyone gets a medal.

I feel sorry for you teachers. You're not allowed to touch the kids; you're almost not allowed to talk to them, otherwise you'll be out on your ear. You're supposed to stand there in the classroom and be abused – allowing the young louts to scream and shout and call you all the names under the sun – and you can do nothing about it. There is no discipline any more with the younger generation. I sympathise with teachers in our education system. When they wake up on a Monday morning and go to school, they have to be looking over their shoulders all the time, which must distract them from their purpose in life – educating people. They have to overcome so many obstacles before they can get round to doing their job.

The police are another group I have a lot of sympathy for. These days, you have to be near enough a saint to be a policeman. The police have to restrain themselves and accept a lot of verbal abuse from people. They are not allowed to react at all; otherwise they'll find themselves up on some disciplinary charge.

When I was a youngster, you respected a policeman. The local bobby might even have given you a clip round the ear and a severe warning. He was an authority to look up to, as indeed were teachers. Nowadays, the police are spoken to like trash and there's nothing they can do about it.

Mr Patel, who owns the local newsagent's, has to put up with a bunch of louts coming into his shop and stealing things. If they get caught, the crime is considered so small that it's hardly worth processing through the system. However, if Mr Patel lost his temper and whacked one of them, *he'd* be the one ending up in prison. When you defend yourself in this country, you're the one who gets prosecuted.

The government says that they're going to get tough on crime. Well, they're not doing a very good job, and I don't refer just to the current coalition government – it harks back to the previous Labour government, whom, frankly, I hold responsible for creating a lot of this benefits/claims/layabout culture with their goody-goody human rights stuff.

Look at the fiasco of the demonstrations in March 2011 against government cuts. Fair enough, people should be free to demonstrate in an orderly fashion, and 99 per cent of them went there to do just that, but the thugs decided this was a good opportunity to have a day out and smash windows and set fire to premises, even to attack the Prince of Wales's car. Then the riots in August 2011 (which started off in Tottenham as a protest after the police allegedly shot a local man) got hijacked into an opportunity to burn buildings and loot shops. After that, copycat riots sprung up all over London and in other towns in England. *I* say the army should have been called in to sort these thugs out in a way that they understand – herd them like animals and bang them up for a year or so in prison. Instead, on the news channels, you heard a series of commentators who started by saying how terrible it is and that 'Stealing and looting cannot be condoned.' And then came the big 'but' . . . 'But, we have to search *deeper* to understand what *motivates* these youngsters, and why they've been *driven* to this kind of life. We have to understand that *poverty* is what's causing this kind of anarchy.'

I am sick and tired of listening to these bloody goody-goodies pussyfooting around the issue – it's a load of rubbish. Poverty is *not* an excuse for criminality. You are dealing with thieving thugs who don't want to work because it's easier to steal or leech off the benefits system.

It's not the fault of the police – it's the fact that they can't fight fire with fire. If they did, likely as not, they would end up being suspended, dismissed or maybe even sent to jail themselves. I think there's a case for a new law to be introduced whereby unplanned wrongful police action during riots or unlawful demonstrations is categorised as *accidental*, bearing in mind that in the heat of the moment, the police might just make a mistake. Such a law would enable the police to go about their duties without the threat of suspension looming. When I was a kid, I came from a poor family and we had to go without. On our council estate the neighbours were just as poor as me, but all us kids were *frightened* into not breaking the law. We were frightened because we knew what the consequences would be. I saw kids who went off the rails end up in borstal and places like that. And people caught stealing or breaking and entering ended up in jail.

We also had a work ethos – you got what you wanted by working hard, not by stealing or cheating. The point is, that's also what 99.9 per cent of the working population believe today – it's just a small minority of thugs that need to be dealt with once and for all. Sadly, however, the magistrates seem to have their hands tied. I really believe it's all to do with the limited amount of prison cells we have available. Well, it's about time we took a leaf out of the Americans' book. They've got a rule in America – they call it 'three strikes and you're out', which means that if you commit a crime for the third time, you're sent to jail for life! And that third crime might even be pinching a Mars bar from a shop. Sounds very draconian, but it's certainly a big deterrent against getting involved in crime.

How come we can spend many millions taking military action in Iraq, Afghanistan and Libya, yet we don't have the money to build more prisons? It is a stupid false economy. Spending money building more prisons in this country (enabling us to house thousands more prisoners) is the real way to go.

And when you've done that, give back the power to the magistrates and the police. Let the person who nicked the Mars bar from Mr Patel's newsagent's get banged up for a minimum of six months. Trust me, they won't do it again. I've spoken to people who have spent some time in prison – away from their homes and their families – and they tell me it's definitely not a nice place to be. However, not until that deterrent is at the forefront of people's minds will it stop them turning to crime.

The procedures policemen have to follow after arresting somebody are so complicated these days, it's no wonder they think the odd villain who nicks a few Mars bars and a can of Coke from Mr Patel is just not worth processing. In this modern age of information technology, with mobile phones, iPads and all that stuff, you would have thought that something could be implemented as a fast-track way of charging people.

What I suggest is very logical. Get nicked for breaking and entering a property – six months. Do it again – two years. Do it again – ten years. Just print a simple menu. Make it known to everybody – no way out, no appeals, that's it. You will solve the crime problem overnight.

Recently, I read in the newspapers that the police are so hard pushed these days (as are the courts) that they've set a new unofficial precedent for people found guilty of crimes relating to drugs. Anybody found dealing, or in possession of, up to £2,000 worth of, say, cocaine, will be able to get off *without* a custodial sentence. Can you believe that joke, or what? If there's a shred of truth in that, then what message does it send out to people? 'Fair enough, I'll do little packages worth £1,999,' or, 'Oh, I see, selling drugs is legal now.' That really *is* how some idiots will view it.

It's not rocket science to implement my suggestion. I don't know how much it would cost to build prisons, but I do know that we could have had loads of them with what we spent on the recent foray into Libya alone.

We need to set new standards and create new careers. Elevate a prison officer's career to a status that anyone would be proud to have and make the job available only to those with good qualifications, such as A levels or a degree. Pay them a good wage and you'll get a better quality of prison service.

And the same applies to the police. How often does some smart-arse lawyer get a crook off a charge? It's because, regrettably, some of the academic brain power within the police department is not good enough. And it's not good enough because being in the police force is not deemed to be a sought-after career. Again, make it a prestigious career by paying well. Raise the entry standard. Reward officers well, in line with professions such as lawyers, doctors and accountants, and you will have a much better police force and, in turn, a much safer and better country for ordinary citizens to live in.

I'm sure people would agree with me that if we spent our money in *those* directions – rather than poking our noses into foreign affairs, which half of us do not understand – Britain would be a much better place. And, more to the point, young people would learn that crime, drug-taking and violence are no longer tolerated in this country.

I will leave you with a funny letter I came across. Many a true word is spoken in jest.

Dear Prime Minister,

Let's put the seniors in jail and the criminals in a nursing home. This way, the seniors would have access to showers, hobbies and walks. They'd receive unlimited free prescriptions, dental and medical treatment, wheelchairs, etc., and they'd receive money instead of paying it out. They would have constant video monitoring, so they could be helped instantly if they fell or needed assistance.

Bedding would be washed twice a week, and all clothing would be ironed and returned to them. A guard would check on them every twenty minutes and bring their meals and snacks to their cell.

They would have family visits in a suite built for that purpose. They would have access to a library, weight room, a pool, spiritual counselling and education. Simple clothing, shoes, slippers, PJs and legal aid would be free, on request. Private (secure!) rooms for all, with an outdoor exercise yard and gardens.

Each senior could have a PC, a TV, radio and daily phone calls. There would be a board of directors to hear complaints, and the guards would have a code of conduct that would be strictly adhered to.

The 'criminals' would get cold food, be left all alone and unsupervised. Lights off at 8 p.m., and showers once a week. They would live in a tiny room and pay £800 per week, with no hope of ever getting out.

Justice for all, I say.

I have to stop writing for a while now, because one of my people in our property company has told me that we've got some squatters living in the flats above some shops we own, and we can't do anything about it. Why? Because they're *entitled* to be there, and it's going to take us three to six months to get them out.

'How did they get in?' I asked. 'They must have broken in – they must have broken the locks.'

'Yeah, for sure, but no one saw them do it, so they're entitled to sit there.'

'What, in *my* building?'

'Yes, in your building.'

Simple as that.

2

'Yo, Mother Chucker!'

**Listening to incomprehensible business jargon, and
the new language spoken by teenagers.**

It's 8.30 a.m. and I'm leaving my house in Essex to battle through
the traffic for a meeting in town. The meeting is with a bunch of
young executives who are going to run me through some new business plan. Obviously I'm interested or I wouldn't be wasting my
time. However, I've been to enough meetings like this to suspect
that I might end up getting aggravated, so I'm bracing myself.
What's not helping my mood is that the journey there is in stop-
start traffic and there are bloody roadworks in places I swear I saw
the road dug up and then resurfaced just a few weeks ago. Anyway,
when I arrive, I'm in no mood for nonsense.

As soon as I get in the room, I see the warning signs. There's a
bunch of lads standing there: some in skinny jeans and woolly
jumpers, others in designer blazers and white, open-collared shirts.
There are piles of PowerPoint presentations on the table, ready to
be dished out to all the attendees. Up jumps the first fellow, who
goes into his ramble.

'We need to remove the low-hanging fruit before looking at the
tougher problems. Let's start with a blank canvas and do some blue-
sky thinking. I've had a brain dump and come up with this business
model. It's all about empowerment . . . we'll develop a bespoke solution. We're going to be thinking outside the box.'

The fellow sits down, looking all pleased with himself, and hands over to another bloke, who's going to explain the actual details.

'We need to maintain our core competences in order to keep our edge in the marketplace and be customer-centric. After evaluating barriers to entry, I've concluded that at launch we'll have first-mover advantage without any need for downsizing. Going forward, we'll need to continue to manage the project proactively and we'll need to update our go-to-market strategy. If we're to survive in this vertical market, we need to do some SWOT analysis to be able challenge the best of breed . . .'

Five minutes later, he's still talking. 'As I've just demonstrated, Lord Sugar, I have all my ducks in a row now and have a solution to empower all our employees to deploy their vision. It's a case of sweating the assets. This is a paradigm shift. What we can ill afford is for this to be incremental. I'll go through the PowerPoint presentation now and will then facilitate a further meeting with you guys once you've digested it, okay? Cool. Let me start with some real joined-up thinking to manage your expectations . . .'

I couldn't take any more of this. 'Oy, oy, hold up a minute. What the *fuck* are you talking about? I have not understood a bleedin' word you've said. If I want a bleedin' business model, I'll go out and buy you some Lego or Airfix! And my interpretation of a vertical market is when Petticoat Lane has run out of space and they're piling the stalls vertically and supplying ladders for the punters to get up to them!

'I tell you what, you could give advice to one of my old school friends, Martin Winje, who runs a licensed brothel in Amsterdam. He's been looking for ways to describe the models – whether the girls are sole traders, co-operatives or managed assets. You'd go down very well there.

'Anyway, will you please speak in plain English and just get to the point so that I can understand what you're going on about.'

'Oh, sorry, Lord Sugar. Yeah, cool, cool, I'll try.'

I don't know whether it's me – whether I'm just too old now or what – but the young executives who are involved in large organisations seem to be an utterly new breed of people with a whole new language. Maybe it's just that I was used to dealing with people who got straight to the point and didn't waffle on. I'd ask them a simple question and get a simple answer. Now you have to sit and listen to a load of waffle, and then try to interpret what they're saying.

I'm convinced that this new type of business speak is simply one-upmanship; these people are simply jockeying for position. It's a kind of statement of how clever an individual is because he or she can string together a load of sophisticated new jargon. Personally, I think they've missed the point. If they want to be clever, they should concentrate on what they've been employed to do, rather than come up with a load of verbal diarrhoea. Maybe I've missed something and I'm in a bit of a time warp. In fact, I constantly challenge myself that maybe *I'm* wrong and that this is what the new world is like and I should accept it.

But then, who wants to plough through a fifty-page PowerPoint presentation? And when did it become the rule that you always have to? Is there some kind of MBA business training that makes young executives believe they can't have a meeting without one?

I often wonder how long these people spend crafting these presentations. It must take hours. Hang on, silly me! We're talking about a large organisation here – don't be so stupid, Alan, they don't do it *themselves*; there's a whole host of workers employed for that. It's much too menial a task for executives such as they.

'Who are you?' I politely ask when walking around this office floor full of executives.

'I'm the PowerPoint expert.'

'Really? Do you do anything else other than make PowerPoint presentations for all your colleagues?'

'No, I'm rushed off my feet.'

'I'm sure you are, but, dare I ask: what has producing Power-Point presentations got to do with the core business of the company?'

What has happened to the old-fashioned ethos of employing people who are productive? In whatever industry or business one is in, one normally employs people to have a specific job that contributes to the end goal. This particular bunch of personnel is tasked with writing presentations.

By the way, the people I've described are all university graduates – not only with MBAs, but some of them with 2:1s and firsts from top universities.

I *must* be right. Either that or I'm going completely and utterly nuts.

It's not just in the boardrooms that I have trouble understanding what's being said to me. Young people seem to have developed another language, which is totally impossible to follow.

My wife forced me to watch the ITV programme *The Only Way Is Essex*. I have to admit it was compelling viewing. But she's killing herself laughing watching these people, while I'm thinking the end of the world is coming shortly.

'Hiya hon, ohmygod, loveyoulots, shu'uuup, you n'wa'I mean,' and those elongated 'hellos'. I'd love to be a fly on the wall in an English lesson in a Japanese school. Can you imagine showing an episode to the students and watching their faces?

And then there are the youngsters.

I have to admit that when trying to talk to my fifteen-year-old grandson, I have to ask him to repeat everything he says. He doesn't finish his words – it's a kind of slurred speech in a completely different language.

A while ago I decided to join Twitter – I'll tell you about that a bit later – and I find it very useful. But I'm bombarded with messages from young people using this other language. It's totally alien to me.

'Yo, mother chucker, your Twitter is boom select! Sick man,' which I am told means 'I love keeping up to date with you.'

And here is a compliment from someone who says, 'Well wicked man! UR a pure legend!!!! Propa Gangsta! UR SO COOL M8!!!' I think that means they like me.

Apparently, phrases such as 'this is sick' or 'you are dope' mean something good. And your 'shorty' is your girlfriend, and 'homies' are your mates.

One thing I've learned from the way that the 'yoot' speak is that everything is *like* something, but it never actually *is* anything.

And, finally, one real beauty: 'E's jammin wif his bredren Nick' means I am socialising with Nick Hewer.

But there's one thing that all these youngsters have in common – uptalking. You know, that tedious habit of speaking in a rising cadence, with an especially perky uplift at the end, so your sentence sounds like a question even though it isn't. It's the kind of drawl you'd expect from Bruce and Sheila in Australia. I'm reliably informed that it's technically known as upward inflection. Well, whatever it is, it gets on my bloody nerves and winds me up. Never mind inflection; it's more like a bleedin' affliction.

Now, you may be thinking, having seen me on TV, that I am not the most eloquent at expressing myself, particularly when it comes to the use of grammar. Point taken, but at least you can understand what I'm talking about!

3

I Am a TV Freak

Why I'm glued to *EastEnders*, the value of reality TV, and whether it will all go wrong for Simon Cowell.

I am a TV freak. I love television. Relaxing in front of the TV is what I do in my spare time. I've often told people that I don't read too many books simply because I read for a living at the office. I must read the equivalent of half a book per day: emails, memos, reports, presentations, news articles and all that stuff. The only books I've read in recent years are technical books on flying.

So what do I like to watch on TV? Well, some would say total rubbish. I do like light-hearted stuff, and some of the programmes I most enjoy watching are things like *EastEnders*, not least because my niece, Rita, appears in it. I admit that *EastEnders* is so pathetically ridiculous sometimes that you do question your own state of mind for watching it but, nevertheless, it's quite addictive.

The younger generation, of course, will not be familiar with what television was like thirty-odd years ago. It's difficult to believe that back then there were only three channels: BBC1, BBC2 and ITV, and twenty-six years before that there was just one channel: BBC. What's more, in those days, TV only broadcast from five o'clock until ten o'clock in the evening. Contrast that to today, when we have hundreds of TV channels to watch 24/7.

My good friend Maureen Lipman, whom we all know as a great actress, is not very happy with modern-day television. She complains to me about the lack of anything like the old-fashioned dramas and situation comedies that used to be the backbone of TV entertainment. She and some of the old hacks, such as Michael Parkinson and, surprisingly, Stephen Fry are all in agreement on what the problem is: reality TV is ruining television.

I, of course, see things in a different way. First of all, what is reality TV? Reality TV is a way of observing people in real life, watching them make mistakes, watching them make fools of themselves, and generally taking the mickey out of them.

Look at the programme *Have I Got News For You*, which gives a comic review of the week's events, during which the brilliantly quick-witted Ian Hislop and Paul Merton take the piss out of everyone from the prime minister to people like me. Now, some would say that that's a 'proper' television programme, but it's actually no better than reality TV in the sense that it preys upon other people's mistakes.

Take it a stage further and look at that very popular programme *Question Time*, hosted by David Dimbleby. It's supposed to be a programme that allows people to air their political views. Politics is generally considered to be quite boring, so why is *Question Time* so popular? It's because the viewers want to see the panellists get beaten up or fall flat on their faces – simple as that. When they allow some illiterate lout in the audience to make an unjustified point to a politician, the point is judged not on its merits, but on how loudly the audience cheers. And the panellists – or contestants, as you might call them – have learned to play the game, by 'tuning' their answers so they get the greatest amount of applause. *I* would ask – how is that different from other reality TV shows?

I admit I watch *Have I Got News For You* and *Question Time*. I think *Have I Got News For You* is very funny and I admire the wit of the guests they have on the show. With *Question Time*, of course, I'm an interested party, being a member of the House of Lords. I like to see which star-struck politician has decided to go on because they want to get some TV exposure. I've often said to Ann, 'What the hell would anyone want to go on that programme for? It's a no-win situation.' *I* certainly wouldn't.

Similarly, I have turned down the opportunity of being on *Have I Got News For You* because I would have no chance against the researchers and the wit of the two resident comedians, who'd have stored up information with one thing in mind – to make me look a right prat.

My friend Adrian Chiles once told me, when he worked for the BBC, that he was invited to go on that show. He thought he should – as part and parcel of the duties of being a BBC employee. However, he told me afterwards how disgusted he was that all they wanted to do was ridicule him. Now, there *is* a devilish side of me that would really like to take up the challenge, though I think I'd need a good stiff drink beforehand to give me a couldn't-care-less attitude on the air. That said, the sensible side of me always tells me to refuse.

What else do I like to watch on TV? Well, obviously I watch a lot of football, and that's courtesy of Sky Television, a company that I'm proud to say I helped bring to the market. I don't like watching football on ITV, but do so if it's an important game. I don't quite know why ITV can't do football, but it was the same when BBC lost their *Match Of The Day* rights a few years ago and ITV took over. It just wasn't the same. One has to laugh, though, at the fiasco during the 2010 World Cup, when ITV accidentally showed an advert just at the time England scored – that has to go down in history as one of the biggest ever TV boobs.

One of the best achievements in my business life was helping to birth Sky TV. I'm sure that if one were to ask Rupert Murdoch, the owner of Sky, he would agree. However, I won't bore you with all the details on how Sky came about; I've spoken about it at length in my autobiography, so if you're interested in how it happened, you can pick it up there.

I admire Sky tremendously for the way they've built themselves up to be such a powerful force in the television market. They are very fleet of foot and have a great understanding of what consumers want. Lately, this has proved true again. They have started a new channel, Sky Atlantic, which effectively shows a lot of the great new programming coming out of America – stuff like *Entourage*, *Boardwalk Empire*, *How To Make It In America* and *Curb Your Enthusiasm*, with the fantastically dry sense of humour of Larry David.

Some of this stuff has been turned down by conventional channels such as BBC, ITV and Channel 4. It's true that *Curb Your Enthusiasm* was once broadcast on one of Channel 4's digital channels, but you had to search hard to find it – there was no way that an ordinary British viewer would stumble across it. I believe that Sky has got the right people and has done a great job for television in the UK.

On the other hand, some of the greatest TV shows *have* come from the BBC. *Fawlty Towers* is my favourite. My wife Ann wonders how I can continually watch them over and over again, but I often put on a *Fawlty Towers* DVD when I'm travelling by plane – I can't get enough of them. What about the episode with Basil and the Germans? TV platinum, I would say. The only thing that has made me laugh as much in recent years is Larry David in *Curb Your Enthusiasm*; though you do need a special understanding of that sort of humour. I guess it's only certain people that would appreciate it – it does tend to have a kind of New York Jewish audience, because many of his jokes send up what people dislike about the so-called Jewish mentality.

Then there's *Only Fools And Horses* – classic stuff. Who can forget the one with Del Boy, Rodney, Granddad and the crashing chandelier, or the one when Del, trying to act cool in the pub, goes to lean on the bar and falls right through it? Absolute TV gold. What a versatile actor David Jason is to adapt himself from the Del Boy character to Detective Inspector Jack Frost.

Back to reality TV – why is it so popular? Some say that it's popular with the TV companies because it's cheap to make and certain TV companies have an agenda whereby they need to drag in viewers in order to sell their advertising. Why go out and spend £20–30 million on locations, camera crews, sophisticated sets and all that stuff when, effectively, you can build a fake house and fill it with a bunch of people arguing with each other and somehow attract the new type of viewer that's out there? Of course I'm referring to *Big Brother*. Personally, I cannot understand what must be going through someone's brain to sit there and watch that garbage.

I'll tell you a funny story. When I built my house in Spain, I installed a television system which included a few Sky boxes. (I know I'm not meant to have Sky boxes in Spain, but I *was* the owner of the company that made them, and I would like to say that I was just out there testing them.) However, like all digital boxes in the early days, they were prone to crashing. We've all seen a box crash – normally the picture freezes, and the way you deal with it is to pull the plug out of the wall and reboot the box. Well, one morning, I came downstairs to find my son Daniel and his wife Michaela sitting in the TV room looking at a frozen picture.

'Sod it,' I said, as I walked in, 'the bloody box has crashed again. Hold on, I'll go and reboot it.'

'No, no, no,' said Daniel, 'leave it – we're watching.'

'Watching?! What are you watching?'

'It's *Big Brother*. Leave it alone, Dad.'

I swear to you, they were looking at a picture of people sleeping in a dormitory. It wasn't until one of the people turned over in bed that I realised it was live TV. They were watching people sleeping!

'Are you a pair of brain-deads or what?! How can you sit there watching this trash?'

All they did was laugh at me and say, 'You don't understand – it's fantastic, it's hilarious.'

And this very same couple, my son and daughter-in-law, have the same opinion about *The Only Way Is Essex*. I alluded to this show in the previous chapter, but let's analyse what it's about. There's a bunch of women, many of whom have false boobs, new teeth and skirts that would just about pass as belts. As for the men, there's one thicko who can't pass his driving test, and another thicko who doesn't know the name of the prime minister. These people are filmed in what is described as 'everyday life' – in the pub, in the café, in the shops, massaging and spray-tanning – and they talk in this flat East End drawl, which I guess only the youngsters understand.

All I can say is this – good luck to ITV, because it's brilliant marketing. It costs virtually nothing to produce and they get millions of viewers. And during the advertising breaks, they are banging in adverts targeted at that particular age group.

'Daniel, Michaela, why do you watch that rubbish?' I asked.

Remember, we're now ten years on from the *Big Brother* incident, so their answer was a little more mature. 'Yeah, you're right, Dad, you're right. It *is* rubbish. It is total, utter rubbish, it *is*. I don't know *why* – we're just addicted. We can't help it; we *have* to watch it.'

And my wife is exactly the same. I watched it to see what all the fuss was about and, as you've read already, I find it quite useful in helping me to interpret this new language the kids speak. But is that TV entertainment? I'm wondering what Maureen Lipman and Michael Parkinson would say about that one, because *their* comments were actually targeted at programmes like mine, *The Apprentice*.

To add further insult to injury, at the prestigious BAFTA awards in 2011, *The Only Way Is Essex* won the only award that was voted for by the public (all the other awards are decided by a so-called expert panel of artistic luvvies). I was so happy *The Only Way Is Essex* won – it made me laugh to think what a smack in the face it for those intellectually talented panellists, who must have been grinding their teeth. And when I looked around the room at the executive producers and other so-called artistic geniuses, the look of disapproval on their faces was a real sight to see.

I have often said to Maureen, 'The market has changed. You have to move with the times. Surely there's stuff on TV these days that you watch?'

'No,' she says, 'I don't. I don't watch anything . . . Maybe the news, and of course I watch *your* programme – only out of loyalty – but that's about it.'

I pointed out to her that if she could be bothered to watch BBC4, she'd see that there is some great stuff out there – even some old-fashioned drama. The series they did about famous old comedians such as Frankie Howerd, who was brilliantly portrayed by David Walliams, was great. There was also the wonderful story of Tony Hancock's life, which showed what a sad, depressive drunk he was. And the life story of Hughie Green – again portrayed brilliantly by that great British actor Trevor Eve – was also fantastic.

I even got a mention in one of those BBC4 programmes, when they did the life story of Clive Sinclair. It showed how the boffin Clive built up his business, and it ended with him saying that he lost it all to some barrow-boy – that was a reference to me.

'Maureen,' I said, after telling her all about these BBC4 programmes, 'a lot of youngsters wouldn't even know who these comedians were, but *you* know who they were, and you'd have loved those shows. What have you got to say about that?'

'Well, who watches BBC4?'

'Well, *you* can, if you want to. That's what it's there for. It's there to bring back the type of stuff that you're saying is missing from modern-day TV.'

But I think that tells the story, does it not? No one watches it. It gets a very small audience. Another great programme, *Mad Men*, started out on BBC4 because it was considered a niche product – but it soon caught on amongst the luvvies. When I watched the first series on BBC4, hardly anyone ever mentioned it. But as soon as it got promoted to BBC2, everybody loved it and everybody talked about it. And, of course, it became an award-winning programme.

TV is all about catering for the masses. Take, for example, the great Bruce Forsyth. What a fantastic fellow – coming up to his ninth decade – and how well deserved his knighthood was. But look where we all saw him first: Saturday-night entertainment like *The Generation Game*. And whilst he had this charismatic way of doing it, he basically took the piss out of his contestants – so nothing has changed. People like to see others make mistakes – they love it. It goes back to the earliest days of silent movies and Laurel and Hardy, where somebody whacks someone over the head and it makes people laugh. Nowadays, Brucie, with a seventy-year span in entertainment under his belt, is hosting one of the biggest shows on the BBC, *Strictly Come Dancing*. Whoever would have believed that a programme about dancing would be so popular? By the way, for those of you too young to remember, the programme is called *Strictly Come Dancing* because originally, thirty-odd years ago, there used to be a BBC programme called *Come Dancing*, but it was a serious programme that showed ballroom-dancing tournaments in the then fashionable dance halls. If you tried to put that type of programme on TV now, people would laugh it off the screen.

Simon Cowell's *The X Factor* and *Britain's Got Talent* – not new. I remember someone called Carroll Levis who had a talent show on TV where the winner was picked by a clap-o-meter (which measured the audience's applause). However, in Hughie Green's long-running show *Opportunity Knocks*, it was the public's vote that decided the winner. So there's nothing new about the *X Factor* concept – what's new is the glitzy manner in which it's presented. What's new is all the schmaltz that goes along with it – talking to the mother, the brother, the uncle, and how it means so much to the person, how they've dreamt about this all their lives and, 'Simon, please, you don't realise what this means to me.' Cry, cry, cry; tears, tears, tears . . . 'I have learnt so much about myself.'

And the auditions beforehand – again, these are simply there for entertainment, with a fair share of losers who can't sing and look ridiculous. But they get the audience figures up – and they manage to get away with all this for five or six programmes before the real show starts.

Then there's the final selection process, out in Spain or America, in some villa, when we watch the painful reduction of the contestants down to the final sixteen acts that will actually enter the contest. The tears, the pathetic decision-making of some of Simon Cowell's assistants, who can't quite pull off trying to create an air of drama as to who's going through and who's going home – you can see that much of it is rehearsed. Nevertheless, it is brilliant TV, the biggest show on television and the biggest money-earner for ITV.

This is what the audience in Britain wants to see so, Maureen (and Michael Parkinson), I'm sorry to say that *your* visions for television are long gone. This is what you're going to have to put up with, and it's not going to get better.

There is, of course, the risk of oversaturation with these reality shows, and in some cases there's a danger that the host (or the owner of the format) feels that they can walk on water. In the case of Simon Cowell, one can't deny his rise to fame and the exceptional success of his TV shows, which serves to endorse what I'm always banging on about – you should expect to get success by drawing on a wealth of experience. Simon Cowell is a classic case of this – he has only been able to get where he is because he started from scratch in the music industry and worked his way up. What he doesn't know about music production and sales is not worth knowing, so he is a very worthy person to be heading up such a show.

But success can sometimes go to your head and you can get on a roll where you start to believe that everything you touch will turn to gold. I, for example, suffered this syndrome in the eighties, when every product I brought out sold like crazy. I got carried away with new products and markets, blindly thinking there would be never-ending success. Instead, things went pear-shaped – and I wonder if Simon's craving for the American market and his absence from the UK market, which made him what he is, will backfire.

He decided not to appear in most of the episodes of *Britain's Got Talent* and got someone to replace him, and he did the same with his biggest show, *The X Factor,* appearing instead in the newly launched US series. He started off by taking Cheryl Cole, one of the biggest attractions of the UK's *The X Factor*, with him; the point being that he's gambling on America and forgetting his home market. Cheryl was quickly dropped from the US show; some say it was due to her wonderful Geordie accent. Whatever the reason, America has proved to be a graveyard for many and we've seen that viewing figures for the US *X Factor* were considered disappointing, while in the UK the show lost out to *Strictly Come Dancing* in the ratings. Simon has admitted he got a bit cocky, and only time will tell if he can turn the shows around.

In a similar vein, and this will make you laugh, the BBC decided to show the UK version of *The Apprentice* in the USA, on BBC America. The response? Wait for it – they said the people there couldn't understand what I was saying, so they put subtitles on screen while I was speaking!

*

Now, there are other types of commentators on TV. I mentioned Stephen Fry earlier. Of course, he's not as old as Maureen or Michael Parkinson, and doesn't really go back as far as they do in the history of entertainment, yet he shares their belief that reality TV is not real entertainment, not *real* TV. Oddly, he seems to have got himself a kind of niche in the marketplace: everybody loves Stephen Fry. It's one of those things that happens in the luvvie-run TV industry. If you say something enough, everyone believes it. 'Stephen Fry is wonderful. Oh, he's fantastic. Oh, he's marvellous. Don't you just love Stephen Fry?'

Well, sorry, *I* don't. It may be because he's had a couple of pokes at my television programme, which he has no right to do. But, more to the point, it's because he's the biggest diva going – someone who is known to throw his toys out of the pram when he can't get his own way; someone who flounced off Twitter saying he wasn't going to do it any more, and then suddenly came back. Okay, the man has had issues in his life, and all credit to him for recognising them and pulling the situation around, but I don't think he deserves to be viewed as this great oracle on modern-day television. Well, I for one don't see him that way.

On the subject of the luvvies, I've come across a lot of them since I've been involved in TV, and they have this wonderful way, as I've already mentioned, of repeating things to convince them-selves that something is good. Indeed, the producers will *always* say that what they've produced is brilliant.

Well, I'm sorry, but in some cases it's not bloody brilliant; some stuff has been bloody useless, to be honest. But no – everything is super. I remember doing a programme for Sky (I can't even remember what it was called, it was so bad) shortly after my first appearance on *The Apprentice*. 'It's fantastic, darling; it's wonderful; it's marvellous, absolutely brilliant. Honestly, you were terrific.'

'Really? I thought it was a load of crap actually.'

'No, not at all, not at all. It's wonderful.'

It *was* a load of crap, and I remember my daughter Louise anticipating the programme, all excited about me being on TV after *The Apprentice*. When she saw it on Sky One, she said to me, 'What the hell were you doing there? It was pants.'

She was dead right. But not according to the luvvies. 'No, we all stick together and we all say that something is brilliant – so it's got to be brilliant, hasn't it?'

Of course, if one doesn't want to watch something on TV, one doesn't have to. And this brings me on to my next subject, which is the advance in modern-day technology.

Do I love that Sky+! Not because I made millions of Sky+ boxes, but because it was the greatest invention, as far as I'm concerned, since the microwave oven; one of the best gadgets I've ever had in my life. And why? Because when I watch *The X Factor* with the wife, I can skip through all the crap. I don't want to know what the contestants' parents think of them, see what it's like where they come from, watch them go back and visit their nans. I don't want to know what happens backstage when they walk off and Dermot O'Leary pats them on the shoulder or hands them a tissue. I'm not interested. We whizz through until the first one steps out and sings. We listen to them sing, we listen to what the judges have to say, and then we move on. Sorry, Mum and Dad; sorry, Auntie and Gran, but you're not coming into my home. In fact, recently, my wife and I both laughed out loud when I announced that my skip through an episode of *Britain's Got Talent* actually condensed it to twenty minutes.

For an ITV programme that starts at nine o'clock, I programme it into Sky+, find something else to do until fifteen minutes past nine, then start watching it from the beginning, skipping past the breaks, and end up finishing the programme at the same time as everyone else, without having to endure the adverts. Sorry ITV, but your adverts are wasted on me! In fact, I remember once being asked to speak at an ITV-sponsored seminar. It was just about the time we were developing the Sky+ box, and I said to the audience, 'You should all go off and get yourselves jobs with the BBC. I believe your days are numbered, because soon these high-technology gadgets are going to be in everyone's homes and people will not want to sit through your adverts any more.'

Of course they looked at me as if I'd just arrived from the planet Mars, and the following speaker totally disagreed with me. Well, he had to, because, let's face it, they were all employed by ITV, which derives its income solely from adverts.

Another wonderful high-tech gadget I have is a Slingbox. Now, I just want to dispel any rumours that I'm trying to flog something that I make – I don't know who the manufacturer is and I've got no interest in them whatsoever, other than to say that it's a great little device. In a nutshell, all I do is stick it on my Sky+ box at home, load some software into my laptop computer and when I go away to places like America, I can get straight into my Sky+ box, watch Sky News live, record programmes on the planner and play them back at my leisure. In fact, it's not often that Ann comments on the gadgets I buy, but she loves this one because while we're away, sometimes for weeks in America, she manages to keep up with *EastEnders*. Previously, she'd have a stack of them to plough through when she got home. A brilliant invention, and when you think about it, quite simple – it's all thanks to the wonderful world of the internet. Everything's possible if you have a high-bandwidth phone line.

TV viewing habits are changing, not only because of Sky+, but also because of another great invention, the BBC iPlayer (and other players that are available for the other TV channels). People no longer worry about missing a programme – they pick it up later on the iPlayer, maybe even at work the following day in their lunch break. The number of viewers of *The Apprentice* on iPlayer is massive. In fact, for the past couple of years, it's been the iPlayer programme with the highest demand.

In another 'watch this space' glimpse of the future, in March 2011, I became chairman of YouView. This venture will lead to the most futuristic TV-viewing experience for all and sundry. It's a non-profit-making venture made up of shareholders such as the BBC, ITV, Channel 4, Channel Five, British Telecom, TalkTalk and Arqiva. The technology will combine the viewing of all terrestrial channels in HD, as well as TV delivered by the internet. To nutshell it, you will plug in your aerial for the terrestrial stuff – plus your internet connection – and you will enter a new world of TV entertainment. One of YouView's biggest advantages is that it will have an electronic programme guide that allows you to go *back* seven days. So if you missed a programme, you just skip back on the remote control and there you have it. No more going to the PC, finding iPlayer, then finding the actual programme – it will all be there on your TV via a simple set-top box. And the good news is that there's no subscription.

4

Don't Knock the BBC

In defence of a fine institution.

Do you really want to see a world without the BBC? I'd like to stand up for them against all the stick that they get from the rest of the media, particularly the *Daily Mail*, and also the government.

The reason for the constant criticism is that the BBC is funded by the licence fee we all pay – the £145.50 a year we cough up. Well, let me try to put things in perspective. £145.50 a year is about £12 a month. Let's face it, some of us pay £60 a month for our Sky subscription, £30 a month for our mobile phone, £20 a month for our internet connection – so we've become used to these types of subscriptions. And when you look at it that way, £12 a month for all those channels, for that great website they have, for their wonderful radio programmes on a multitude of stations – you've got to admit, it's fantastic value for money. And nobody should complain how the money is spent.

I have a mad idea, which I've expressed at times to the BBC. I've said to them, 'You know what? If I were in charge of the BBC, this is what I would do; this is my fantasy. I'd tell the public, "Okay, you don't have to pay if you don't want to – it's voluntary – but, because we're now in the digital age, if you don't pay, then you won't be able to pick up the programmes on TV. So the choice is yours: you pay, you see; you don't pay, you don't see. All right?" And how could this be achieved? Easily, because Sky TV has proved that digital television can be encrypted in such a way that you can produce TV sets and boxes each of which has its own profile, with channels that can be enabled or disabled.'

Now, if that happened, all the arguing would go away. The *Daily Mail* would have to cut down their news output by fifty pages a week, as they wouldn't be able to have a go at the BBC. And politicians like Jeremy Hunt would be out of work because the public would be able to decide for themselves whether or not they wanted to watch the channel.

Just stop a minute and think about how we all take the BBC for granted. We get in our cars, turn on the radio and listen to some of those great radio shows or the news and traffic information. We also listen to the radio at home – it wakes many of us up in the morning. On TV we watch *EastEnders*, *Strictly Come Dancing* and of course the superb *BBC News*. We see *Match Of The Day*, as well other great sporting events like Wimbledon and the Grand National; and on top of this there's the BBC website, which is one of the most informative I've ever seen. And all this for twelve quid a month! I would say it's the greatest value out there.

Who runs the BBC? Who's the governing body? Do you think it's the BBC Trust? Not at all. Do you think it's Ofcom, the body that's supposed to oversee all media companies? No.

It's the *Daily Mail*. The *Daily Mail* puts the fear of shit up every single BBC executive. They can make a mountain out of a molehill. Take good old Bruce Forsyth, for example. When he turned eighty, the BBC was guilty of buying him a cake to celebrate his eightieth birthday. Can you believe that this warranted a full-page spread in the *Daily Mail*? How outrageous it was that in these dire economic times they were wasting licence-payers' money on buying Brucie a birthday cake! Oh, and another terrible thing – Jana Bennett, the once Director of Television, went somewhere in a taxi, which also cost a few quid.

Television is all about entertainment, and in the entertainment business you throw parties and you buy people thank-you presents. You'll always find the luvvies at some bash somewhere – it's part and parcel of being in TV and show business. All the other TV broadcasters do the same. I wouldn't like to tell you the lengths they go to to entertain; I wouldn't like to tell you how much some of their executives spend on hotels, restaurants and bars to entertain the talent they're trying to lure to their networks. And not only do they entertain the talent, they entertain their agents, to try to get them to persuade their clients to accept contracts.

In fact, the biggest hypocrite going is the *Daily Mail*, which employs people to sell space to advertisers. I often think that what I might do one day is buy ten shares in the *Daily Mail* (or the company that owns it), then turn up at the annual general meeting and demand to see the expenses of the people who take advertisers out for lunch or invite them to parties, launches and other jollies, because, 'As a shareholder, that is *my* money they are spending.' It's no different from the ridiculous fuss they made over poor old Brucie's birthday cake.

Then there's the brain surgeon Jeremy Hunt, the current Culture Secretary – the man who, when in opposition, objected to me being an adviser to Gordon Brown's government, the man who protested that, as an adviser, I shouldn't be on BBC television, as this may be considered political. What a load of rubbish. As anyone who's ever seen *The Apprentice* will know, there is nothing in that programme that can be construed in any way, shape or form as political. Nevertheless, these political animals love to make mountains out of molehills.

Get this. Jeremy Hunt made a statement that, wait for it, the BBC website is *too good*! Yes, he's had complaints from his mates at News International. They say that the BBC, which has an unfair advantage over commercial ventures as it's funded by licence-payers, has too many people working on the website's news department and that the news they are giving out is *free*. How are we, at News International, supposed to exist when we're trying to *sell* our news online and the BBC is giving it away for nothing?

And Hunt agrees with them! 'Now, BBC, you're doing too good a job with the tax-payers' money. Stop it! Stop doing such a good job! And, by the way, how dare you pay Jonathan Ross an alleged £6 million a year on a three-year contract? It's outrageous.'

No, it's not outrageous. He was being paid that money because he is a talent, a talent that the BBC wanted to keep. It's the same reason footballers get paid a fortune, though Jonathan is much better value. Simon Cowell most probably gets paid a similar amount of money for being on ITV (though I don't know for sure). And so it is that the BBC is not allowed to pay top money for talent any more. This will inevitably result in the BBC becoming merely a breeding ground – such talents will come to the BBC as unknowns, learn their trade and flourish and, just like footballers, they'll move on to someone who does pay top money, like ITV.

I worry about the future of the BBC under the current government, which has a bee in its bonnet about wanting to control finances. One can't help but think that the government is being pressurised by organisations such as the Murdoch empire. Now, I don't blame Rupert – he's a good friend of mine and always will be – but he's the last person on earth I'd have expected to complain about competition. He's never seemed to worry about it in the past – and he's had his fair share of people attacking him for trying to monopolise the media, so he knows what that's all about. With the greatest respect to him and his organisation, it seems to me that this is a case of the pot calling the kettle black.

It certainly seemed as though the message had got through to the government that Rupert was not a happy bunny when that genius Vince Cable got mugged off by a couple of female *Telegraph* journalists posing as constituents. They recorded the Business Secretary saying how he was going to scupper the Murdoch deal to take over BSkyB. His genius statement included this: 'I have

declared war on Mr Murdoch and I think we're going to win . . .
I didn't politicise it because it is a legal question, but he is trying
to take over BSkyB.'

Although the paper didn't run those particular comments, the
recording was leaked to the BBC's Business Editor, Robert Peston.
Needless to say, Cable got stripped of that particular responsibility
and genius number two, Jeremy Hunt, took over control of the
BSkyB takeover. He gave it the go ahead in March 2011 but was
forced to postpone a final decision in the wake of the phone
hacking scandal that hit the *News of the World* in July – more
about that later. Eventually the scandal escalated, and such was
the pressure on Murdoch, News Corporation withdrew its bid
for BSkyB.

5

Janet and John, Get a Bloody Job

Why I blame parents for spoiling their kids, and a letter of advice to my eleven-year-old self.

How many times have you been trying to have a conversation with your child or grandchild and noticed they've perfected this technique of giving one third of their attention to you while simultaneously watching the television and answering a text or a tweet? At the same time, there's a screaming mum or dad asking them why they haven't cleaned up their room.

I was once at a seminar, doing a Q&A with a bunch of about 700 people who ran their own small businesses. A woman in the audience threw a curveball with a question unrelated to the business in hand, but to do with the future of youngsters. At this point, I went off at a tangent about the youth of today, and it made the audience laugh when I started ranting on about evolution – how reptiles, over millions of years, have adapted the colours of their bodies so that predators don't eat them. Then I took the example of the half-man half-ape and how he has evolved. The reason I cited him is because his head was stooped, and it prompted me to say that I fear that, in thousands of years' time, a child will also have a stooped head and that one arm will be in front of their face, holding an iPhone. And the ends of their fingers will have developed into small, pointed tips rather than fingernails.

I'd like to be a fly on the wall in the future – but since I won't be there, this is how I imagine we'll look.

While on the subject of youngsters, there is a stark difference between the way children were treated when I was a kid and what we see today. What I've seen from the way that my children have been brought up, and indeed from the way that *their* children have been brought up, is that kids are totally naïve when it comes to understanding the real world. They simply don't have the work ethic that was instilled in people of my generation. Of course, in my case I can't blame my children because I ended up becoming a very wealthy man, but the problem doesn't just lie with people of wealth; it seems to me that all parents have a similar problem these days.

Too much is laid on for youngsters. I've had young kids ask me,

'What do you reckon, Lord Sugar, an iPhone or a BlackBerry – which one should I get?' And they know their parents will shell out for one of them! In my day, you'd be asking yourself how you could make a few quid to be able to afford something like that.

Nothing brought this home to me more than when I heard my eight-year-old grandson explain that one of his pals at school was going on his first holiday with his first passport. My grandson could not believe it. Why? Because, since the age of two, he has done more travelling than Michael Palin. I recall telling him that his mate's mum and dad already have to come up with loads of money, which they work hard to earn, to send their son to a private school – it's something that they want to do for him. I explained to him that they could have sent him to a state school and saved lots of money to spend on other things, and that his mate's parents are normal-salaried people and can't afford to go on holiday. He was fascinated that his mate had never been on a plane and that he was going by train to Disneyland Paris.

Back to the lady at the seminar, her question was: 'My twin sons are twenty-one years old now. Can you suggest what they might do, or what I might tell them to do for a living?'

My reply was: 'It's too late, I'm afraid. You look like a very nice lady and I'm sure that you love and care for your children dearly, but I'm willing to bet, not knowing you at all, that your kids have never had to fend for themselves. I'm guessing you're not a person of great wealth, but that your priority in life has been to make sure your kids have everything. I bet they've got the Nike trainers, iPhones, iPads, Lacoste polo shirts . . .' The lady was nodding at me as if to say I was right. 'Well, I'll tell you what I would do, madam – I would have a little sit-down with them and say, "Right, you're twenty-one years old and your father and I have looked after you very, very well. Now, there's the door – clear off out there into the real world and go and earn some money of your own."'

I blame the parents. They are just as bad as the kids, who are under tremendous peer pressure. They get laughed at in school if they are wearing cheap trainers from Asda instead of Nikes, and if they don't have a Lacoste logo on their polo shirt they are considered plebs. They compare notes with each other as to what they've got and what they aspire to get. Each material possession is a status symbol that makes them cool and someone to look up to; hence the pressure put on the parents to make sure their kid is happy and can compete. It's sickening. I intentionally used the word 'compete' in this context. It's a word one would normally use in describing participation in a competition or sport, but in this case it's simply keeping up with the Joneses, as they used to say.

I told the audience that parents should go back to old principles, even if the kid is driving them mad asking for new clothes or the latest Xbox. The kids should be tasked to work for these things, rather than just getting them. Fair enough, you can splash out for a birthday or Christmas and all that, but these kids want something *every week*. If I wanted something, I had to save up for it myself. When my kids, who were born to a wealthy man, wanted something, I told them to get a Saturday job in McDonald's – which they did. My daughter always reminds me that getting her regular pocket money out of me was like getting blood out of a stone – well, bloody good job too. I can tell you, I was very conscious of not letting them grow up as spoilt brats. My wife and I succeeded there, I can assure you.

At that point, the audience erupted in applause. I'd obviously touched a nerve. This was 2011 and I was talking to a bunch of people for whom, it seemed, reality had finally hit home. I have to say that this bunch was well tuned in. They'd had their reality check, and when I went on to tell them that, if you want something in life, you have to go and get it yourself, there was more rapturous applause.

*

In the audition process for *Junior Apprentice*, the production people often tell me how surprised they are at the amount of young people who aspire to go to university. With no disrespect, in my day many teenagers did not have the aptitude even to be considered. I guess, in this day and age of multiple-choice exam papers, it's easier to get some qualifications and therefore put yourself up for university. Or could it be that going to university is a way of wasting three years before realising you have to face up to reality and get a bloody job to support yourself? *I* think so, in many cases. It's basically a period in their lives where they can lie about and enjoy themselves.

But, of course, let's not go *straight* to uni. No, no, no – got to have a gap year to recover from the exhaustion of getting a place. Maybe a year away in Australia, with Mum and Dad sending cash every month or so. All this to recharge their batteries and brace themselves for the three years' hard graft ahead at uni – or is it for the social life?

Who do I blame? Again, the parents themselves. They have allowed it to happen. And why has it happened? Because, to use a famous saying from Harold Macmillan, 'You've never had it so good.' Got to have a microwave, got to have a dishwasher, got to have a washing machine, three tellies in the house and possibly two cars. That is what people strive for these days. Well, you can't blame them, but there is one thing missing – and that is to tell the children that all this is achieved by hard work. Unfortunately, this part of the message is not transmitted.

In my opinion, the place to instil this is at primary school. Parents should understand that this is an important part of the curriculum, and the six- and seven-year-olds should be told the commercial facts of life, like so:

Mummy and Daddy have jobs which pay them money. Mummy works in a shop. She stands behind the counter and sells things. Daddy works in a factory that makes the things that Mummy sells. Uncle Johnny drives a van that takes the stuff from Daddy's factory to Mummy's shop, and Mrs Brown next door goes to the shop and buys something from Mummy. So where does the money come from to pay Mummy and Daddy?

Well, it's very simple. Daddy's boss buys some stuff for £10 and sells it to Mummy's shop for £15. That means he's made £5. And because he sells thousands of these things and makes £5 on each one, he is able to pay Daddy (and Uncle Johnny, the driver). Mummy's shop takes the product at £15 and sells it for £20 to Mrs Brown, and Mummy's boss takes all those extra £5s and pays Mummy. And then Mummy and Daddy come home with the money they get from the shop and the factory and they have to buy food for the house and pay for the electricity that runs the light bulbs, the television and the washing machine. And if they didn't have jobs, you wouldn't be able to watch television, you wouldn't have a washing machine and you wouldn't be able to go on holiday.

This could be a new edition of the Janet and John books.

And so, little ones, as you make your way in this wonderful world, *you* might work in a shop or a factory one day, or if you're very clever, you might be the boss of the factory or you might even own a shop, because bosses tend to have more money than Mummy and Daddy have.

That, of course, put in very simplistic terms, is my dream scenario. In reality, little Tommy or Jenny would come home and tell their mum and dad what they'd just been told, and the parents would be down at the school the next morning, claiming that their children had been traumatised and demanding that the teacher be suspended under some new human rights EU legislation that's been brought in – mental abuse, or something like that.

Some youngsters today have a real wannabe mentality. They want to get themselves on television and become 'famous'. This is the darker side of all those reality TV shows, which can create overnight 'stars', albeit Z-list ones. Let's face it, we have seen some very talentless people who are perceived to be succeeding in a TV career. This seems to blind some young people to the fact that these examples are one in a million and, regrettably, they shift their focus from mainstream life and pursuing a regular job or career.

On the other hand, I may surprise some people when I say that I have a lot of admiration for Katie Price (once known as Jordan). Now, before you shut this book and chuck it away, indulge me for a moment. She has, of course, had some issues in her private life, but be under no illusion: she is a grafter and is very smart. She has made herself a fortune with her magazine deals, books and TV appearances. Trust me, she knows exactly what she is doing and why. She has worked the system well. I know that one day, when she's a bit older, she will cringe at some of the things she did in her youth, but don't we all?

The same could be said for the Beckhams. David worked hard to hone his talent as a footballer and continues to work hard to enhance his public image, all of which has brought him rich rewards. At the same time, he's become a fantastic role model for youngsters by demonstrating that you don't have to get drunk or take drugs to be cool. I say well done and good luck to him. His wife, Victoria, who was once in the The Spice Girls, has also grafted well. I think she even admits herself that she doesn't really have a wonderful voice, but she was in the right place at the right time and has moved on to do other things. The Beckhams have to make hay while the sun shines, while they are still relatively young. And if they can manage their success and fame while at the same time being sensible, decent family people, then that's a great lesson for kids.

I am amazed by today's drinking culture, with young people waiting all week for Friday to come. Then, on Friday night, they go out and spend a fortune, with just one purpose – to get blind drunk, fall over, vomit on the pavement and abuse the police. They start off by downing shots such as tequila, swallowing them one after the other as if they were taking medicine – they don't even taste it. It's not uncommon for them to consume a whole bottle in one night. The cost to the police service and the NHS is massive. The ambulances that have to be called out to take these drunks to hospital would be better deployed being on standby for genuine emergencies.

I say charge them a £200 fine on the spot and give them a £500 bill from the hospital. And if they are violent and whack a policeman, bang them up in prison for a month. I don't know how one would deal with the logistics of chasing down debts from these animals, but it could be done, one way or another. They could be asked to attend court if they don't pay and given a custodial sentence. It's got to be the only way. All this talk of putting the price of alcohol up or stopping low-priced alcohol being sold in supermarkets is not the solution. Some of these thugs will just go out and steal so they can drink. Plus, putting the price up disadvantages those who enjoy drinking in moderation, and why should *they* pay the price?

And, I'm sorry to say, if the picture you had in your mind was of the louts being male, think again – the girls are just as bad, if not worse.

People often ask me, in my role as the host of *The Apprentice*, what advice I would give to the young Alan Sugar. So here is a letter I would write to my eleven-year-old self:

Dear Alan,

Thank you for your letter. I understand that you're interested in going into business. I've carefully noted some of the little schemes you've been up to lately to make yourself some pocket money and, quite frankly, they seem rather enterprising. You yourself are surprised that some of your schoolmates don't do the same – the most probable reason is that you have some kind of instinct they don't have. Your pals may turn out to be

*doctors, scientists and accountants, but it seems to me that you
have got a bit of a commercial brain on you. You see things that
others don't see, and that is a talent.*

*I'm sure I'm right when I say to you that if you aspire to be
something you can't be, you won't succeed. You might like
music, for example, but I bet you can't play the piano. I'd go
so far as to say that if you were locked in a room with a piano
teacher for a year, you'd still not come out as a concert pianist.
You might be able to knock out a quick rendition of 'Roll Out
The Barrel', but you'll never in a million years have the talent
that's needed to play in the Royal Philharmonic Orchestra,
because those who do have that particular talent are born with
it. It is this reality you need to grasp hold of. You've got to
recognise what you're good at and what you're not good at, and
focus on the good. Don't try to be something that you're not.*

*But let me put to one side for a moment your aspirations of
being a businessman and talk about the pitfalls of trying to
run before you can walk. Now, I'm sure that you mess about
in school with all your mates, and sometimes you might get
distracted. You might make people laugh; you might even be the
class clown. In doing all this, you're wasting some of the most
valuable time in your life. Well, here is a wake-up call, a reality
check. You have got to go to school – you're only eleven, and
the law says you have to stay there till you're at least sixteen.
That's it – get over it; it's not going to change. And, by the way,
it's free. You might think some of your teachers are idiots, but
actually they have dedicated their lives to trying to educate
people. And the words that come out of their mouths should be
like gold dust to you. And whilst this might be the most boring
letter you've ever received, my advice to you is: suck everything
in – use your eyes and your ears and keep your mouth shut.
Don't mess about in class because, I promise you, as sure as*

night follows day, you will be kicking yourself later in life for wasting five years messing around with your pals and ignoring what's been given to you for free at school.

I know that you like particular subjects to do with finance and advertising, but when it gets to what you perceive to be boring subjects like English or French or maths, you tend to tune out. Well, don't. If you ever succeed in business, there'll be nothing worse than being stuck in a meeting one day, in France, sitting there like a dummy, while other people are getting their points across.

'Oh, this is really boring, boring, boring,' you must be thinking. Well, I'm sorry about that, but maths is important, English is important. I'm not suggesting that you go on to become a rocket scientist or anything like that, but mental arithmetic and expressing oneself correctly in the English language are going to be very important to you in the rest of your life.

By the way, the fact that you really enjoy other – less crucial – subjects than maths and English is not a problem. In fact, you will notice that you excel at the subjects you really like – and that, young man, may be your first clue as to what direction you should focus on in the rest of your life.

Well, that about covers your schooling, save to say that you will need to make a decision whether you can leave school having reached a level of education that's good enough for you to go forward and do what you want to do, or whether you feel you want to be some academic and go on to university. But just like the concert pianist I referred to earlier, you have to be a special person to excel in the sciences or the arts. And from what I gather, looking at your letter to me, you seem to be a bit of an enterprising busybody, perhaps not cut out for what you may perceive in the future as a boring existence.

But enough of that. Now I want to tell you something else. Be a nice person. Learn to be respectful to your elders. Respect the law and don't be a lout. Temptation is one of the worst things in life. I guess in your school there are a few bigshots – usually, they're bigger lads (or girls) who tend to have an audience around them. They might even be bullies to a certain extent, and people seem to be in awe of them for some reason or other. Carefully stand back. Look at those people and ask yourself: what is it about them that's so special? Maybe it's that they're funny; maybe they're clever; maybe they're streetwise. Fair enough, you can admire them for those reasons, but when you've seen through all of that, you might also realise that, actually, they're not so special at all. And I can tell you from my experiences, young man, that many of these people will turn out to be losers in life. You need to be your own person. You need to turn your eyes away from things that you know are wrong. The most frightening thing for me as an adult is to see young people like you lured into bad habits such as drugs, alcohol, gambling and crime. You do not want to go there – trust me. You're too clever for that – I sussed that out from the letter you sent me.

Be a good person. Be good to your parents, your brothers, your sisters, your uncles and aunts. Be a nice neighbour. Be firm but polite. Have an opinion, by all means, but don't discount the fact that people older than you have seen a lot more in life that you have yet to come across.

You might like to put this letter away and open it up again in twenty-five years' time. If you do so, I promise you will see that my words were true.

Yours truly,
Alan Sugar

Oh, and here's another question I get asked all the time: would the young Alan Sugar succeed in *The Apprentice*?

Yes, if I were a twenty-year-old candidate on *The Apprentice*, I would walk it.

6

DON'T Tell Me I'm Fired!

Answering some commonly asked questions about
The Apprentice, and why I'm glad I don't use the F-word on TV.

One of the questions most frequently asked of me is: when I meet the candidates for the first time in the boardroom – in episode one of *The Apprentice* – do I instinctively know which one is going to win? The honest answer to that is no.

It's just the same in life when you meet someone for the first time. You should not form an opinion of them immediately; the longer you have to deal with them and be involved with them, the more time you have to make a true judgement, so I'm not one for knee-jerk reactions. Neither am I one for listening too much to what other people think about an individual. So many times when I was younger I'd meet someone new whom I already hated! Why did I hate them? Because somebody had told me they were no good – they were a liar, a twister, a shyster, or just not a very nice person. So I'd often have this preconceived idea before the person even opened their mouth. With the benefit of experience, I now know that this was totally wrong and should never happen. So don't form an opinion about somebody because of what you've heard, and certainly *never* form an opinion about someone from what you've read in the newspapers.

I've also learned that, as the show progresses, you see people start off like a house on fire and then fall by the wayside. Then you see some who start off very slowly and flourish later on. I don't often get it wrong in the elimination process, and I stand by the fact that those who are left in the final few episodes are the real contenders – no doubt about it.

I might fancy some person as a finalist in the early stages, but I'm wise enough to know not to block out the others. And, yes, every single year, throughout the course of the process, I *do* change my mind just like the weather. But isn't that what it's all about – giving people the opportunity over a period of twelve weeks to show what they can do? Wouldn't every employer like to have twelve weeks to interview somebody and set them tasks before they employ them?

Thousands of people apply for *The Apprentice* every year and, because of the strict BBC guidelines on compliance, we have to make sure that everybody across the country gets a chance of entering, and that's why the auditioning process takes a couple of weeks. Candidates come to our Manchester, Birmingham and London venues for interviews. Thousands upon thousands of people are interviewed by the production company (with assistance from some human resources experts) and eventually we get down to 150 contenders, who are invited to supply more detailed CVs and are sometimes invited back for further interviews. At this stage, I am informed about some of the contenders simply by way of their CVs and a few photographs. And though it's rather difficult to do, we finally get down to the sixteen candidates whom we feel are suitable for the process.

Even before we do that, it is important to inform the candidates about what they're letting themselves in for. We get in touch with them and remind them that they're going to be spending a considerable amount of time away from their family life. This is something that I would find very difficult to do. In fact, when I used to travel to the Far East in my earlier Amstrad days, being away from my home and family left me with an awful hollow feeling. And this has affected some people who have entered *The Apprentice* process in the past. Therefore, it's very important for us to ensure that they fully understand this and have a kind of cooling-off period in which they can have a really good think about it, to consider that, if they're successful in the process, they could be away from home for quite a few weeks without any real contact with their families. Having given the potential candidates this warning, we have had a few people, quite understandably, politely pull out.

On top of this, we ensure that the candidates are healthy and have no problems in their lives. They are told in detail what to expect once they're seen on TV and how it will change their lives. We advise them that the media will hunt them, and in some cases their family and friends. Again, sometimes, quite understandably, some of them decide to pull out at this stage.

Of course, with *Junior Apprentice*, we had an even stronger duty of care to make sure that the young people, sixteen- and seventeen-year-olds, were treated correctly and not exploited. We followed the strict compliance guidelines, which specified the hours they were allowed to work, the accommodation they were allowed to stay in, and a lot of other stuff.

And hats off to the BBC and the production company, Talkback Thames, they laid on a mentor and confidant for each of the candidates, who were treated with kid gloves. I'm happy that no criticism whatsoever could be aimed at the BBC or the production company, or indeed me, for exploiting young people. The programme turned out to be a blinding success, so much so that a new eight-episode version was commissioned.

And so, based upon this very painstaking process of elimination, we end up with our sixteen candidates (or twelve, in the case of *Junior Apprentice*). I emphasise that I have still not spoken to any of them at this point. I meet them in the flesh for the first time when they come into that boardroom in episode one.

I guess many of you who watch the programme would say, 'How is it that the candidates make the same mistakes year after year? I mean, you would imagine that, like us, the viewers, they have seen the programme before – yet it seems they never learn and fall for the same old stuff every time.'

I can explain this very simply. The tension that is created in them by their desire to succeed makes them think and act irrationally sometimes. What fascinates me more is that they don't seem to cotton on to the fact that if your team wins, you survive, so you need to be a team player rather than jockey for position. But the opposite tends to happen. As viewers will know, after a task has been set, a lot of the contestants spend time undermining the project leader, undermining the task in hand and being nonproductive. Yet if they were to just do what they're told to do – focus on the task and work together as a team – they would be winners, and *none* of them would be fired.

What am I thinking in that boardroom when I see the same mistakes being made time and time again? Well, of course, it is very frustrating, but sometimes I'm also very surprised when someone pulls a rabbit out of the hat, selling an amazing amount of goods or coming up with a fantastic advertising campaign. So there are surprises in both directions.

The success of *The Apprentice* is a bit mind-boggling. In fact, people can't understand why each year the audience grows, or at least maintains its very high level. It's mind-boggling because, after all, as some people say, it's the same thing every time: you set them tasks, they run around in the street, buying stuff, selling stuff, pitching, advertising – we've seen it all before. The thing that keeps it fresh is that the candidates are all different, and one of the greatest things that the BBC and Talkback Thames have done over the years is to not fall into the trap of trying to replicate the types of candidate.

We've had some fantastic contestants over the years – people such as Paul Torrisi, Saira Khan, Tim Campbell, Tre Azam, Syed Ahmed, Stuart Baggs ('the brand') and Kate Hopkins. The public loves these sorts of characters, but the biggest mistake one could ever make in auditioning new people is to try to replicate them – viewers would see through that very quickly. The good news is that the programme has new characters every year, and it never fails to amaze me the fascinating array of people you come across.

Each series creates a new character. Take my dear and loyal associate Margaret Mountford. She decided she was going to give up *The Apprentice* because she wanted to further her academic studies, and a lot of people were sad to see her go; indeed, to this day, a lot of people still say they miss Margaret. But she has been replaced by another wonderful character, Karren Brady. Now, you couldn't have two more different personalities: Margaret has her famous expressions and sharp snipes, while Karren has a different way of going about things, bringing her wealth of business experience into play. Both are great assets to the programme, but each are very different.

Now, some people say that the people applying for *The Apprentice* are just TV wannabes, and it's true to say that, at the audition stage, we do get a fair share of these. But over the years we've become very experienced in sifting these people out. Nevertheless, being on TV does have an effect on you. It's human nature, I suppose. You get to like seeing yourself on TV; you get to like the fact that people recognise you, and you want more of it. Indeed, some of the candidates who didn't win have succeeded in a media career. Saira Khan, for example, has had a few television shows of her own. But, generally speaking, the apprentices have been there for the opportunity to win the prize of the £100,000-a-year job working for me.

The past winners have done quite well and, on average, have stayed with me for over two years. In most cases, they have then gone off and started a business of their own – and of course that's what it's all about.

I'm quite happy with that because my reasoning for wanting to do *The Apprentice* in the first place was as a follow-on from the work I was doing trying to promote enterprise – speaking at schools and universities to try to instil an enterprise culture into young people. I find that *The Apprentice* is a way of doing that in a light-hearted way. One of the main reasons I continue to do *The Apprentice* is because of the junior version. I think it is so important to capture that audience and inspire them. I kind of get a kick out of it, thinking I'm doing a good service for the younger population. It fascinates me to see how enterprising and bright some of these youngsters are, and I'm constantly, but quietly, searching for something in them that echoes what I had in my early days. It *is* very rewarding.

There is no question in my mind, and indeed it has been stated by politicians, that *The Apprentice* has made business and enterprise something young people aspire to. Everywhere I go, I am surrounded by young people who stop and talk to me, telling me their ideas, telling me how much they love the programme. They talk about some of the tasks that are set, the mistakes they see people make, how good some of the candidates are, which ones they like, which ones they hate. The programme has performed a service, without a shadow of a doubt and, for that reason, I'm happy to have been involved in it. I know for a fact that in most schools now, though it's not part of the official curriculum, groups of students are set *Apprentice* tasks which last over a period of weeks. It has become a common practice, and I get lots of letters from schools asking me to send a signed poster to congratulate the winning teams for their efforts. This tells me that what I had in mind – to inspire the young – is paying off. It *must* be if schools use the process so frequently.

On the subject of inspiring the young, I'm glad that during filming I've restrained myself from my sometimes impatient behaviour – unlike some other TV personalities! The tremendous influx of celebrity chefs has brought a couple of even more short-tempered characters to our screens. I think the bubbly Jamie Oliver was one of the first of the new generation of celebrity chefs that kick-started the cooking revolution on TV. Whoever would have thought that watching someone prepare food would be interesting? But it is! And, again, I guess it's relatively cheap to produce a programme like that. I think Jamie has done a fantastic job. Contrast his cheerfulness with the more temperamental Marco Pierre White or the loud-mouthed Gordon Ramsay. Why do people watch his shows? Do people tune in to see an exquisite dish being prepared, or are they reality shows and is the appeal really the sensationalism of what goes on behind the scenes in the kitchen, with Gordon Ramsay effing and blinding at people and them screaming back?

Now, I could be leading with my chin here, as people might say, 'Hey, Sugar, isn't that a bit hypocritical, as you're always bawling out your apprentices?' However, if you watch carefully, you'll see that I never use the F-word on TV. I'm pleased about that because, as I've said, a lot of *Apprentice* fans are youngsters, and I consider myself a bit of a role model. I just wish people like Wayne Rooney would wake up and realise that they have the power to be the same.

By the way, *Masterchef*, another successful cookery show, has been made into an elimination process similar to *The Apprentice*. What started out as a BBC2 programme has now become prime-time viewing. It has grown bigger and bigger and has become more popular.

I have been asked many times whether I've thought about making a *senior* version of *The Apprentice* for people who have been made redundant and are finding it hard to get a job because of their age. It's an interesting concept and it *is* workable. On the other hand, I wonder whether, with far more mature people, you would get that level of competitiveness and impulsive naïvety that contributes to the entertainment value of the main series. Personally, I doubt it, as they would be grown men and women who, shall we say, have mellowed. More to the point, there would be too much Sugar on TV, and the BBC would not be up for it for that reason alone.

On a more light-hearted note, it also seems *The Apprentice* has become the subject of sweepstakes within companies, where the office staff bet on who's going to win. I am told that productivity on a Thursday morning can be affected, as staff discuss the previous night's episode. Well, there's no harm done and it's nice to know that people are getting some enjoyment out of it.

Apart from the satisfaction I get from the impact of *The Apprentice*, I would be a liar if I said that I didn't like the way that I've become famous and recognisable in the street. And I have to say that the majority of people that I bump into are very complimentary. Of course you get the odd idiot, normally a drunk, who shouts out, 'You're fired!', which is pathetic – as if I hadn't heard that a thousand times before – and my response usually makes them shrink and want to hide themselves away, particularly if there are some onlookers around who've seen what a prat they've made of themselves.

But even that is better than being recognised by some of the thuggish Spurs fans I encountered when I was chairman of the football club – all I got there was abuse.

You can play the fame game as much as you want to. I do go to certain functions or places where of course I will be recognised. I don't do it deliberately and I do keep the number of those visits down. However, there are some people who play on their fame and parade themselves around for the sole purpose of being recognised, chased and photographed. In fact, there are quite a lot of people out there like that. I saw a very funny message on Twitter from Peter Jones from *Dragons' Den*, communicating with Duncan

Bannatyne. Peter suggested that Duncan, a man who can afford to fly by private jet, flies by Ryanair or EasyJet not because he wants to save money but because he enjoys being seen as the celebrity amongst the other 200-odd passengers! Rather humorous, I thought at the time but, you know, many a true word is spoken in jest.

More recently, Ann made me laugh when she told me that she was at the shopping parade in Chigwell, in the newsagent's, paying the bill. In the shop was Joey Essex, the dumb twit from *The Only Way Is Essex*. He was there on the pretext of buying a bottle of water, but Ann said that anyone could see from the way he was standing and looking around that he was waiting to be recognised. How funny is that? Pathetic too.

In fact, one of the reasons I quite like going to America is that no one knows me there. I can walk into a supermarket and have a look at all of the things on offer. I can go into the big department stores and walk around and keep up to date with modern-day products – the latest technology, for example – and no one will bat an eye. I don't want to come across as a snob, but unfortunately I can't do that at the moment in the UK because the salespeople come up and pester me. They start schmoozing and talking a load of patronising bollocks. Not only is it embarrassing, it's a little bit sad, because I always have to be on my guard. The mischievous media love stories like, for example, 'Spotted – Alan Sugar tries on a bright-red shirt with yellow dots.' Not that I would ever buy such a shirt, but you get my drift. Of course, you'd say and I'd say, 'Who cares?' But some of the media are so pathetic that they write about trivia like that. This aspect of being famous is not so good, and that's why in America, or in the rest of Europe, I enjoy being able to walk around freely.

I can tell you with all sincerity that fame has not gone to my head. I am very conscious of not wanting to talk down to anybody or ignore people I knew in the past. I hate the type of person who does that, and I have to say that no one could ever accuse me of being like that. I still mix with the same group of friends I've had for many years, some of whom I've known since I was sixteen years old. I have not taken on a load more media friends, apart from those whose company I genuinely enjoy, and those are a very limited few.

Another enjoyable side of the TV business has been to see how the programme is physically put together. This is a science in itself and it has fascinated me to watch these professionals putting it together. It may be interesting for you to hear that each and every episode of The Apprentice can have up to 130 hours of film – all this to produce a one-hour programme.

Why is there so much? Well, we have camera crews following the two teams around on the streets while they're on a task, as well as camera crews at the locations where they're doing their business deals or presentations. We have camera crews following Nick and Karren, a camera crew back at the house and, of course, a camera crew in the boardroom. All that footage adds up.

Multiply that by the twelve episodes and you've got thousands of hours. All that footage is stored on what is effectively a giant hard-disk drive, then loaded into an editing suite. And eventually, bit by bit, word by word, it is examined and edited by some very talented people, who shrink the programme down to one hour.

There are things, as I said in the previous chapter, that I could never do – for instance, become a concert pianist or a great artist. The editing team provides another example of a talent I don't have – the ability to see how piecing together footage of the candidates with some film of a plane going through the sky leaving a trail, the moon rising over the horizon, or light glistening on water with ducks going by will add to the drama of the programme. These behind-the-scenes people are part of what makes

The Apprentice the most professionally polished piece of entertainment.

Because I've been involved in *The Apprentice* for about seven years, I've seen the same people each season working on the programme, and it proves what I am going to be banging on about in this book – how experience, consistency and hard work pay off. I've seen people who started off as young junior directors take more senior positions because not only have they learned what to do but, more importantly, they've learned what not to do. They know what works and they know what doesn't. *The Apprentice* is an award-winning programme – in fact, I think that we've won every single national television award going, except of course the one dished out by ITV. I'll leave you to work out why perhaps that one has eluded us.

So, is *The Apprentice* a reality TV programme? Well, I guess it may be, since it's based on real facts and real-life situations. Everything you see is unscripted and unplanned. Of course, the tasks have been developed and well thought out in consultation with me; however, every word that comes out of the candidates' mouths is their own. The same applies to everything I say, and indeed everything that Nick and Karren say. So I will concede that it's a reality TV programme, but one firmly based on business.

Do onlookers like Stephen Fry think it's good value? No. Do people like Stuart Rose and Terry Leahy, the ex-CEOs of Marks & Spencer and Tesco, think it reflects business reality? No. They say, 'That's not business.' In fact, Stuart Rose once said, 'If I spoke to my people like that, I'd be given my P45.'

I wonder whether that's a bit of sour grapes. Ann sometimes tells me that I shouldn't worry about it. 'You are exactly what you're like in real life on that television programme – you're not acting, and people *like* you. Some people get a bit jealous of you and would like to be in your position on that programme, and when they come out with these jibes it's really their way of saying, "I think I could do a better job."'

Well, plenty of people have tried to do a better job. There have been lots of copies of *The Apprentice*. Of course, they can't copy the format exactly because there'd be legal problems. However, some of the commercial channels have tried to put on some very similar programmes, and they've failed. Do I get some feeling of satisfaction over that? Well, I guess I do, simply because they are competition and a threat, but I only have to watch the first episode of a copycat *Apprentice* to know it's doomed. And it's doomed because it lacks the polish, the professionalism, the precision and the hard work that goes into making a first-class television programme.

I've learned by now not to worry about snipers, but you can imagine how angry and frustrated I was when I was accused of using *The Apprentice* for political reasons. It was such nonsense. And this brings me on to a modern-day issue in television known as product placement. Now, the BBC, of course, has to be very careful that somebody like me doesn't do a television programme in order to promote my own business. You may have noticed that there has never been any reference to any of my companies on the programme – their names haven't been mentioned or shown on the outsides of the buildings. I've never spoken about our products in specific terms – and this is all because of compliance at the BBC.

I don't have a problem with this. I think it is absolutely right that a television programme should not in any way promote a person's product, be it mine or anyone else's. However, I did have one row with the BBC during the first series. I was told that the BBC's compliance department was worried that I had an e-mailer phone on the boardroom table. 'Oh no, Sir Alan, you can't have a product you manufacture in the show – that would be against compliance rules.'

I replied, 'Whose boardroom is this meant to be?'

They responded, 'Why, yours, Sir Alan.'

I said, 'Do you expect me to have a competitor's phone on my boardroom table, rather than a phone I manufacture?'

Realisation dawned. 'Oh, right, Sir Alan – see your point. That makes sense now.'

I remember having rows with the production company in series one of *The Apprentice* about the use of my friend Mr Al Fayed's Harrods. They insisted that the Harrods brand name could not be shown. I said to them, 'This is getting ridiculous. Harrods is a British institution – everyone knows Harrods, like everyone knows Rolls-Royce. And that's why you like showing me riding around in my Rolls-Royce. You have to draw the line somewhere, otherwise I'd have to ride around on a golf cart.'

The same rules about promoting products exist in many of the commercial channels. However, new legislation came out recently whereby product placement *is* allowed, in recognition that the commercial TV channels need to be able to enhance their revenues – not least because the Sky+ advert-skipping factor may have started to hit home.

In America, product placement has been going on for a long time. Simon Cowell was seen on *American Idol* sitting at the panellists' desk while in front of him was a large glass bearing the Coca-Cola logo. Serena Williams somehow manages to put her Gatorade bottle in front of her when she's interviewed by the BBC at Wimbledon. I'm surprised that the BBC haven't put a stop to this but, then again, I'm often surprised at how naïve the BBC is sometimes.

When I first heard about the compliance regulations, I was told that I could not show anything to do with my businesses in *The Apprentice*. I accepted it and understood the concept, but it sent me on a little mission. I started to notice that on programmes like *EastEnders*, when the camera zoomed in on one of the character's mobile phones, as they often do when they're showing text messages, the brand name Nokia kept showing up all the time – or so it appeared to me. Mischievous Alan started to write letters to the compliance people at the BBC, stating that while *I* was playing by the rules, I'd like to know why Nokia phones were being shown every single time a character was calling or texting someone. It was my opinion that this was not at all deliberate on the part of the BBC, but that perhaps somebody was doing some kind of deal.

I also noticed, when I was watching Ricky Gervais's *Extras*, the appearance of a laptop computer – a business which, of course, I'm in. I saw the brand name Mesh on the rear of the computer, in a position where it doesn't normally appear on commercial products in the marketplace. In other words, it looked like a label had deliberately been placed on it. In fact, it looked pathetic; you could actually see it was a sticky label. I'm probably the only one who would have noticed such a minor detail because, as I say, I have this little hobby of checking out BBC programmes where products are deliberately placed.

Again, let me exonerate the powers that be at the BBC by saying that, bearing in mind the thousands of programmes they produce, they can't be held responsible for a couple of people who might be doing the odd deal here and there. And when I say deal, I don't mean actual money changing hands. Instead, perhaps, in order to keep costs down, items like computers might be donated for free, as long as the brands are shown.

I must have started World War III at the BBC, because it seemed as if Nokia phones were immediately removed from *EastEnders*. As for *Extras*, there were only two series, which had already been transmitted, so that matter was closed.

I have to say that the production company who make *The Apprentice* are so on the ball on this subject that they meticulously ensure they can prove they paid commercial rates for anything that could be construed as product placement. It is amazing how many people approach both me and the production company and ask whether we could include certain products or services.

Nevertheless, my stalkers at the *Daily Mail* tried to stir up trouble in the seventh season of *The Apprentice*, when we had an episode where the apprentices had to produce some mobile phone applications. This was an excellent task; very topical and in keeping with the twenty-first-century technology used on the show. Of course, it's a no-brainer that to perform this task the candidates would have to use mobile phones throughout the show. Devices were used from BlackBerry, HTC and Apple and, indeed, as part of the show, the consultants chosen to help the candidates used Apple laptops as development tools. Indeed, when the show was broadcast, an array of these laptops was shown, each bearing the famous Apple logo on the rear.

Despite the variety of machines used, the *Daily Mail* decided they had struck gold because, several months earlier on Twitter, I had declared that I prefer a BlackBerry to an iPhone. I think they were hoping to find that the use of a BlackBerry on the programme was deliberate product placement, arranged by me! They tried every trick in the book. They phoned BlackBerry and my companies to see if there was any commercial link between us, to see if I was being paid anything or getting any special favours – all to no avail. Despite that, they made fools of themselves by publishing a stupid article suggesting the BBC was guilty of product placement in respect of BlackBerry, when in fact it was clear for all to see that there were loads of shots of other manufacturers' products.

The fact remained: how the hell are you supposed to make a TV programme about applications for mobile phones without showing the phones?

I look forward with interest to seeing how product placement will be gradually introduced as part of TV programming on the commercial channels, and whether it is abused. Are we suddenly to see, in *Coronation Street*, for example, the use of famous branded foods and drinks? Will the judges on *The X Factor* be allowed to display Coca-Cola glasses on the table? Will Louis Walsh be able to wear a great big Rolex watch or Kelly Rowland an outfit bearing the Chanel logo? I guess it's a case of watch this space.

My skipping the adverts when using Sky+ is really going to kick in big-time soon, as I've also heard that in order to help boost the revenues of commercial companies, advertising breaks are soon going to be allowed to become longer – up to five minutes. More power to the elbow of Sky+ and the new YouView devices, I would say, but it also means that when production companies make a programme for transmission (on a commercial channel) in a one-hour slot, the actual content of the programme, which is currently forty-six minutes, will drop to something like forty minutes, while twenty minutes of it will be advertising.

Now, here's a cause for concern. BSkyB and other broadcasters make loads of money from advertising and they might start to realise that by providing the means to skip adverts, they're shooting themselves in the foot. The worrying thought is that, in this digital age, it *would* be possible for BSkyB or any other broadcaster to implement adverts in such a way that it's not possible to skip them when a Sky+ recording is played back.

So there is to be less real content and more advertising in TV shows. I think that says it all. In fact, the recent programme with me and Piers Morgan kicking around in Florida (and in my old council flat in Hackney) contained so much good material that ITV, at the last minute, extended it to be a seventy-five-minute programme, in order to net around sixty minutes of actual content.

There are some things about being on TV that I don't like. For a start, I don't like getting up at five o'clock in the morning to meet the apprentices somewhere on location to set a task – that's for sure. I'm not a happy bunny on those days and I end up feeling I should apologise for being in a real strop to the production people, who work relentlessly.

I don't like hanging around waiting for things to be ready for filming, though I do realise that this is because they are perfectionists and want to get the lighting and the conditions just right. They want to get just the right shot of the candidates having their post mortem in the café, or answering the phone in the morning.

Another thing I don't like, believe it or not, is all the luvvy bashes, award ceremonies and all that stuff. It gets on my nerves and I can't be bothered to attend most of them. Sometimes I'm persuaded to turn up when the programme is up for a prestigious award, many of which, as I've already stated, we have won.

I'm also pestered to go on every single panel show and chat show. Again, I turn most of them down, with the exception of Jonathan Ross's programme, because I like Jonathan and I get on with him. I think he's very funny, and of course it does help promote the programme when a series is about to start. Since Jonathan left the BBC, I went on Graham Norton's show once, because he's another man whom I admire tremendously – he is brilliant, absolutely brilliant. I have never met anybody with such a quick wit. And, again, that guy is not scripted – he's as fast as lightning. I love his humour – it has just the right balance – and that's why I agreed to go on his show.

But, in general, I don't really like participating in shows where there are other, to put it bluntly, big egos. On Graham Norton's show, I had the misfortune of being there at the same time as the comedian Lee Mack. And whilst the programme that was eventually broadcast was relatively well edited, the fact of the matter was that each and every time I tried to open my mouth, Lee Mack jumped in, interfered and demolished my flow of words. He was doing his best to disrupt me in front of a live audience, something I'm not used to. I'm sure he was doing this because, as a comedian, old habits die hard and he couldn't help himself.

On one of the Jonathan Ross shows, I had the bad luck to be there at the same time as that funny comedian Johnny Vegas. What made it worse was that I'd said to Jonathan, 'How about if I bring the wife along and she sits in the green room?'

He thought it was a rather nice idea. 'Yes, let the public see Lady Ann – why not?'

Well, I really felt for her because, while I was on stage talking to Jonathan, all I could hear was Johnny Vegas shouting across the studio, interrupting what Jonathan and I were saying, shooting his mouth off and making stupid remarks, interfering in the programme and embarrassing poor Ann, who's a very shy person. Fortunately, the editing of the programme cut out most of it, but it is disruptive and another example of how other celebrities jockey for position when there's a television camera about, in order to show themselves doing what they're supposedly best known for.

Adrian Chiles, who became a household name on *The One Show*, has become a pal of mine because of the great work that he did on the *You're Fired* programme. I went on that show a few times during its infancy, and they called me back for the last show he did before he left to go to ITV. I remember having a joke with him, saying that I'd been sitting around in the green room waiting to come on and there were pictures plastered on the wall of all the guests that he'd had on the show since it started – and the only one that was missing was me! And I was one of his first guests. It got a few laughs and it helped bid him a very fond farewell from the BBC.

All in all, I don't mind helping my new-found television friends out but, generally, I will turn away most of the opportunities. I now know that putting together a bunch of big egos is trouble. That's why I decided not to do *Celebrity Apprentice* anymore. I did do a few, but the celebrities were such a handful. Now, you'd have thought that people in TV would know that the power of the programme lies in the editing, but no – throughout the making of *Celebrity Apprentice*, the contestants were constantly pushing each other out of the way to grab the limelight, always trying to position themselves at the forefront of things. It was quite amazing to see the hissy fits and the throwing-the-toys-out-of-the-pram episodes. It was a phenomenon I'd never seen in the main *Apprentice* series, but these people, who considered themselves celebrities, would not put up with certain things. They'd have constant arguments amongst themselves and take immediate dislikes to people in their teams. They were a really hard bunch to control, and although the whole thing was being done for charity, I was astounded at the amount of rows and backbiting that went on.

So that is why I don't appear on many other shows. And before anyone tries to have a snipe at me, I'm honest enough to tell you that I will appear on certain programmes if it's to my advantage. Indeed, when I decided to write my autobiography, I was dragged around to a few shows I wouldn't normally appear on, mainly to publicise the book. Sorry about that, but at least I'm admitting it.

People often ask me, 'When will you give up doing *The Apprentice*?'

I'll give it up when I no longer enjoy doing it, or when I feel that the programme is not delivering what it set out to. Of course, there's also a certain phenomenon we often see on television, when the key actors or writers decide they no longer want to do their very successful show because they feel that either the character they've created or the theme of the programme will become repetitive and boring – so they decide to get out at the top.

One example of this was Ricky Gervais with that great show *The Office*, which ran for two series plus a Christmas special. He then decided he was no longer going to do any more of them – he'd made the point. I'm sure he wanted *The Office* to be a classic series that would go down in history, which indeed it has. John Cleese did the same thing with *Fawlty Towers*, of which (though it seemed like more) there were only twelve episodes. And they most definitely *were* all-time classics. It's interesting that, despite it being one of the greatest ever sitcoms, it was originally turned down by the BBC. What's more, Cleese said it would never have even got off the ground at ITV. There's a message there: if you have a vision, persist with it rather than give in to the wet blankets who say, 'It won't work.' Rather like I did with *Junior Apprentice* when the BBC initially turned my idea down.

Now, I'm not sure that one could apply the same reasoning to *The Apprentice*, but then again, a hard commercial fact is that if or when its audience starts to drop off, the media will create a groundswell of ill feeling. They'll start by sneering that it's losing its audience, then they'll moan that it's becoming boring. And, usually, when that happens, the broadcaster will shut it down, just as Channel 4 did with *Big Brother*. It just so happens that when the seventh season of *The Apprentice* kicked off in May 2011, the first episode drew in a record audience that peaked at 8.4 million viewers, which was more than a million up on the previous year. So maybe it's not yet time for me to throw in the towel.

If I *do* throw in the towel, I won't be desperate to get back on TV. One of the side effects of reality TV programmes like *Strictly Come Dancing* and *I'm A Celebrity, Get Me Out Of Here* is that they have enabled broadcasters to take advantage of what I would call the regeneration of old celebrities – or you *could* call it the deployment of the Z-listers. As we have witnessed over recent years, people who were once famous as, for example, footballers or TV personalities suddenly appear again on our screens. I guess, from their point of view, they don't *know* anything else apart from the business they were in, and they need the money as they're no longer employed in their conventional roles. I'm fortunate that I don't rely upon my television appearances for an income, but these people *do* – and from the broadcasters' point of view, they can get the talent relatively cheaply (compared to the going rate they'd have to pay for top-class, fashionable talent).

I suppose that for most people who've been involved in the

entertainment industry all their lives, being on TV is a bug. It's in their blood; it's something they're driven to do. One can imagine old-time Hollywood stars, in the winters of their lives, sitting back in their parlours and watching the films or shows they appeared in. I can't see me ever doing that. Obviously I *do* see the programmes I'm involved in before they go on air, but I'm not one of those people who sits and watches them over and over again.

Maybe in my old age I'll pull out series one of *The Apprentice* and sit back in the retirement home, Zimmer frame to one side, and watch the young Alan Sugar on TV. Who knows?

7

The Tiny Fork Diet

My weight gains and losses, and my latest diet innovation!

Over the course of forty years – and I'm not kidding you here – I must have put on about thirty stone in total! Not all at once, I should add, but I've yo-yoed up and down in weight at various times, on some occasions gaining as much as three stone – and then losing it.

Fortunately, my weight gain has never got too out of hand. I spend a lot of time in America and it's awful to see so many obese people there – particularly children. Even in the UK, obesity has become a big problem. Recent figures published by the government state that up to 80,000 people are on benefits and unable to work because they are obese. This, of course, is also a drain on the NHS, with obesity-related illness estimated to cost the NHS £4.2 billion a year. I found out that in August 2010 alone there were 42,360 incapacity benefit claimants with alcohol addiction, 37,480 with a drug dependency and 1,800 who were obese.

Obesity, as anyone who knows about putting on weight and having a craving for food will tell you, is a disease, no different from alcoholism or an addiction to cigarettes or drugs. It is interesting to examine why people get this way. Is it, as some have suggested, that the advertising of fast food by certain retail organisations has encouraged unhealthy eating? I believe there was a big row in the United States a few years ago involving McDonald's, where lawyers jumped on the bandwagon to bring some semi-derisory court cases against them, blaming the incapacitation of their clients (due to their excessive weight) on McDonald's marketing.

Psychologists will tell you that it is hard to work out what goes on in the minds of people who suffer with obesity caused by overeating, or indeed of those who suffer from the complete opposite conditions – anorexia and bulimia. Psychologically, overeating and anorexia are two sides of the same coin.

Nevertheless, putting psychological aspects to one side, there is a responsibility for fast-food companies, parents, schoolteachers and the government to instil in people the necessity to be careful with what they eat.

To a certain extent, governments worldwide have attempted to bring these matters to the attention of consumers. Take food labelling, for example, where 'nutritional facts' printed on the packaging is now a mandatory requirement. To counter any negative perceptions, food companies have jumped on the bandwagon with some labelling of their own, to try to imply that their foods are more healthy – 'virtually fat-free', 'low salt content', 'sugar-free'. (I bet those of you who are not enjoying this book wish you were Sugar-free right now!) Yet despite that, I believe that most people are not conscious of what makes them put on weight.

I can speak with authority here because I often used to ask myself, 'What is it that's making me put on all this weight?' Eventually I realised it was almost always associated with my state of mind – stress or aggravation. Some people say that when they're aggravated and have problems, it puts them *off* eating – no such luck in my case. It's the first thing I do to relieve stress – turn to food. On the other hand, when I have no problems, when I have a clear head and I'm happy about things in life, then I don't eat to excess. I'm sure any psychologist would say that I've hit the nail on the head in that it's all to do with my mental state.

To make things worse, I'm one of those people who only have to *look* at food to put on weight. Unfortunately, my children have the same genes, and my wife is the same. We look enviously at other people who are as skinny as rakes but eat as much as they want! I've asked many doctors why this is, but none of them have really given me a good explanation other than: 'Well, it's their metabolism; it's the way they are made.' Perhaps this is one of life's mysteries, which one day will be cracked. If someone could find the chromosome that distinguishes between people who can eat as much as they want without putting on weight and the likes of me and my family, and then come out with some genetic engineering treatment, there'd be another Facebook or Google fortune out there to be made.

I'm lucky that I have the willpower to lose the weight efficiently when I put my mind to it. My resolve sometimes shocks and amazes onlookers who, having not seen me for a five- or six-week period, discover that I've taken the weight off again. I suppose I am blessed with a determination to get things done. Once I make up my mind to do something, that's it – I do it. Is that because of my personality? Possibly. I remember, as a kid, being a dunce at maths. I used to muck about and joke around in class. One day, however, reality hit home when I realised that without a maths GCE, I had no chance of getting a serious job. At the same time, my teacher, Mr Grant, announced that we were about to embark on the complex subject of calculus, and even the boffins started to huff and puff in anticipation of the difficult times that lay ahead. I took this as a sign that calculus was tough and decided to turn my mind to it. I got it straight away and, to cut a long story short, I became the calculus king of the class – to the amazement of Mr Grant, who had given up on me years earlier. The same might be said about the recent pilot's exams I passed. My wife can't understand why I put myself through all this learning so late in life. I do it because it's a challenge. I don't *need* to do it, as I'm not a commercial pilot and I don't depend on it for income, but when asked why, I say, 'Because it is there to do.' It's a matter of engaging your mind, as well as having the grit and determination not to fail. That's what's needed to achieve most things, and I guess the same applies to going on a diet. It's all in the head.

The food companies spend a fortune researching how to make foods low in calories or fat. There is talk of using nanotechnology to genetically modify foods so that they taste the same but contain no salt or no fat. Interestingly enough, a recent survey on this sub-ject received in a negative response. I guess the sensible among us know that eating things that have been engineered or tweaked can't really be good for you in the long term, even if they taste identical to the original version. All the same, I am guessing that Coca-Cola sell as much Diet Coke and Coke Zero as they do the regular stuff.

As well as the so-called slimming foods themselves, there are the organisations, such as WeightWatchers, and there are hundreds of different diets out there (usually accompanied by books, CDs and DVDs) based on the dieting theories of various 'experts', such as the Grapefruit Diet, the Atkins Diet, the F-Plan Diet, the Cambridge Diet, the GI Diet. My wife Ann and some friends have tried these out, but when you cut through the smoke and mirrors of these so-called magical diets, it all boils down to some form of discipline – for example, not mixing carbohydrates with protein – or they are simply low-calorie diets in disguise. So, on the basis of not liking bullshitters, I've never tried these diets, as my semi-technical mind saw right through them. However, one thing I've learned is never to try to impose my thoughts on others who believe in them, because if it makes them happy to go about things in this way, well, good luck to them, if they get to achieve their goal in the end.

So, to put it simply, my view is that you can forget about buying the latest diet book because they're all trying to repackage very simple principles – it's all about what you stuff in your mouth and how many calories you burn per day. A doctor once explained to me, very meticulously, that an average man naturally burns 2,000–2,400 calories a day. Let's take, for example, an office-bound person who doesn't do much exercise – if that person eats 3,000 calories a day, they *will* end up putting on weight. And the only way that person can lose weight is to take in fewer calories than their body burns. The doctor also told me that every 3,000-calorie deficit equates to a weight loss of approximately one pound. So, in simple terms, if a man who burns around 2,200 calories a day sticks himself on a diet of 1,200 calories a day, in three days, theoretically, he will lose a pound, and in thirty days he will lose ten pounds. This, of course, assumes he has the willpower to maintain an intake of 1,200 calories a day.

At this point, I would like to state the obvious and make it clear to everyone that I'm not a doctor. I'm not dishing out medical advice, so anything you read here on this subject, you will need to go and check out with your own doctor or get a professional opinion. I'm merely expressing my own opinion and sharing my own experiences here, so I don't want any ambulance-chasing claims in the future – there is my arse-covering disclaimer in black and white.

So what regime have *I* adopted over the past years to keep a relatively constant weight? Well, it comes down to simple arithmetic in the end. I like food, but you can't get much for 1,200 calories. In fact, you can't get much for 2,200 calories, so even if you *do* manage to get down to your target weight, you're constantly battling to make sure you don't stick it back on again, as I did with the yo-yo effect I mentioned earlier.

This is where exercise comes in. For the past few years, I've been a big cycling enthusiast and, going back further that that, I've always liked playing tennis – singles rather than doubles. I also tried golf once, and I have to say I'd rather watch paint dry. To me, it's just boring. Then again, if people love it and get enjoyment out of it, good luck to them – I'm afraid it's not for me, hitting that little white ball around in the burning-hot sun, hanging around and arguing with people about whether you can go on the green or off the green. It makes me laugh when people say, 'It's good exercise; we don't use a golf cart or a caddy – we walk.' Yeah, they might walk, but then they go into the clubhouse and stuff their faces full of sandwiches, crisps and beer.

As well as exercising, I have become a walking encyclopaedia on the calorific content of food products. I can look at a tableful of food and know what I should eat and what I shouldn't eat, and exactly what numbers are going in my mouth. But it's amazing how uninformed some people are. I remember my long-time colleague Bob Watkins deciding that he would go on a bit of a diet. We often used to go to the Far East, where we would work very hard during the day. In the evenings, however, to put it bluntly, we used to stuff our faces with a load of Chinese food (or steaks if we were in Japan) and a little bit of booze as well. And we were both susceptible to weight gain. Bob decided one morning that he was going to start on a diet. We were in Taiwan, at breakfast, and he ordered not one, but two glasses of fresh orange juice.

'This is my new regime – this is healthy stuff,' he told me.

I said to him, 'You're right, it is healthy; but, Bob, you've decided you're going on a 1,000-calorie-a-day diet, and you're about to consume about 250 calories in orange juice alone.'

He pooh-poohed that one. 'Nah, you don't know what you're talking about – this is healthy.'

Well, he had his own way of going about losing weight, and he succeeded in the end but, like me, he was also fond of his food and I think he suffered the yo-yo effect over the years.

Weight became my topic of discussion on many occasions – I must have bored the pants off people when I was on a diet, telling them what I was up to. I remember that to incentivise some work colleagues I would have a bet with them that they could not lose weight. The foreman at our Southend factory, Norman, was, to say the least, a rather chubby chap. I remember once at a staff Christmas party suggesting he should lose some weight. His wife told me that he had tried everything, but he just couldn't get his head around it. I told him that if he lost five stone in a certain period of time (I know it sounds a lot, but he was a *big* boy), I would buy him two new suits. He jumped at the challenge and, to be fair, he did it – he'd been incentivised to cost the boss some money and make me look a mug. The shame of it was that a few weeks later the trousers were at the tailors being let out – 'Just a tad,' said Norman at the time.

As I've said, it always surprises me how uneducated people are about food. They say, 'I'm not going to eat much; I'll just have a salad.' It turns out to be a ham and cheese salad, drowned in some kind of thick, creamy dressing. Well, sorry to tell you, mate, but that's not healthy. I mean, it's not bad – it's not as bad as, say, Kentucky Fried Chicken – but what you're eating there adds up to about 800 calories. The dressing alone is most probably about 350, never mind the ham and cheese. And, oh yeah, there are a few lettuce leaves as well – okay, you're right about those; they *do* contain very few calories.

I don't agree with diets that say that all you should eat is pro-tein – eggs, fish, meat – which you're not allowed to mix with carbohydrates. The trouble with that is, once you do, you've messed the whole thing up. I don't go along with that regime because, from experience, I have concluded that, when you finally do lose the weight, you need to be free to have a bit of everything – you cannot exclude yourself from enjoying life, otherwise you will never suc-ceed in maintaining a steady weight.

I've adopted a principle based on a seven-day plan. I'm not fussy about which days are which, but there will be at least four days out of my week when I will remain under the 2,200 calorie mark, and I will set that against perhaps a weekend or a night out when I can indulge myself beyond the 2,200 calorie mark – in other words, I keep within a total of 14,000 calories per week. And no, I don't cut out bread and sweets and all that stuff – I have a little, here and there. One thing that works in my favour is that I've never really liked desserts. Ann will vouch that, even in my plumpest days, I never had dessert after dinner at home or in a restaurant – the problem was that I used to eat too much of the other stuff!

Laying off the booze totally is impossible, but there's nothing wrong with the odd drink every now and again. I could not become a complete teetotaller, as I tend to have days when I will drink wine or spirits. Drinking can be a danger, mind you. The French word *aperitif*, I believe, means appetiser, and if ever the French got something right, then that was it. I find alcohol to be a massive appetiser – it makes me eat more than I would normally. Therefore, whenever we are out for dinner, I'm mindful not to have a drink at the bar first. Sometimes I'll start off with sparkling water or something boring like that, and switch to wine partway through the meal.

In my constant battle for self-discipline, exercise helps tremendously. For example, when I go on a sixty-mile bike ride, I burn an additional 3,300 calories (beyond the normal 2,000 calorie burn per day). In this way, I can make space for a slap-up meal. So if I did three sixty-mile bike rides during the course of my seven-day/14,000 calorie plan, this would allow me nearly 24,000 calories over the course of the week.

All a bit scientific? Well, not really – it's simple maths. Though, having said that, you *do* have to know the calorific content of everything you eat. If you're interested, go into WHSmith and buy yourself a calorie book – there are loads of them out there – which list the calorific content of all food, from branded products such as ready-meal or tin of baked beans to natural ingredients like fruit. Or, better still, get into the habit of looking at the labels of the stuff you're eating. It's all there in black and white, but be careful – they can be a bit tricky. They sometimes just show the calorific content for a 100g portion of the stuff, or for what they call a 'serving' (bear in mind that the pack may contain, for example, four or five servings), so I'm afraid the maths comes into it again.

I also have another principle and that's the 'Is it worth it?' factor.

What do I mean by that? Well, it's simple – even if you are teed up for some blowout, you need to decide whether the stuff in front of you is worth it. If not, reject it. Please excuse me, Chief Rabbi, but two Cumberland sausages, perfectly cooked, three rashers of best Danish bacon and some HP sauce in half a loaf of French bread – now, that little lot might come to 1,200 calories, but that *is* worth it! That is, as opposed to some poseur chef's Speciality of the Day, a 'chicken pot pie' that turns out to be a microwave-heated monstrosity which, when you pierce the so-called puff pastry, disgorges a load of white goo with traces of small cubes of chicken and a hint of something red that might be pieces of carrot, plus some brown thing that looks like an imploded mushroom, all simulating what the dog sicked up the other day on the carpet – also circa 1,200 calories. Now that's *not* worth it. This might touch a nerve with the owner of the restaurant, whose name I won't mention (in case I get sued), but who will recognise what I am saying.

Here's a little summary of what I steer clear of: fatty meats, chips, fried stuff, cakes, cream, sugar, butter, cheese, milk, chocolate – all of these are high-fat-content items. The things I tend to eat are: fish, chicken or lean meats, lots of salad, fruit, steamed vegetables such as broccoli, spinach and carrots – and there's nothing wrong with the odd jacket potato or boiled potatoes, just so long as they're not fried. I've got used to having sandwiches without butter, maybe with a tuna filling and a bit of salad. I've found you don't need butter and you can get used to doing without it. It is a killer, as far as I'm concerned. And some of these so-called low-fat spreads are still nevertheless *fats*, and you should steer clear of them too. You're better off not using any of them at all.

I personally cannot drink coffee or tea with no milk, so I use low-fat milk and only put in a little. I also use one of those Sweetex tablets instead of sugar, and I definitely avoid the plate of biscuits that always seems to be on the table at business meetings. I do tend to drink fizzy drinks like Diet Coke, which admittedly can't be that great for you. If you can get away with drinking just plain water, that's better still, but I guess you've got to have some sins in life.

So why is it that I'm conscious of my weight? Well, it's because I want to feel good about myself. I hate it when my clothes become tight because I'm overweight. I hate looking at myself in the mirror. I also hate being out of breath from being overweight. On the other hand, you feel just great when you've managed to get down to a reasonable fighting weight. These days, with all that exercise and a good diet, my doctors are fascinated that this sixty-four-year-old fart has a resting heart rate of forty-eight beats per minute and perfect blood pressure. When I have my six-monthly check-ups, my blood tests all show normal levels, so I must be doing something right.

I tell you – this is no bullshit now – I was in America last year and I had a little accident on my bike and banged my shoulder. I found a doctor to look at me, which is a feat in itself in America, as they're all frightened you're going to sue them. Anyway, to cut a long story, the guy decided he was going to put me through the full monty. Instead of just looking at the bruise or asking for an x-ray, he started doing an extensive range of tests. Ann sat there watching. After he took my heart rate and blood pressure, he looked a bit puzzled. He told me that there must be something wrong with his equipment, and would I mind waiting a while until he brought in another machine from a different cubicle. After repeating the test, he asked me, 'How old did you say you were?'

'Sixty-three.'

He called in one of his other doctors. 'Look at this – this man's got a heart rate of forty-eight beats per minute and he's sixty-three years old.' He turned to me. 'What do you do?'

'Cycling.'

'Well, you must be Lance Armstrong!'

It was funny and nice to hear, and it made Ann laugh, but the bloody quack was useless. He ended up giving me an injection in the shoulder, which was not needed. It was a total waste of time – I shouldn't have bothered.

I am not so foolish as to believe I'm going to succeed in maintaining my weight level for ever. I'm old enough and wise enough to have learned, from my forty-odd years of yo-yoing up and down, that it could happen again. For instance, I was watching Spurs on TV the other day. We were 2–0 up, but the other team was making a comeback – every time they scored, I jumped up and grabbed some biscuits and crisps that were on the table. And, do you know, at the time, I don't think I was even aware of what I was doing. I think that tells it all – nervous eating. And if you watch Spurs long enough, you'll end up bloody well exploding sometimes.

Here's one of my latest tips, which I'm currently experimenting with. I was at a restaurant the other day and was served one of my favourite dishes, clams in a tomato sauce. The restaurant supplied me with a miniature fork, which you use to prise the clams out of their shells. I took quite a liking to this little fork, and a thought suddenly came to me – if I retained the fork for a while longer and used it to eat the main course that was coming up, it would take me much longer to do so. I was thinking about this because my family and I are very fast eaters. I often notice, when sitting in a restaurant with other people, that I have completely wolfed down what was in front of me while everyone else is still halfway through.

It occurred to me that if I ate more slowly, then I might feel full up sooner and not eat the rest. And so I embarked upon my new scheme, using a standard knife to cut up the food and a small fork to eat it. The results were that it certainly *did* slow me down – you simply can't get the same quantity of food in your gob. And, amazingly, even though I was conscious of why I was doing it, I *did* have that full-up feeling when there was a third of the meal still on the plate – so it works!

Now, my dear wife Ann, bless her, comes from a warm, homely Jewish family. When she cooks, we often say she cooks for a hundred, not for ten. And when she puts stuff on your plate, there's usually enough there for three people, let alone one.

She means well, but I often say to her, 'Please, for God's sake, put half on there. Leave the rest over there on the stove and, if I want some more, I'll go and get it.'

But she *can't*. She can't resist it. And that's where my small-fork trick comes into play. Of course, I realise that, no matter how much the small fork slows me down, if I still ate everything on the plate, there would be no benefit. However, as I've mentioned, it transpired that eating more slowly made me realise that I was already feeling full up after only half a plateful was down my gullet – and that was the sign for me to stop.

Ann now thinks I'm totally nuts, as I've asked her to go out and buy six of these forks for me to continue my experiment. Little does she know that I'm going to take them with me to certain restaurants we frequent. Of course, the waiters might end up calling for someone with a white coat to take me away and, yes, I am getting a little eccentric, but I think I've hit upon something here – The Tiny Fork Diet!

Try it. You'll get bored trying to plough through your plate of food with a little fork – so much so that it might tire you out. What's for sure is that it will slow you down and give you the opportunity to feel full up before it's too late and you've shovelled the lot in.

Am I a bit mad? Probably. Eccentric? Possibly. Getting worse as I get older? Yes, definitely. But they say there's a bit of madness in everyone. Some people even say it's a sign of genius. I don't know who those 'some people' are, but I'll go along with them and say that maybe they're right.

And here's a bit of lunacy in itself – why have I even told you all this? Well, it's because once I've put it down on paper, people will read this part of my book and take a look at me to see if I've kept my weight down. It's another way of forcing me to stick to my regime!

8

What Happened to Wholesome Food?

Overpriced poseur gaffs, good old-fashioned Italians, and
how I'd perform as a restaurant owner.

I guess the concept of going out for dinner is not just about filling
yourself up with food – it's more about having an enjoyable evening
with family and friends in a nice atmosphere, as well as enjoying
the speciality of the restaurant. The reason that some of these
restaurants exist is that they are supposed to produce dishes that
you would not normally be able to achieve at home. So it's a com-
bination of ambience, an evening with friends and, obviously, the
food.

Well, that's the theory anyway, but it's not always the case. Over
the years, since I've become a well-known personality, I've had
cause to frequent many restaurants, both at the invitation of other
people and because I've wanted to try them out myself. Some of
the restaurants are very good, whilst others are complete and utter
garbage – overpriced poseur gaffs, where the food takes not second
place, I would say, but fiftieth place. Why are these overrated places
so popular? It's because they are places 'to be seen at' rather than
because of the food they produce.

One such place, where in actual fact the food is not too bad, is
The Ivy. This is a restaurant in the centre of London's Theatreland.

The Ivy has positioned itself as a meeting place during the day, at lunchtime, for those in the theatre and media business. It's carved itself out a little niche in the market, and the place is always packed out with the usual suspects. It's quite hard to get a reservation unless you are well-connected, and sometimes some of the Z-list celebrities put themselves on the waiting list weeks in advance, just to be seen sitting around amongst television and film producers and newspaper editors. It is a real poseurs' gaff, no question about it.

I recall one funny occasion when Piers Morgan invited me for lunch. It was at a stage in his life when he had just, in his eyes, hit the big time. I think it was when *Britain's Got Talent* was first airing on television, so Piers felt that he needed to parade himself at The Ivy. When I met Piers there, he was already seated. He'd chosen what he considered to be the best position in the restaurant, with his back to the wall, so he could look outwards at all the media luvvies. That day, the great Michael Parkinson was dining there, and we even came across Lorraine Heggessey, who was boss of Talkback Thames, the company that produces *The Apprentice*, *Britain's Got Talent*, *The X Factor* and many other shows.

Now, in order to understand this story, you'll need to appreciate that Piers, once he got on TV, became a bit of a bigshot. He loved quoting audience figures and all that type of stuff, and he was rubbing in the fact that *Britain's Got Talent* had 10.5 million viewers. He'd be sending me texts all the time, pointing out that *The Apprentice* only had 7 million viewers, so he was already more famous than me on television. His pathetic banter would go on and on, and I, in my customary way, used to slap him down by reminding him that the viewers might possibly be watching the other panellists, Simon Cowell and Amanda Holden, plus, of course, the guests on the show. To give him the benefit of the doubt, I said I would divide his 10.5 million viewers by three, which was being very generous, and pointed out to him that the number of viewers solely attributable to him was much less than I was achieving on *The Apprentice*.

Even as I tell you this story now, I'm feeling a bit pathetic myself – getting sucked into this childish argument – but the reason I mention it is so you can get the picture in your mind that Piers Morgan thinks he is more popular than me on TV.

Anyway, while we were sitting there having lunch, some shaven-headed, loutish-looking person, the sort you wouldn't expect to see in The Ivy, walked over to our table, ignored me, shook Piers's hand and said, 'Hello, Piers, you're the man. You are great. You're a wonderful fellow, top bloke,' and then walked off. It was so pathetic – you could see that Morgan had either asked or paid the guy to come over and do it. I don't know whether he really meant it seriously and hoped that the other diners at The Ivy were looking on, or just wanted to spring it on me as a joke! When we finished lunch – and he'd finished parading around the restaurant, shaking everybody's hands and talking to Michael Parkinson – we finally walked out of the restaurant together.

The funny part of this story is that The Ivy is right opposite St Martin's Theatre, where the famous play *The Mousetrap* is playing. It was just before an afternoon performance and there were around seventy young girls in school uniform lining up to go in. They spotted me and started screeching and shouting my name out, right in front of Piers. What a wonderful moment! Perfect timing.

But getting back to the main issue here – the poseur gaffs – are they worth it? Well, as I said, that particular restaurant, The Ivy, is actually not bad for lunchtime, snack-type food but, more to the point, it's a place where people go to meet.

There are a host of other restaurants in the West End of London which have been bought up in recent years by one individual, Richard Caring. He owns some famous places, such as Harry's Bar, Annabel's, Scott's, J. Sheekey, George, Le Caprice and, indeed, The Ivy.

Now, I don't blame this fellow for doing that; it's obviously a very astute business move for him. He's had the foresight to buy up all these very famous restaurants and I assume, though I may be wrong, that he runs them under one main holding company. There is, however, one issue, and that is that if you go back to the thing that made those restaurants great, it was most probably the individuals who founded them and what the restaurants actually stood for in terms of cuisine, atmosphere, etc. But now some of the signature dishes, like Le Caprice's iced berries served with hot white-chocolate sauce, are now served at the other restaurants too. Again, I don't blame them for doing that, but the diners will surely see through all this and think that they're eating at a chain like McDonald's, so I don't think this principle ought to be applied to established restaurants, which should really have their own character.

All of which leads me to the point I'd like to make. Are these types of establishments ones that should be owned by a conglomerate? Do they lose their character and individuality when they're all owned by the same boss and all run, from a financial point of view, in the same manner? I think they do.

Now, this gentleman acquired The Ivy and opened something called The Ivy Club, and he made it quite exclusive. I became a member, as did many of my friends and colleagues. It was a very impressive environment. The layout of the restaurant, the bar and the general set-up were great. There was just one problem – in my opinion, the food sucked. And it wasn't *just* my opinion; it was also the opinion of a couple of friends of mine, who, quite separately, came to the same conclusion. I found it so unacceptable that, unusually for me, I instructed my bank to cancel my annual membership. What a crying shame that the place had achieved the right atmosphere and ambience, but had got the food so wrong – terrible!

But do the type of people that go to these places care? Does the owner care that he's lost a sixty-four-year-old fart like me who's interested in food? No, not when he has the younger jeans-and-open-collared-shirt brigade who sit there spending a fortune drinking in the bar while their stick-thin designer girlfriends peck away at a lettuce leaf. Perhaps *I've* got it wrong. He's probably laughing all the way to the bank and needs me like a hole in the head. I actually want good food – sorry about that.

He also owns another restaurant, Scott's, which is great; the food is good, no question about it. That's because they have stuck to the old tradition of Scott's, which was known for its seafood. A great restaurant and a great atmosphere, it's become a very sought-after place to be seen by the category of people I mentioned earlier, as well as a load of celebrities. It's a regular haunt of Simon Cowell, for example, who loves it, and I've bumped into him a couple of times there.

They've got a technique I would like to share with you. It goes like this. When you phone up to try to get a reservation, they tell you they are fully booked. Now, you may think that could be true, but if you keep phoning up and they keep saying they are fully booked, they get themselves the reputation of being a place that everyone wants to go to. You end up going to their website, trying to book for three or four or five weeks' time, almost desperate to get in. Now, to be fair, and I'm going to be honest here, with my title and my popularity as far as being on TV is concerned, dropping my name will get me in more often than not. But on one particular occasion, a friend of mine, whom I hadn't seen for a long time, wanted to go out to dinner and requested we go to Scott's. He asked me to make a reservation for four, which I told him I'd do. I called up the following day and got one of those answering machines where you have to keep pressing buttons. I finally got through to an actual person who was taking reservations. They told me that they were awfully sorry, Lord Sugar, but they were fully booked on Saturday night and there was nothing they could do about it, but they'd put me on a waiting list.

Bearing in mind that they normally get me in as soon as they hear my name, I believed them. I called again two days later and they told me they were still fully booked and I was still on the waiting list. On Friday I called once more and got the same story. At this point I decided I would give up. I called my friend and told him that I couldn't get in there so I'd booked another of my favourite restaurants, Scalini, the Italian restaurant in Kensington. I said I'd meet him there at nine o'clock on Saturday night.

Now, my friend is a bit of a persistent fellow and he really wanted to go to Scott's. Unbeknown to me, he had been beavering away on the phone on the Saturday morning and he'd found out the name of one of the managers, called him and given it all the 'Lord Sugar wants to come and blah, blah, blah.' Next thing I know, he calls me at five o'clock on Saturday and asks me whether I would mind if we went to Scott's instead of Scalini, as his girlfriend really wanted to go there.

I said, 'That's fine by me, but how did you manage to get a reservation? They've turned me down all this week.'

He said, 'Well, you know, I mentioned your name and I gave them a bit of stick, and they eventually gave us a table for four.'

Now, this is the bit that will interest you – when we got to the restaurant, I went up to the maître d' and said to him, 'What was all this bollocks about not being able to get a table? I phoned three times and I was told that you were full up and you'd put me on the waiting list and all that stuff, but my friend here called you and you got him in! What's going on?'

'Oh, I'm so sorry, Lord Sugar, big misunderstanding, blah, blah, blah.'

When we sat down, I was further aggravated to see four or five empty tables – this was at nine o'clock on a Saturday night. I was so aggravated that Ann said to me, 'Calm down. Stop it. Don't get angry.'

However, me being me, I couldn't resist, so I called over the

maître d' again and said, 'Can you please explain to me why you
gave me a hard time, telling me there were no tables available –
and I called *three* times – when there are five empty tables?'

He said, 'Well, sometimes people don't turn up, Lord Sugar.
And sometimes people come early and they finish early.'

'No,' I said to him, 'that's total bullshit! Total load of bollocks!
This is all a game, isn't it? A game of telling people they can't come,
in order to create some kind of must-be-there atmosphere.'

He was caught bang to rights and was embarrassed, to say the
least. 'Let me give you my personal card. Call me directly next time
and I will make sure you get a reservation.'

'No problem, don't bother. Obviously the team you had on
during the week were given their instructions to play the game, and
it didn't work out.' But not being one to hold grudges, I've been
back there since and have had no problems getting in.

In any case, I guess it's a marketing ploy, and I suppose you
have to give credit to the person in charge of the group's marketing.

Now, Harry's Bar, another one of the group, is a great restaurant, and to be fair they have also kept their tradition going – but
they've had a very funny business model. It is an Italian restaurant,
or at least it claims to be. However, whenever I've taken Italian
guests there over the years, they've been confused about the menu.
It is, to say the least, totally incomprehensible. It's written in Italian,
fair enough, but no one can recognise anything, including the
bemused Italian guests I've taken along. What's the game there?
Very, very simple – you're too embarrassed to ask what the dishes
actually are, then the waiter comes over and tells you what the
specials are for today, rattling off four or five dishes. And nine
times out of ten, everyone goes for the specials. A rather clever
ploy, I would say.

I assume the nightmare for any restaurant is to have a massive
menu with everything on offer needing to be available and fresh,
so could it be that, by pulling this little stunt and having 90 per

cent of your customers choose from the five special items that the chef is concentrating on that night, you've made life much easier for all the staff? Now, let me make it perfectly clear: this is a first-class restaurant and the five specials are superb. Also, the rest of the stuff they serve up beforehand by way of appetisers and things like that are very special. So in this case I believe the integrity of the restaurant has not changed, although it is owned by the new conglomerate, and all credit to them. I hadn't been there for a long time, but when I did recently, we had an exceptionally good meal.

The real poseur restaurants aren't necessarily the ones located in the West End, but those whose reputation comes from being owned by some famous chef. Sometimes these places just try too hard by serving some really obscure dishes that verge on the ridiculous. It fascinates me that the punters fall for it; they always seem to be jam-packed and have a tremendously long waiting list.

I have to admit that I have fallen for it too, only to be faced with a menu, thankfully written in English but describing the crazy dishes which are the hallmark of the restaurant – dishes such as sweetbreads on a bed of beetroot and liquorice ice-cream, complemented by turtle urine jus! Okay, I've exaggerated a bit there, but I think you get my drift. When this stuff turns up – and sometimes you need a magnifying glass to see it – to be fair, it looks like a work of art, with a sprig of some green shoot sticking out of it and a lot of coloured dressings around it. But once you've finished admiring the way it looks, you're left with approximately two forkfuls of something which, after looking around the room, you just stick in your mouth and swallow without tasting – a bit like putting a peg on your nose when taking medicine. The reason I take a quick look around the room is to see if anyone is looking at me with the same thoughts in their mind or whether I need to put on an approving look instead of one of shock!

Afterwards, of course, you are all supposed to say how

wonderful it was, because you're too bloody embarrassed to tell the truth and say, 'What a load of bleedin' rubbish!' Needless to say, I do not frequent those places any more.

Whatever happened to good old-fashioned wholesome food? The first restaurant I remember going to with my wife was called Topo Gigio. It was originally in Great Windmill Street and then it moved to Brewer Street. It remained consistently good, a brilliant Italian restaurant, so much so that, no matter how well I had done personally and financially over the years (bearing in mind I'd started dining there at the age of twenty), it was a regular place for the wife and me and our friends to dine. Not anymore though. When we went there a couple of years ago, we were bitterly disappointed to find that the boss, who happened to be the son of the original owner and whom I first saw as a little boy sitting on the stairs in the restaurant, had decided that he needed to change the menu away from the Topo Gigio tradition to some kind of nouvelle-cuisine-type stuff. It was the end of an era for me. I shook his hand and looked him in the eye. He could see my disappointment. It was the last time I went there.

Why did he do it? The place used to be packed, so what was he playing at? Was he seduced by this trend for making microscopic plates of food, reducing his menu from the original fifty or sixty items that they were famous for down to maybe ten or fifteen? The wine list had also changed. It was now all high-priced wines which, to be perfectly honest, one couldn't distinguish from the old favourites we used to have.

It turned out to be not only the end of an era for me, but also for Topo Gigio. I drove by there recently and the place was closed down, with a 'To Let' sign outside. It was such a shame to see the demise of this once-great restaurant, with its long and colourful heritage. Does that tell a story?

I think the traditional Italian restaurant is dying off in Britain. Some great restaurateurs, such as Mario from Signor Sassi, Valerio at Scalini, and Sandro, who used to run Barbarella, are a dying breed.

It does make me laugh when I meet these guys and talk to them about the way our American cousins have decided to interpret Italian food in a manner which only they can. The Americans will claim, of course, that there are a lot of Italians who came over from the old country to start up Italian restaurants in America, and that they are the experts. However, the trio I just mentioned will tell you that some of the names of the dishes in these American restaurants mean nothing – they are thought up by second- or third-generation Italian-Americans who have created names which just sound a bit authentic.

I know that, in Florida, a place we visit quite a lot, there are hundreds of Italian restaurants, but the menus always seem to be the same, and everything is plastered with marinara sauce. Now, this thick red goo is supposed to be a sauce that originated in southern Italy. It's made of tomatoes, garlic, herbs and onions, but there seem to be many other variations, including olives and other spices. When I talk to the trio about this, they tell me that this thing does not exist – 'marinara' is not the name of a sauce in Italy, it's used to describe a dish that includes some seafood, like spaghetti alla marinara, which, literally translated, means mariner's spaghetti. They say the only tomato sauce an Italian should refer to is salsa al pomodoro or pummarola. This red goo seems to be the staple diet of all Americans who eat Italian. They slap it on everything – fish, chicken, meat, pasta, as well as seafood.

I've often tried to take some of the waiters in these restaurants to task, particularly those who'd have you think that they're Italian. Here's the funny thing – half of them are from Brazil or Puerto Rico! One day, whilst in a jocular mood, I asked for my own concoction of special Italian sauces. I told the waiter I would like some pasta with Al Capone sauce, Mussolini mussels and some Berlusconi cheese on top. He, of course, looked at me as if I'd just arrived from the planet Mars and asked me to clarify what I was talking about.

I looked surprised and asked him, 'This is supposed to be an Italian restaurant and you've never heard of Al Capone sauce, Mussolini mussels and Berlusconi cheese? Is this an Italian restaurant or not?'

He called the head waiter over and asked me to explain it to him, at which point I told him not to bother – just serve up the goo.

I often wonder why the Irish immigrants to America didn't come up with a food tradition of their own. Perhaps if they'd got in ahead of the Italians, they could have invented some *green* goo – the Yanks would go for it, I'm sure.

In stark contrast to the microscopic portions served by some of the poseur restaurants I described earlier, in America, a plate of food is meant to feed the whole of Africa. It's far too much for any single person to eat. So much so, the doggy-bag practice comes into play on most occasions, and you'll see many of the diners walking out carrying half the stuff they've just been served, so they can heat it up the next day. Just the thought of heating that goo up is enough to put you off.

It's funny when you come across Americans who say they went to Italy and they didn't enjoy the food. And France? They think they've been poisoned. Funnily enough, they say that Britain's not too bad. Typical Americans.

There's one particular restaurant we go to in Florida where they really go over the top trying to replicate a high-class Italian restaurant, but the waiters are a couple of Jewish fellows from Brooklyn and, as I said, some immigrants from Puerto Rico or Brazil. On one occasion, the head waiter came over and started to read out the list of specials for that evening. He asked, 'Have you ever had a dining experience with us before?' and proceeded to tell us exactly how they cook everything in such detail that, by the time he'd finished his spiel, we'd forgotten every single thing he said. I wouldn't have minded if the intricate detail the waiter went into was reflected in the excellence of the food – but no. Slap the goo on overcooked shellfish that tastes like rubber on a bed of pasta.

Now, I might be being totally unfair about American cuisine because, to be perfectly honest, my main experience of it has been in Florida. I guess there will be people out there who will say I'm talking a load of rubbish. 'You should come up to Boston'; 'You should come to New York'; 'You should come to San Francisco.'

Well, maybe they're right, but then maybe they really *don't* know any better. Perhaps they don't know what food is about. Perhaps, because they're American, these dishes are all they've known throughout their lives, so they think they're great.

I've never been able to eat certain shellfish, such as lobster or giant prawns. I don't know what it is, but I seem to have some sort of allergy to it. In the early days, my wife would say to me, 'It's all psychological; you're talking a lot of nonsense.' But there was one occasion when I proved her wrong by tucking into a risotto dish which we found out afterwards contained lobster. I became violently ill and no one could understand why – until we found out what was in it. From that moment on, I think she believed me. Now it's 'Don't eat the lobster, Alan!'

Ann likes all that stuff, but she complains bitterly about the way it is cooked in America. She reckons it has this chlorinated taste about it. I pointed out to her that it means that this food has not been caught locally; it has probably come from some other location and been kept on ice. And what does American tap water taste like? Chlorine. So I'm guessing the taste of this ice has been absorbed by the food.

I would now like to share with you a couple of my party tricks for when I get bored stiff in these restaurants. There is one particular old family-owned Italian restaurant in Florida that is quite good.

You know the food is fresh because of the time it takes to arrive after you've ordered it. In other words, they cook it to order rather than having a big pile of it sitting in the kitchen somewhere.

One of my favourite dishes is clams in a light tomato and garlic sauce – small clams, I should add, known in Europe as *vongole*, as opposed to the larger monsters sometimes served up. What's my party trick? I arrange the empty clam shells in a pattern and send them back to the kitchen, to the delight of many of the waiters and the chef.

Another party trick is to challenge people to balance a wine cork on the edge of their glass. They fall for it hook, line and sinker. Of course, you can't do it; it's impossible. Sometimes I challenge people to bet on whether *I* can do it. They get so excited (as it's impossible to do) that they'll bet me a fiver or a tenner. What's the trick? Get two forks, stick them into the cork on either side, then balance the cork on the edge of the glass. It will sit there in stable equilibrium for ever; so much so that, if you pick up the glass carefully, the cork and the two forks hanging from it will remain in place.

And my final party piece, when I'm really pissed off with a restaurant, is to use some of the horrible thick gooey sauce on the plate to write a message. It reminds me of the old days, when one of my aunts used to make pretty pictures in the tea leaves at the bottom of her cup. But this is a bit different. By carefully crafting the thick goo (and possibly a bit of mashed potato), I can then use my knife to write a message, such as 'The food is crap.' It makes the waiters laugh. I'm not sure what the chef thinks – I imagine he couldn't care less.

Anyway, at least my antics make my grandkids laugh – they are my best audience. Ann just shrugs her shoulders. I suppose I'm a bit of a nutter really.

*

I can't write about restaurants and not mention the effect VAT has had on the industry. Imagine the old Italian hacks, who started their restaurants many years ago, being told that from now on they had to charge 12 per cent (that was then; now it's 20 per cent) on top of the normal bill. They would go nuts. In an industry with so much cash flying around, many businesses, I have to say, tried to avoid VAT and got themselves into hot water with the authorities, in the same way that some hairdressers did. I heard stories that Customs and Excise (as it was called in those days) used to plant people in the restaurants to take note of how many customers had come in, and the next day they would raid the place and ask for all the bills.

The effect was that the cost of dining went up, bearing in mind that you would leave a tip and would now have to pay VAT as well. It did affect the trade for a while but, like all things, we just got used to it. On the other hand, the food one buys in supermarkets is still VAT-free at the moment, so there's an anomaly when it comes to hot takeaway food and sandwiches. This is further complicated by the fact that, if you buy a sandwich or a hot dish and sit down to eat it in the shop, you have to pay VAT. On the other hand, if you take it out and walk down the street eating it, you don't.

It seems that the retailers have had enough of this nonsense, and the likes of Prêt à Manger, Starbucks and McDonald's have taken the matter to the European Court of Justice to get a ruling that it should not matter whether you eat inside or out.

I love it. Apparently, a small trader in Germany who ran a burger van went on a crusade, as he was being asked to charge VAT to people who sat on a chair next to his van to eat their burger, while not charging those who stood up to eat. I think he won his case and that's why the big boys have jumped on the back of it. So watch this space. The courts are going to have a hard time changing the German ruling. If it goes through, the revenue authorities will have to refund millions. I can see my old mate Valerio, who runs Scalini, pounce on this and have standing areas in his restaurant.

So what are my favourite restaurants? Well, I have a few, and I have to say that, as usual, the wife is right. We used to travel from home up to the West End regularly on a weekend, but the traffic has got so bad that she's made me face up to the fact that sitting in a car for an hour and a half, crawling through frustrating traffic, only to end up being served a load of tutt is not really worth it. So we only tend to go to West End restaurants on special occasions, or on weekdays when I'm up there on business anyway.

However, some of our local restaurants are very, very good. In particular, I'd like to pay tribute to one of the greatest Chinese restaurants I've ever eaten in. And trust me, I have spent a lot of time in Hong Kong and China. I'm referring to the Roding Restaurant in Abridge, Essex, where Thomas was the boss for thirty-odd years and only recently retired, handing over the reins to his capable staff. I can still picture him as a young man, and I find it hard to look at old Thomas now, who must be the same age as me, and realise that this is the same bloke.

The quality of the restaurant is so consistently good that some of my friends who actually live in the West End come out to *us* on a Saturday night to enjoy what I believe is the best Chinese restaurant in the world. Obviously people will disagree with me, but a lot of Essex people do agree. Some of them get a bit inebriated and Thomas has a wonderful solution for pre-empting any arguments about the bill afterwards, particularly about the number of bottles of wine or bottled water that the customers ordered – this is possibly a business lesson he's learned from bitter experience. What he does is line up the empty bottles by the side of your table, so that if there's any argument like 'Oy, what's this, four bottles of wine?

We never had that much,' he simply points to the four empty bottles on the floor. Job done!

And then there's a great fish and chip restaurant in Ongar, simply called Smith's, a family business that originated in Loughton. What's the secret of that restaurant? Fresh, wholesome, interesting, basic food. And it's packed out every weekend.

And, most recently, there's part of our real-estate portfolio, the famous King's Head pub, right opposite where I live in Chigwell. It came up for sale, and when my son Daniel brought this to my attention, we decided to buy it out of some sort of local sentiment. The intention was that we would completely refurbish it and find a tenant to occupy it, because Chigwell needed a really good restaurant. Daniel went on to find this very young, enterprising man called Dylan who had a small restaurant in Buckhurst Hill. His speciality was kebabs, a kind of mixture of Turkish and Greek food. This little place in Buckhurst Hill was jam-packed, so Dylan grasped the opportunity of starting up this massive restaurant, called Sheesh, which opened in February 2011.

It has been a blinding success, and the reason again is quality. Believe it or not, it is very healthy, fresh food at reasonable prices. I reckon it will go down as one of the better restaurants in Essex. It was interesting to watch this young man work so hard while the redevelopment of the building was going on. It took a good nine months, and he threw his heart and soul into it. I have not experienced, in recent years, anyone working as hard as this fellow, and he deserves to do tremendously well.

I was so impressed by young Dylan that I couldn't resist mentioning on Twitter that his new restaurant was opening in Chigwell – just to give him a bit of a kick-start. Because I did this, there are many people who, to this day, believe that it's *my* restaurant. No matter how many times I tell them the contrary, they cannot get their heads around the fact that we are merely the real-estate owners. I still get messages on Twitter saying, 'Went to your restaurant last night, Lord Sugar – fantastic!'

I've given up telling them it's not my restaurant, but it conjures up an interesting thought. Can you imagine *me* as an owner of a restaurant – with my limited patience? Imagine how I'd deal with people complaining about the food taking too long to come? It would be like *Fawlty Towers*, when Basil would clip people round the ear and be downright rude to customers who asked quite reasonable and civil questions.

Yeah, I think I've got the message there – it's not for me.

9

Merlot Schmerlot

Why wine waiters annoy me, and visiting a French vineyard with Nick Hewer.

Part of the enjoyment of dining out is to drink a nice wine, but there's one thing that really winds me up. I wonder if you've noticed the following practice carried out by wine waiters in many restaurants. (By the way, I should say that this is not exclusive to America; it's universal – it's part of the business model of some restaurants, and it's quite annoying.) The waiters constantly top up the wine glasses of the diners, the idea being that, whilst you've been eating and chatting, you've been sipping away. Before you know it the bottle is empty, so you're encouraged to order another one.

Apart from anything else, it is particularly annoying when they pour out too much white wine and it loses its chill. I am always pulling up the wine waiters on this. It further winds me up when you are in the company of a guest who is driving home and just wants a little wine, only to have their glass filled to the brim.

It makes me sound a bit stingy, but that's not the case – I always reassure the waiter that we'll be ordering extra bottles, and in many restaurants I eat and drink at they already know this. So what's even more annoying is that, after telling one waiter off, the head waiter comes over and does exactly the same thing – grabs the bottle and starts pouring. I have trained the waiters now in some of the regular gaffs I go to. They now know to leave the pouring to us and stay well clear. In fact, out of the corner of my eye, I often notice them stopping other waiters who are about to commit this crime.

On a recent visit to one of our regular restaurants in Florida, I noticed the wine list had changed and one of the wines I normally chose was missing. I asked the waiter if he could send me somebody who knew about the wine list and he told me that he was going to send over the sommelier.

'What?' I said. 'What are you going to send over?'

'The sommelier, sir.'

I have to admit, it was the first time I'd ever heard this word. It sounded like he'd said, 'Sole meunière', which is a classic French dish consisting of sole which has been filleted, dredged in flour and pan-fried in butter.

'Sole meunière?' I said, surprised. 'I didn't ask for fish, I wanted the wine waiter!'

The poor fellow had a bemused look on his face. Maybe it's me. Perhaps I'm the heathen, I don't know, but I'd never heard that word before.

Anyway, along came this tall, suited gentleman with a rather snooty attitude to ask whether he could help me. I told him that the wine that I normally chose didn't seem to be on the list. He started to explain that he felt that that particular wine was no longer appropriate for the restaurant – that year's vintage had been disappointing, so he had decided to remove it. What a load of cobblers! He was a real American bullshitter and, as we Jewish lads would say, 'What does he know from schmaltz herring?' (Don't try to understand that – it's a very Jewish thing.)

Now, perhaps it's me, but I think all these American wines taste the same – the red ones are syrupy, sweet and thick, and they have been tuned to suit the American taste. Having been a regular visitor to Florida for over thirty-five years, I've decided to stick to a wine that is reasonably priced, since they're all much of a muchness – Napa Schlappa, Merlot Schmerlot, Zinfandel, Cabernet

Sauvignon – all these bloody names I've never heard of. Actually, I *have* heard of the Cabernet Sauvignon and Merlot grape varieties, which both originated in France, but the Americans have totally murdered the taste. Flash bottles with coloured labels, gimmicks, plastic corks – what have they done to the great wine tradition? And if you ask for an Italian or French wine, well, you need to take a mortgage out. They are ridiculously priced, probably to prevent you buying them because the Americans want to sell their Californian tutt.

Having said that, the irony is that the Yanks, bless 'em, in recognition of the massive market for wine, seem to have groomed the single most important wine critic, or guru, in the world. Robert Parker's opinion can influence wine prices and make or break a vintage, or even a château. Imagine one man having that much power. And imagine, particularly, how French vineyard owners must feel, especially those with a long family tradition behind them. In France there are still 9,000 growers in Bordeaux alone – little family-owned-and-run châteaux, each with different-tasting wines. When an American gives his so-called words of wisdom, they must feel sick!

I recall, when I went to stay with Nick Hewer at his house in France, that we went to a small family-run vineyard and tasted at least three different red wines. The owner went to great pains to explain how they change the taste by varying the size and volume of the casks and by using different woods – now *that's* wine-making. Compare that to the mass-production vineyards in America, with their giant mechanical presses and enormous aluminium storage towers.

On another visit to France with Nick, we went to a large vineyard where the younger generation had taken over. Here, a rather enterprising young man explained that he had decided to join the bandwagon after going to America to see how they mass produce wine. When he returned, he kitted out his facility with all the large machines and set up a fully automated production line. I asked him why he had moved away from tradition. He simply told me, 'If you can't beat 'em, join 'em.'

When I suggested to him that this surely wasn't what his family had intended so many years ago, he told me that he did it to survive. What's more – and this is a big point – he told me that he takes grapes from other people, so they're not even all grown in his vineyard. He has simply turned his place into a commercial wine factory, and it was sad to see.

He also showed us, as if to admit he was cheating a bit, a part of his premises where they still use the old methods to make some 'real' wine, in a smaller area of the vineyard. He also let us see the very antiquated process, the beautiful copper coils and boilers in which they made the traditional Armagnac his family was known for. He took us to a large, old, barn-style shed where there were barrels of Armagnac stored, some going back to 1947. Well, at least *that* made our day, as the sight of the modern-day stuff had left us depressed.

This says it all: when you walk around the supermarkets in Florida, you'll see a French red wine called Fat Bastard. Now, what are they saying there? Is it some form of marketing that makes you want to buy it just to taste it? They've even got the French catering for the American palate. And it doesn't make any difference; it all tastes the bloody same!

I have seen some good restaurants ruined by their obsession with pushing wine as their main business model. In France, near Nice, there was a famous restaurant, La Chaumière, which had been run by one family for many years. It had an interesting policy of providing a kind of set-meal programme with many courses, including beef cooked in an open fireplace. The wine was on a take it or leave it basis, meaning that they plonked two bottles of red and one bottle of white on the table. They were in plain bottles with no labels and it was fantastic stuff. The family sold the business to some bloke, who changed the whole thing around. He reduced the quality of the food – it lacked the freshness of the previous regime's – and he introduced a wine list where the cheapest bottle of wine was 150 Euros, and it was crap. The place went downhill fast. We tried it a couple of times and, like many others, didn't go back. Fortunately, the family has bought it back and the change is like night and day. I think the moral of that story is that people don't like to be ripped off. It's not the money, trust me; it's the way they went about it.

10

What Makes an Entrepreneur?

**Answering the eternal question 'How can I succeed in business?'
And please don't ask me again.**

In my seminars, one of the most frequently asked questions is
'How can I succeed in business? I want to be in business – tell me
what to do.'

It's quite annoying when you are asked such naïve questions.
And I'm fed up being asked to make up a boring list of my top ten
tips – which is another very annoying question I get asked by every
journalist. I think practical explanations are always best. Here are
some stories of how I grew my business. And I hope you can see
what I am on about. I should state up front that these stories appear
in my autobiography, but I didn't analyse them there in the same
way, so even if you've read and memorised that book, you'll still
find plenty of good advice here!

I have often been asked to define what an entrepreneur is.
It's a difficult question. My stock answer has always been that an
entrepreneur cannot be grown; a person is born with entrepreneurial
spirit within them. My letter to the young Alan explains it best,
with my example of the concert pianist (see page 58). In my view,
that analogy applies to entrepreneurial talent.

Having said that, entrepreneurial spirit does lie buried in the
subconscious of many people, and it takes day-to-day opportunities and experience in business for it to actually flourish. After all,

no budding concert pianist suddenly sat down at a piano one day and started playing Grieg's Piano Concerto – someone must have spotted their ability, and the person themselves must have had a love and affinity for music and spent years practising.

Now, I've spent my business career giving good value for money, and I hope never to deviate from that ethos. On top of that, I've always been an honest trader, so I'm going to make it perfectly clear that reading this chapter is not going to turn you into an entrepreneur. You either *have* something or you don't. You can read a hundred books and you're still not going to be able to spot opportunities if that instinct doesn't exist within you. And neither, as I've famously said in the past, can you walk into Boots and buy a bottle of entrepreneurial juice that will suddenly turn you into a genius.

So what I hope I can achieve in this chapter is to coax something out of your inner being to assist you in prospering in your business life. It is fair to say that most of the stuff I can tell you about is based upon the experiences I've had over the past forty-seven years in the businesses I've been involved in. This means that my comments will relate mainly to manufacturing and trading, as well as marketing, selling, contracts, deals, etc. One has to recognise, of course, that there are loads of other businesses which I've *not* been involved in, particularly those in the service industries and those relating to the booming e-commerce market. Nevertheless, the principles remain the same in many cases.

Let me take you back in time.

Hello, what's this? A load of workmen, big lorries, plumes of fire and loud drilling – when did this all start?

As a kid of around eleven years old, I spent a lot of time looking out of the window of our top-floor council flat in Clapton (in the London borough of Hackney). It was a relaxing pastime watching the traffic and the people go by. There were no Xboxes or Nintendos then – not that we could have afforded one if there had been.

On one particular day in the late fifties, the roads in Clapton were being resurfaced and I was excited to see all this carry-on. A crew had arrived and started to dig up the road. I was glued to the window, watching the workers with all their machinery, fascinated by the sights and sounds of it all – the flames and the clattering of pneumatic drills as they loosened the surface and dug it up. I'd go down to the street and watch them more closely. I'd chat with the workers and ask them what they were doing.

The removal of the old road surface uncovered a base layer of wooden blocks set into the ground in a herringbone pattern. New road construction techniques no longer required these blocks, so they were discarded. The workers showed me the blocks, which were impregnated with tar, and they chucked a couple on to their fire – they burned like a rocket. Bingo! Why bingo? Well, read on.

There was no central heating in the flats in those days. If you needed heat, you lit a coal fire. Lighting a coal fire at home was a specialised job. You could buy firelighter strips, but for poor, working-class people like us they were considered a waste of money. Instead, most people bought little bundles of wooden sticks which were packaged in rolls and sold by most general hardware shops. As an eleven-year-old, I was sent by my mum to Mr Braham's or Mr Morris's shop in Upper Clapton Road to buy these sticks – they sold for the old sixpence a bundle (2.5p in today's money).

Why am I telling you all this? Well, if you haven't sussed it by now, you *certainly* need to read on and try to learn.

First of all, **you need to be able to spot an opportunity and turn it to your advantage.**

Wooden blocks impregnated with tar ignite immediately – and they were being chucked away by the workers! Coming up is one of my first business ventures, or, as some would call them, my cheeky childhood schemes. And crazy as it might sound, it all stemmed from, of all things, road construction. Yes, bingo! It occurred to me that these discarded wooden blocks could be made into firelighting sticks. I could cut the blocks into bundles of sticks and flog them to Mr Braham and Mr Morris as being far superior to the ordinary ones they were selling.

After I'd cut up some blocks and tied together a few bundles with string, I went round to Mr Braham and asked him if he wanted to buy some. He looked at me as if I were nuts. 'I've got enough of this stuff out in my backyard – why would I want any more?'

I knew he'd have a fire going in the back of his shop (as I'd once worked there on a Saturday), so I chucked on one of the sticks, which burst into flames. He looked at me and smiled, as if to say, 'You little sod – how did you do that?'

Threepence a bundle was the price he said he'd pay and, within two days, I'd converted all the stuff and taken it to his yard. The other kids were on to this like a shot, but they didn't have my sales skills.

I stacked the bundles in the corner of the forecourt where I lived, but the next week I ended up giving away loads of bundles to the neighbours, as by now the stuff was getting nicked. There was, of course, a limit to how many of these blocks I could deal with. What I had stashed away was minute compared to what was available, so you can imagine my frustration when I saw my wooden gold being carted off in lorryloads, just to be dumped somewhere.

Anyway, in the end, the bigger boys in the flats got in on the action. They started doing the same thing and sort of muscled me out. 'That's it, mate, it's over for you. Get out of the way, we're taking over.' I wasn't too sorry though, as it was a lot of hard and dirty work to make a relatively small amount of money.

Nevertheless, I learned an important lesson. I think it was Karl Marx who said, 'Catch a man a fish, you can sell it to him. Teach a man to fish, you ruin a wonderful business opportunity.'

And I learned something else: **you mustn't be complacent.** Any products, services or ideas you come up with won't last for ever – you have to move on. Even if you are blessed with foresight and are a bit quicker than the next person, it won't take too long for others to catch on, and up will spring the competition.

I mentioned earlier how entrepreneurial talent resides in you and how it comes out at certain stages. As well as the example of my fire-sticks, which endorses this, please indulge me one more time as I tell you an old story.

At around the same time, when I was eleven, next to our council flats there was a rag-and-bone merchant who would go round collecting items such as old iron and other metals, clothing and material. He'd pay scrap value for the stuff. In his yard was a sign saying, 'Wool 5s per lb [five shillings per pound of weight], cotton 1s 6d per lb [one shilling and sixpence], brass and copper 2d per lb [tuppence].' Playing out in the street, I noticed people taking items in and getting money in exchange and I wondered if I could get hold of any stuff so that I too could make some money.

It was during one of my other ventures – car cleaning – that I found something. In the back streets of Clapton, some of the big Victorian houses were converted into small garment factories, with rooms full of machinists. One day, while cleaning the factory boss's car, I saw in the front garden some open sacks of material trimmings, ready for the dustman to take away. When I went inside to collect my 1s 6d for cleaning the car, I asked the boss what was in these sacks and he explained they were remnants of the material used to make the clothes. Bingo again! I asked him if I could take some, and he said I could. The sacks were bigger than me, so I went back to the flats and got our old pram. I loaded on two sacks and took them round to the rag-and-bone man.

Here was my first experience of getting 'legged over'. Unbeknown to me, the sacks contained gold dust as far as the scrap merchant was concerned, as the material was wool. The bloke took one look at this eleven-year-old and said, 'What you've got in those sacks is rubbish.' He weighed the stuff on his scales and said, 'I'll give you half a crown [2s 6d] for the lot.' I took it. Naïve – stupid, you might say – but half a crown was a lot of money in those days.

The next week, after cleaning the boss's car, I asked him what kind of material was in those sacks. When he told me it was wool, I was furious – I should have got at least £1 10s for those two sacks. I took a scrap of the material to the rag-and-bone man and confronted him. 'I've just been told this is wool – you told me it was rubbish. I want some more money or I want the two sacks back,' I yelled at him angrily. I won't tell you what he said to me. He slung another two shillings at me and told me to clear off.

'I can get loads more of this stuff and I'm going to find another rag-and-bone man to sell it to!'

He just laughed and virtually threw me out.

Another side of me came out now. I was wound up and angry. I wasn't frightened to speak up, but short of grabbing hold of him or kicking him, what could I do? He was a grown man and I was an eleven-year-old shnip.

I took the time to mention this example because it's one that shows you how you can be diddled out of a deal; the point being that such an experience makes you more streetwise. **You need to learn to recognise the dodgy people out there who don't have the same principles as you in life or in business.**

In both of the above stories, I spotted an opportunity and turned it to my advantage. To summarise on the fire-sticks, if I hadn't been inquisitive and chatted to the road-diggers, they wouldn't have shown me how the tar blocks burnt. I knew about the plain ones available in the shop and I knew how hard it was to light a fire and get it going. I saw the worker chuck the tar-impregnated block on to the fire and it burst into flame. Conclusion: no need to buy expensive firelighters and a cheap and easy way to start a fire. If I'd never started fires and had never bought plain sticks, there would never have been a deal – it was my *experience* that gave me the opportunity. The killer point here is not just that the sticks burnt easily; I configured them into a bundle and made it easy for Mr Braham to get the plot straight away. I didn't just go in there with a tar block and say, 'Do you want to buy some sticks that I can make from these?' I pre-empted it, so that his decision to buy was fast-tracked by me showing him something he understood – he wasn't forced to *imagine* anything.

As for the rag-and-bone-man story, his sign registered in my mind – people were getting money by bringing him old stuff. I didn't react there and then and go searching for stuff to sell him; it wasn't until I stumbled upon the wool cuttings that I put the two things together. I think the message here is that you never know when something stored in your mind can come into play as far as business is concerned.

It is clear from these examples that, as a kid, I was able to absorb things and store them in my mind and, when opportunities came about, quickly spot them and act fast. I was always very inquisitive, poking my nose into things to gain more information.

I hope that in documenting some of my activities as a youngster, you'll see the importance of storing information and having experience as well as a little expertise. More to the point, you can see the entrepreneurial spirit in me, and how it started to come out. Hopefully, this may have sparked off something within you, and you see something similar in your own nature.

Other incidents from my early life taught me important lessons that any entrepreneur needs, one of which is: **you have to master**

the art of presentation and salesmanship. One example from my childhood days is when I used to help one of my brother's friends, Manny, on his stall in Chelmsford Market. Manny sold foam rubber bits and pieces, which people would buy to make cushions. It was at Chelmsford where I first experienced the amazing salesmanship of some of the stall holders. The man on the stall next to Manny's sold towels and bedding, and he attracted a crowd of people by piling his items one on top of another, creating a perception of value for money. He'd start his patter by letting the crowd know the high prices of these items in the shops.

I was fascinated by his spiel. 'There you are, two big bath towels, three hand towels, four flannels, five pillow cases, three sets of sheets. I'll throw in two pillows and, wait for it, a wonderful full-size blanket. Now, the lady over there – put your hand down, love – I don't want twenty-five pounds, forget twenty pounds, forget fifteen, don't even think about ten. The lady over there – put your money away, dear. Now, I want *five* – hands up – five pounds the lot.' The customers couldn't hand over their money quickly enough.

Even though this bloke was just selling towels in the market, I can assure you he is no different from the suited and booted executive with a fancy PowerPoint presentation trying to sell Rolls-Royce engines to Boeing. The commodity may be different, the environment may be different, but the presentation and selling skills are exactly the same – and don't let anyone tell you other-wise.

When choosing a career path, one mistake I made was thinking I could do something I was inevitably not cut out for. I came from a working-class home where, historically, it was assumed that everyone in the family would go and work in a factory. I, however, was from a new generation and my parents recognised that education would perhaps offer new avenues career-wise. I wanted to pursue a career in science and become a professional in some way or other, making me the first professional in the family. It took me a long time to realise that I was not really cut out for this. This is a really important lesson for everyone to learn: **do what you're best at.**

It's funny how people with vast experience can spot what you are best at, while you can be blind to it. The headmaster at my primary school recognised me as a young man of enterprise. In my final year there, when I was about eleven, we had an 'open day'. I was chosen by the head to present the school's work to the visiting parents and dignitaries.

It came naturally to me, explaining in detail the work on show. Knowing me, I imagine I was offering *too much* detail and maybe repeating myself. While I was talking, I could see people smiling and whispering to each other – they were smiling at this little kid who was a good presenter. The audience included the Lord Mayor and an array of visiting secondary-school headteachers (one of whom was Mr Harris, my future headmaster). Clearly Mr Harris saw I was already set on the path to what I've been doing for the rest of my life: selling, presenting and marketing.

As I mentioned earlier, I wanted a career as a professional. The subjects I enjoyed most in secondary school were science and engineering. Sometimes I would bump into Mr Harris walking through the corridor. He would look up and say something like 'Hello, Sugar. How are you doing in the commerce and economics division?'

'No, sir, I'm in science and engineering,' I'd say.

'No, no, no, surely you're in commerce and economics?'

'No, sir, science and engineering.'

'No, no, no, no, no . . .' And he would wander off, shaking his head.

It seemed that Mr Harris had it in his brain that that's where

I should be, despite my passion for chemistry, physics, metalwork and technical drawing.

Having seen hundreds, if not thousands, of boys pass through his school, Mr Harris obviously recognised that I was a commercial beast, despite the fact that I wanted to pursue science and engineering. That in itself tells the story. I've seen lots of people in life who are good at certain things, but aren't satisfied pursuing a career in their area of expertise – instead, they believe they are *businesspeople*. I have come across many examples of this with people I've employed, who have tried to flex their muscles in the business world. The sad fact is: they're simply no good at it. They're good at what they were trained to do – engineering, law, accountancy – but watching them flounder in business has led me to believe that you should stick to what you know.

Ignoring Mr Harris, I left school with some GCE qualifications and decided not to go on to do A Levels, simply because I had a desire to go to work and earn some money. Stupidly, my target at the time was to have a car, in order to be in the same league as some of my friends.

My first job was at the Ministry of Education and Science – science being the key word. Naïvely, I had visions of being involved in scientific experiments – missiles, rockets and the like. The job paid £32 per month – £8 a week, in East End terms. On my first day I walked to my desk in a large open-plan office while the other people glanced up for a moment to suss out the new boy.

To say these people were boring would be too kind. The highlight of their day came during the tea break, when they'd debate the virtues of using Marvel powdered milk as opposed to conventional milk that might go off if you kept it for two or three days. Scintillating stuff, as you can imagine.

Eight quid a week was all well and good, but it wasn't enough for me to keep up with my mates. I saw the job at the ministry as something of an investment, so that one day I would end up not having to worry about income. In the meantime, I needed to supplement my earnings. I'd kept my Saturday job, plus a few other ventures, and it was a rather weird situation – I was earning less from my career than I was from my sidelines!

I asked my boss, after we had merged with the science part of the Department of Education and Science, whether I could get myself into a department where I could do something more interesting than compile educational statistics. 'Mind your own business,' was the reply, 'and get on and do what you're told to do.'

That was the final straw. I realised this life wasn't for me. I looked around at some of the people there, particularly the older ones, and realised that I didn't want to end up like these robots, pushing a load of boring paper around.

I left and took another job in clerical statistics at an iron and steel manufacturer, with a view that one day I'd become a cost accountant, but that was boring also. The staff there took a liking to me and, when we chatted during the moments of boredom, they would often tell me that I was wasting my life in this job, doing what they were doing.

In a nice sort of way, they said, 'Look at us – we've got houses and mortgages and children, so we need the job. But you're young – you're at the time of your life when you have no responsibilities. You should be getting out there and doing other things. If *we* had our time over again, we'd be in sales.'

They, just like my headmaster, were right – I could by now tell that my temperament was not the same as theirs. I was never going to be a bookworm, dealing in boring figures. I needed these two negative experiences to realise that I was cut out to be a commercial animal.

I noticed an advert in the *Evening Standard* for a travelling-salesman vacancy. The firm was called Robuck Electrical, manufacturers of tape recorders and record-players. I loved electronics as a kid, so I thought this looked quite promising.

I was seventeen years old, so one of the attractions of this job was that it came with a minivan. Well, beggars can't be choosers. I would need the van because I'd be carting around sample tape recorders and record-players.

I flew through the interview. The boss was very impressed with me, although he was concerned that I was only seventeen and lacked experience. But, again like my headmaster, he spotted something in me. I think he sussed that I had the instinct for selling. He wrote to me the next day offering me the job and telling me to turn up in three weeks' time, when I would meet all the other recruits.

Here is the big point: **I finally took a job that I liked and had an interest in.** And that's what people must do first and foremost, rather than enter a profession because it's the fashionable thing to do. I decided there and then that I wasn't going to become a professional – my true calling was to become a *salesman*.

I was now taking up my third job in less than two years since leaving school. We did some sales training and I watched another four guys do their pitches. Observing them, I picked up a few tips. Later in the day, I pitched, and put a smile on the boss's face. 'Well done,' he said. 'Very good, young man. If you do it like that, you're going to do well.'

You'll recall my example of how even an exceptionally talented kid can't just sit down at the piano and start playing Grieg straight away – well, this was the same thing. The boss saw something in me and coaxed it out, and I learned by watching others. The point is – the raw talent was there.

No bullshit, within three months I was the top salesman at the firm. When I think of it now, the sales territory I had – the whole of London – was massive. It was the biggest commercially intensive area in the country, and it had been given to this seventeen-year-old!

But I'll share with you another experience that gave me a smack in the face that would toughen me up for my later business life. I walked into an electrical retailer's shop in Stamford Hill, near where I lived, and told him that I was Alan Sugar from Robuck.

'Robuck? Who are they?' he said.

'The tape recorder company.'

'Oh yes,' he said. 'I'm so pleased to see you. I've heard about you and I've been wanting to see you. Tell me what you've got to offer.'

I should have known from this warm welcome that something was wrong. I showed him a tape recorder and he said, 'Excellent.' He bought six. This was the easiest sale I'd had so far. In fact, it was *too* easy; too good to be true – he didn't ask any of the usual questions.

I was very naïve. What followed would never have happened to me later in life, after gaining a bit of experience. I called on him a week or so later to see how he was getting on. 'Great,' he said. 'I've sold a few of them already. In fact, I'd like to order another four.'

A month later, the shit hit the fan. I was asked by Robuck's credit controller to go down to the shop and chase payment. When I got there, it was closed. Empty. I went to the shop next door and asked, 'What's happened to them?'

The chap told me, 'They've done an LF, son.'

'LF? What's an LF?'

'Long firm, mate, long firm.'

'What's a long firm?'

A long firm turned out to be an organisation that buys loads of stuff on credit, then sells it very quickly and cheaply, with no intention at all of paying the supplier. At Robuck's expense, I'd learned a tremendous lesson in life.

To be perfectly honest, I had no perception of chasing money or worrying if the company would get paid. Typical of a salesman, I just wanted to sell and was oblivious to things like payment, so this was a bit of a wake-up call at the time. Although it wasn't coming out of my own pocket, the episode was an embarrassment, as you don't want your firm to lose money. For sure, I would be very conscious of getting paid in the future. But I was to come across this same culture when I employed salesmen later in life. You need to get to know the people you employ and see if they're honest or full of shit.

In those days, although there were some multi-retailers, the radio and TV retail industry was fragmented into hundreds of individual retailers who owned one or two shops. It was around this time that one of the most important realisations in my business life came to me. I seriously suggest you absorb this next message – it led to a big breakthrough. Here I was, spending all my time visiting individual retailers who owned one or two shops. The decision-making process of the individual in charge was an important one – I had to put in a lot of effort to sell to them, and in the end they might buy one or two tape recorders. It occurred to me that chain stores such as Currys had about 150 shops in my sales area. If I could get at the bloke at the head office of Currys who makes the purchasing decisions, I could see it would require the *same* amount of effort to persuade him to buy for *all* of his shops – I realised I'd have to talk my heart out in the same way to sell one or one hundred pieces. And so, as the decision process of the buyer is the same, **the key is to be in front of the person who has more buying power.**

I contacted Currys' head office and eventually managed to get through to Michael Curry, one of the bosses. I reported this back to my boss, who gave me a real bollocking, telling me that I shouldn't have contacted such a big retailer. He told me it was out of my league and that things like that were *his* domain. Then he said, 'You actually got through to Michael Curry?'

'Yes.'

'How did you manage that?'

'Persistence. I phoned about ten times and kept leaving him

messages.' Here is another lesson. Secretaries are in place to block calls from people the boss doesn't want to talk to. They'll make all sorts of excuses; they'll take your number and promise to call you back, or ask you to explain to them what you want, so they can fend you off. I played along with the secretary and her promises to get back to me – of course, she never did – and over the course of two weeks I must have called ten times, till, in the end, she had to put me through.

It taught me another lesson: **you have to have some kind of daily discipline in your work life.** In those days I had a simple diary. Each time I called Currys and got a knockback, I would write, two days on in the diary, 'Call Currys again.' This manual diary process was to stick with me all my business life. My discipline was to view the pages each day and deal with the reminders. If I had to list which factors contributed to my success in business, I would say that this discipline thing ranks highly as one of the major bullet points. It's a quality that's needed by every person who embarks on business on their own account.

When I finally got hold of Michael Curry, I managed to get a verbal okay from him to offer some of his managers my tape recorders. I'd won the jackpot. Why? Well, there's nothing better than investing buying power in a bloke who normally has to rely on head office to send him stock. Most shop managers relish the chance of picking products to sell other than those foisted upon them by some buyer sitting in his ivory tower at head office.

This was a great opportunity to prey on the managers. Once they'd been told that their boss had given them the okay to buy, it was like giving a kid a pound and telling him to go to the sweet shop. It was the easiest sell in the world. I gave up dealing with the other retailers for a while and concentrated solely on Currys branches. I must have sold at least fifty or sixty machines to the various branch managers, and I was looking forward to receiving my commission at the end of the month. But when I looked at my payslip, I was shocked to see my commission was not what I was expecting. Fair enough, the long-firm sales were deducted, but on the upside, I'd sold fifty-odd units to Currys.

I called up the boss and said, 'What's going on?'

He told me he'd cut the commission on Currys, as their head office had cottoned on to the fact that I was selling to them. They wanted a lower price, which he had to give them. And because of that, he decided he would reduce my commission to a quarter of what I was getting when I sold to small retailers.

I told him it was bang out of order, since I'd spent the whole of the month plundering these Currys stores. Had I known there was no money in it for me, I wouldn't have bothered spending my time talking to all these branch managers. I had effectively opened the door to Currys for Robuck. I was quite angry. 'I'm not working for you any more,' I said as I walked out of the office. 'You've cheated me.' I guess this was the first real dispute I ever had in business.

When I got home that night, my mum told me that the boss had called a few hours after I'd stormed off, wanting to speak to me urgently. I got hold of him and politely told him that I would think about returning, but I reiterated my disappointment at not being paid the full commission on the Currys deal.

I was so pissed off with Robuck that in the end I decided to leave. I noticed an advert in the *Evening Standard* placed by the electrical wholesalers R. Henson & Co. They were looking for salesmen to sell electrical goods, and the job came with a car. I contacted them and went for an interview

I told the boss I wasn't interested in working for peanuts. I wanted a minimum of £20 a week, clear of tax, as a basic, plus some commission structure. Twenty quid a week clear was a lot of money in those days. My next question was 'What car have you got for me?'

He told me he had a Wolseley.

Wow, a Wolseley! That was a great car, real quality. I couldn't believe what I was hearing. I had visions of pulling up at my flats and parking the Wolseley out the front, in Upper Clapton Road. It would look out of place amidst the Ford Populars and Ford Anglias. I grabbed the job. It turned out that the Wolseley was a Baby Wolseley, an oddball of a car – it looked a bit like a Beetle with an elongated bonnet – *and* it was second hand. Still, it was better than a minivan.

I duly resigned from Robuck.

I spent the first couple of weeks with Henson out on the road with the boss's son, learning the ropes. Then, on the Friday of the second week, I collected a bunch of samples to put in the boot of the Wolseley, so I could be off and running the following Monday morning.

Working for this mob was a great eye-opener. Naïvely, I believed that their products were stock items which I could continue to sell. I soon found out that this was not the case when I successfully sold some Remington razors to the department store, Gamages – I ended up getting a rucking from the boss! He called me into his office and told me that I shouldn't have made promises of being able to supply 200.

That's when I learned they did not manufacture anything. They simply bought parcels of items from various places; there was no consistency in the product range.

In a way, it was interesting because there were always different products coming along. Some weeks we had electric fans, transistor radios, mini tape recorders and loudspeakers; other weeks we'd get a parcel of Hoover toasters or Remington razors.

As time went by, I could easily identify which customers would be interested in the new items. One day I was told there was a parcel of 250 Hoover toasters coming in.

I called one of our customers and told him that I had 250 Hoover toasters.

'What price are they? What's the model number?' he asked.

I told him to hold on, asked Henson Senior and relayed the

details down the phone. I sold the toasters on the spot, in front of
the boss, hung up the phone and said, 'There you are, they're sold.'

I never got any praise for doing deals. Who knows? Maybe I
picked up *my* traits from them. Maybe that's how business was in
those days. It was certainly miles away from the schmooze culture
that exists nowadays, with bosses or managers spending half their
time dishing out insincere compliments at seminars and off-site
meetings, talk-ins and away days. What a load of bollocks, I say.

Working for Henson, sometimes I would literally do the deal,
deliver the goods and collect the money. On one occasion, they'd
bought thousands of seven-inch vinyl records under the Blue Beat
label. Blue Beat was a kind of Jamaican music popular during the
sixties, but the producers had overcooked it a bit and we had boxes
and boxes of these records lying around waiting to be sold.

Fortunately, I'd had dealings with customers in Brixton's Cold-
harbour Lane. One of them, Clint Atkins, a big, burly black guy
from Jamaica, was a real character. Clint couldn't consume the
volume we had, but he liked the product. I knew he had contacts
with other retailers in his community and, sure enough, he gave
me some tips on places in Brixton and Streatham where I could
sell them. I did quite well. Here is an example of a niche product
and targeting the market where it's most likely to sell – in this case,
it was the Jamaican community. Again, you can see me using my
stored information. As soon as I saw this stuff, it was another bingo
moment. I immediately knew a client who'd buy them and, more
to the point, who'd know where I could sell more of them.

This next story is pivotal, as it led me to decide to start working
for myself. A few months after we sold out of the records, I visited
a customer and couldn't help notice some Blue Beat boxes piled
up in the corner of his shop. I'd had nightmares about those bloody
boxes, so spotting them was easy, even though these ones weren't
bought from us. I asked the man, 'What are you doing with those
records there?'

'Don't ask!' he said. 'I got lumbered with these things. I thought they were a good idea, but basically it's Caribbean music and my clientele are not into it. Plus, I don't have the facilities to put them on display or play them, so they're the most useless commodity you can think of. I'd just like to get rid of the blooming things.'

'How many have you got?' I asked.

'About 10,000.'

'How much do you want for them?'

'You can have them for a hundred quid.'

I asked him if I could use the phone in his office to call my boss. In fact, I called Clint, who was always asking me if I could get any more, and did a deal with him. The difference in price between what I bought and sold them for was £80. Now, considering I was earning £20 a week plus commission and this transaction had been done in a quarter of an hour or so, I thought this was a fantastic bit of business.

I told my boss that I'd found some records, bought them and sold them, and that £80 was the profit. To my shock and amazement, he said, 'You should have sold them for much more.'

I was devastated. 'I make twenty quid a week plus commission and I've just made you £80 in the course of a day – is that all you've got to say?'

'But you knew the price of the records was much more, so why did you sell them so cheaply?'

I could not believe I was getting a bollocking. I walked out terribly upset at this situation.

I am going to stop here for a bit and go back in time, as what I'm about to explain will demonstrate another important thing I learned. It has to do with partners.

It was working Saturdays in a chemist's shop that prompted a new business venture. I'd become something of an expert in cosmetics and toiletries, as a result of selling them. In fact, I often say that if I hadn't gone into the electronics industry, I would have gone into cosmetics. I used to drive the boss mad with my questions, I was so inquisitive. At that time, a 'Flaming Red' Rimmel lipstick would sell for 1s 6d, but the Lancôme equivalent was 4s 6d – three times the price!

'Tell me,' I said to the boss, 'these look the same to me – why is one 1s 6d and the other 4s 6d?'

'Advertising,' he said. 'They're both made of the same stuff. There *is* no technical justification, apart from a flasher wind-up case.'

As well as absorbing how people would buy stuff based on the prestige of the brand and the advertising, I was fascinated by what the cosmetic products were actually made of and how cheap the ingredients were. Take hair lacquer, for example. It was effectively industrial alcohol with something called shellac dissolved into it; the theory being that as soon as it's sprayed on to a warmish surface, the alcohol evaporates, leaving the shellac to hold the hair in place – quite simple, when you think about it.

I called a meeting with a couple of my friends, Steve Pomeroy and Geoff Salt. As young fellows, they had expressed an interest in enterprise as part of their banter with me. I told them that cosmetics was a bit of a mug's game and that perhaps we should start a little business making shampoo and hair lacquer. Steve's family's business was lemonade, so they knew where to buy bottles and labels. I could source the ingredients to make the hair lacquer and the shampoo – a soap detergent with a little bit of perfume in it.

Having convinced the two lads we should enter into business, we slung fifty quid each into the pot and formed a brand name – Galsté – made up of our three names: Geoff, Alan and Steve.

I found a hairdressers' wholesale supplier, and we bought gallon drums of shampoo, hair lacquer and some green, gooey setting lotion. Then we designed a small label, which Steve had printed, and we set up a bottling plant in the basement of Steve's house.

Armed with three products in our range, the next task was to go off and sell them. Geoff, who claimed to be a good salesman, had the task of calling on chemists' shops and other general stores to see if he could get any orders. And although Steve was considered to be the expert on supplies and manufacture, I was the one who had to sort out the filling of the bottles. So, come to think of it, Steve wasn't really tasked with anything!

I asked the boss at my Saturday chemist's job to stock some of the bottles on a sale-or-return basis. He always chuckled when he heard about my ventures and was happy to agree. Naturally, when people came into the shop, I would recommend *my* shampoo and hair lacquer, and managed to persuade a few punters to part with their cash. Unfortunately, Geoff and Steve weren't as enterprising as I was and, after a couple of weeks or so, they had zero sales.

One Saturday night, when we were out, we discussed the project and recognised we were not doing very well selling to shopkeepers, so we decided we would try to sell the stuff in East Street Market in south London. The next morning, Steve took his firm's van and we drove to the market, laden with all this gear. The market inspector found us a spot at the end of the market strip, as one of the traders hadn't bothered to turn up. I can picture it now: a large stall with just three products on it! It didn't look very inviting and was made worse by the fact that all three of us were manning such a sparsely populated stall. We didn't sell much that Sunday and, when the market closed just after lunchtime, we went home with our tails between our legs.

I persevered for two or three more weeks, with little success. I decided to spruce the stall up a bit by selling other products. I turned to a supplier who made household cleaning materials such as bleach and pine disinfectant – similar to Dettol. I laid out the stall nicely, with all the products lined up beautifully, including the bottles of pine disinfectant, bleach and toilet cleaner. However, as these were not well-known brands, the move wasn't that successful.

One day, out of sheer frustration and laziness, I decided I wasn't going to bother spending time setting the stall up neatly, so I just chucked the whole lot on in one big pile. This created some excitement amongst the shoppers, who thought that there were hidden bargains to be had. People delved in, looking for buried treasure, and the stuff started to sell like wildfire. Even though it was the same stuff on the stall, when the bottles were neatly lined up, these unbranded products were of no interest to the passing customers. Bottom line: the same stuff at the same price but presented in another way can suddenly start selling. This tells a story on its own.

My friends lost interest in getting up at six o'clock on Sunday mornings, so I ended up being the only one to go to the market. I chucked all the stuff on the stall and a crowd gathered round, as usual. One lady stepped up and asked for six bottles of the shampoo. This was like manna from heaven to me.

Taking a leaf out of the book of the bloke at Chelmsford Market all those years earlier, I went into one: 'There you go, ladies and gentlemen,' I said. 'There's a lady who's bought our shampoo and now she's back. Look at that – you can't get a better testimony than that. Good stuff, isn't it, dear?'

'Oh,' she said, 'it's not for me – I use it to wash my dog!'

You've never seen so many people disperse so quickly.

In the end, we dissolved the business because of the lack of interest of my two partners. I was left with a pile of unsold stock, which I kept in the bicycle shed I had at the flats.

The message here is that I'd thought of an idea. I had the expertise in cosmetics, Steve had the expertise in getting bottles and labels, and he knew the manufacturing process, while Geoff was supposed to be the super salesman. However, the other two didn't have the passion to continue and gave up. They didn't share the responsibility at all and left it to me. It was a lesson learned:

if you have partners, they have to bring something to the party. To be honest, these two didn't. From then on, I learned to do everything myself.

Coming back to the decision to break away and work for myself, I will walk you through my thoughts at the time. Earlier, I mentioned the electrical wholesaler Henson's Scrooge-like manner. As I continued to work for him, my thoughts increasingly ran along the lines of: 'Here I am riding around selling this stuff, which basically is purchased from third parties. On some occasions I do *all* the donkey work – picking up the boxes from the importer, delivering them to the customer, collecting the money. And I don't even get thanked for it. I get my wages of twenty quid a week clear and a bit of commission here and there, but that's it.'

Once again, let me underline the fact that £20 per week plus, say, £5 commission and another £10–15 from my sidelines was a hell of a lot of money in 1966–7.

Some weeks, one of my sidelines (my friend Malcolm and I were refurbishing and selling TVs) brought in as much £30–40, but I couldn't always guarantee Malcolm's participation, so the amount I got from these windfalls wasn't consistent. Nevertheless, selling something for myself that brought in £30–40 made the £20 I got for working five days a week, on the road, reporting to a boss, look stupid. And then, when I remembered the £80 I'd made for Henson in a single day . . . well, that tipped the scales.

One Friday night, I came home and I said to the family, 'I'm going to start working for myself. I told the boss today that I'm leaving.'

My father looked at me as if I were mad. 'What do you mean, you're going to work for yourself? Who is going to pay you on Friday?'

That was an expression I've never forgotten, and it really

summed up his whole outlook on work and life: 'Who is going to pay you on Friday?'

I told him that *I* was going to pay myself on Friday.

If you're going into business, you need to examine your motivation. Ask yourself, 'Why don't I just get a job? Why do I want to be in business myself?'

Now, in my case, it was very simple. I watched my father struggle as a factory worker and saw that it was the ethos of the family that, once a person came of school-leaving age, they would simply move on and become a factory worker in the same way. I wasn't prepared to live the life my family lived, and I recognised at a very early stage that I would have to do it myself and not expect any hand-outs.

Yes, money was the motivator, but I'm not obsessed with money. At the time, it was about making sure I was self-sufficient and had plenty of money so that I didn't have to rely on anyone else. And that is what drove me to be in business on my own. That was *my* personal position – others may have a different reason. Some people may come from quite wealthy backgrounds and may wish to start a business simply because they're interested in achievement and want to prove they can do it themselves, without relying on hand-outs.

The next thing to consider is the *kind* of business you're getting into. Here's the biggest point: simply jumping out of bed one Monday morning thinking, 'I've got an idea – I think I'll go into business' is a complete joke. And that's another thing that annoys me – the amount of letters I get from people (or questions at my Q&As) saying, 'Lord Sugar, I want to go into business – what's the best business to be in?' A total joke. **You have to have experience and, more importantly, a *passion* for the business you wish to enter.**

In my case, as you've seen, I didn't start my business until I had accumulated some experience at the expense of others by way of the previous jobs I'd had. I also had a passion for electronics and technology, which had interested me from a young age. I was to go on and find out that it was this love for the electronics industry that drove me and my colleagues to try to keep thinking up new ideas. I didn't enter this business simply because it was fashionable or 'a good idea at the time'. And so, when I receive letters from young people who say to me, 'Dear Lord Sugar, I'd like to start an airline – can you tell me how I go about it?', you can understand why it winds me up.

If, after weighing everything up, you do decide to go for it then, once in business, **keep control of your costs and know exactly where you are going and how you are doing.** That was my priority, and I checked on a daily basis. To do this, I used the most primitive and mundane of methods – I simply worked out each day how much I was spending on petrol and other expenses and compared it to the gross profit margin I was making on the stuff I was buying and selling.

I set myself targets. In those days, my target was to earn £60 per week. Whilst that might sound ridiculous in this day and age, in 1967, I would guess that £60 per week was equivalent to more than £2,000 per week now.

Of course, in my example, it was simple. By subtracting how much I paid for something from how much I sold it for, I could work out how much money I was making. Of course, I do recognise at this juncture that not all businesses are to do with buying and selling. A recruitment agency, estate agent or consultant, for example, will make no money at all until they have been commissioned to do so, and so starting a business in those sectors is completely different. However, the principle of regularly checking how you're doing is an important one.

When you're analysing your new venture, the most sobering

question you can ask yourself is 'Why *me*? What's so special about me? What's so special about *my* business or the service I'm going to provide that potential customers can't get anywhere else?'

Let's be honest about this. The world is not waiting for you! There are plenty of other suppliers or individuals already out there doing what you have in mind to do, so you have to ask yourself what your speciality is. What is your hook? What is the reason your potential client is going to buy from you? In the case of an actual hard product you have in mind to produce, is it unique? Has it been around before? Are you going to sell it simply because you are much cheaper than your competitors? Are you going to sell it simply because it has greater specification or a unique feature? If you're going to open a shop, what's the big deal? What's different about your shop compared to the one down the road?

If you're going to start an employment agency, who cares? There are thousands of them out there. What's *your* speciality? Why should the human resources manager of your potential customer deal with you? **Unless you face up to the fact that you've got to have something special, you are going to fail and be bitterly disappointed in the marketplace.**

Now, you may throw that back at me and say, 'What was so special about *you*?'

Having just read the story of how I started in business, clearly there were other people out there doing the same as me, people who had lots more money, resources and contacts than me, so I guess my unique point was my determination and my salesmanship, as well as my ability to spot bargains and have in mind who to sell the stuff to. Obviously these were entrepreneurial and enterprising instincts coming out – and, fine, that may be the most unique thing about you and your business.

Oh, and by the way, on top of that, you'll need to **be prepared to put in a lot of hard work, and show a dogged determination not to give up if things aren't going well.**

11

You Can't Skip the Hard Work

Why I'm fed up with businesspeople moaning about the banks
and the government instead of relying on themselves.

I am personally sick and tired of listening to so-called entrepreneurs complaining about how the banks and the government are not helping them in their businesses. I put it down to the fact that the average thirty-five-to-forty-year-old believes that the commercial world we have lived in for the past fifteen or so years is actually the *real world*, when in fact it has been Mickey Mouse Disneyland stuff. It has created a real expectancy culture.

Cast your mind back to the late nineties, when a new generation of business person came into being. Wearing a pair of designer jeans, a lovely blue blazer and white, open-collared shirt, a bottle of Evian in one hand and a PowerPoint presentation in the other, he'd walk into a bank, mention the words 'dot com' and walk out with five million quid. Job done.

Well, we all know what happened there, and we all know what happened around 2008 in the latest economic crisis. The problem is, we've seen some glowing examples of success, like the young bloke who founded Facebook, and similar young entrepreneurs who came up with Google, Amazon and the like.

The fact of the matter is that they are one-in-a-million success stories. Unfortunately, however, young people aspire to be like them. There is nothing wrong with that, but there is a lack of realism in thinking you will be the one in a million who pulls it off. The result is that the old, traditional ways of starting a business have gone by the board. The new generation now expects to come in at what I call the top-floor level. They want to skip the hard work, the back-to-basics, the graft at the coalface. They want to jump into the top position, and they expect that someone's going to lay on the cash for them to do it. To be fair, they've seen it happen on a much smaller scale in the £5 million 'dot com' example I just mentioned. And during the 2000–06 era, the banks were lending irresponsibly to anybody who had the hint of an idea – hence the expectancy culture.

But, hold on, someone's turned the lights out. It's 2008, and I went to the bank and they said no! The bloody government must do something about this immediately. Those banks are terrible.

No, not really. They're not terrible at all, because, as I remind people at my seminars and also in my speeches in the House of Lords, when I was a young man, *I* went to the bank, naïvely, with my hand out, asking for some finance.

They asked me, 'Do you have any collateral? Do you have a balance sheet that shows assets? Do you have a history of profits?'

'No,' I said. 'No, I don't.'

'Well, clear off then, because we're not interested.'

And *that*, I'm afraid to say, is how the market has changed in recent times. Thankfully, banks have gone back to the old-fashioned way of lending money. You need to put up some collateral or you need to show you have a successful business that's profitable or has some assets, and then they will lend to you. After all, that's what they're there for; that's how they make money themselves.

However, the problem is that the younger generation these days don't realise that you sometimes have to start a business from scratch. If you don't have any collateral, a rich uncle, or any assets to hock, then you really need to set your sights much lower when starting your business career. And trust me when I say that you *will* make mistakes. The mistakes will be small ones, but they will hurt because it's your money, not someone else's.

There are lots of famous businesspeople in our country – for example, Richard Branson, myself and many others I could mention – who started in humble circumstances and came up the hard way, taking the knocks as well as the positive things. We all realised that if we wanted something, we had to go out and get it ourselves and not rely upon anyone else.

One incident from a business seminar I held when acting as an adviser to the government sticks in my mind. Some fellow stood up and said, 'Lord Sugar, I think my bank is *outrageous*. They asked me to put up some collateral – they suggested I put up my house in order to borrow some money. It's outrageous!'

'Outrageous?' I replied. 'I want to ask you something: why should they lend you money and gamble on you when you are not prepared to gamble on yourself?'

There was a stunned silence in the room and a lot of murmuring: 'Bloody government . . . useless . . . you're not giving us the message we want to hear.'

'Exactly, I'm not giving you the message you want to hear; I'm giving you the message you *need* to hear. And here *is* the message: Disneyland is over, folks. If you want something, you get it yourself. And if you've got no assets or collateral, don't expect the bank to dish out money, because it's over. The days of irresponsible banks are over. We all know they got a good slapping, and we, the taxpayers, have had to bail them out and take large shareholdings. Yet now you're suggesting that they become irresponsible again and start lending money to lost causes. And I can tell you, I've listened to a lot of lost causes here in this audience today. I can see that you don't like what I'm saying – but I'm sorry, it's the truth, so face up to it.'

After all, why should a bank lend money to an individual with no track record and no previous history in business? It does infuriate me when people say, 'How dare the bank ask me to put up my house as collateral!' What a total joke. *How dare the bank ask you to put up your house as collateral?* Why not? If you're not prepared to risk your house, why should the bank be prepared to risk *its* money on you?

As I said earlier, in recent seminars in 2011, I've met a different bunch of people who've got past that mental block now. Many of the 2009 audience have fallen away; the ones who survived have had a wonderful reality check.

It's interesting to watch a bunch of people in front of you and see their expressions changing. I pride myself on being able to speak in a language they understand. It gets the point home about what old-fashioned banking methods were, which are what they're reverting back to these days. I go to great pains to explain to them that when I got into business in a bigger way, and I went along to the bank – to ask them to assist me in providing the cash flow to enable me to take on more orders – they taught me a very good lesson, a lesson which I have never forgotten. I didn't like what they said at the time, but they were spot on.

'Let me look at your balance sheet, Mr Sugar,' they said. 'You're in the electronics business; you make electrical goods – hi-fis, TV sets and all that stuff – fine. So, how much stock do you have?'

'About half a million pounds' worth.'

'Okay. How much of that stock is finished goods and how much of it is in components?'

'Oh, I would say about £400,000 is in components – bits and pieces, screws, nuts and bolts and electrical parts – and £100,000 is finished goods.'

'Okay, well, here's how the bank looks at all those screws, nuts and bolts and electrical components. We value them at zero.'

'What are you talking about? Are you mad? I've got chips that

I bought from Motorola at six quid each! How can you say they're worth nothing?'

'I'm sorry, Mr Sugar, but a chip is only good if it's inside a finished product. Now, as for the £100,000 worth of finished goods – we value them at half that.'

'What are you banging on about – *half value*? They're worth much more than that. The £100,000 is the factory price – I wasn't valuing them at retail price.'

'Yes, I know, Mr Sugar, but you see, in a fire sale, if you ever went bust, and I'm sure you won't be going bust, that's what we would be offered for them – zero for the components and about half the factory price for the finished goods. Now, let's move on, Mr Sugar. How much money is owed to you by your customers?'

'Erm, about £750,000.'

'Okay, and would you categorise those customers as grade-A customers – the likes of Dixons, Comet, Boots, WHSmith, etc?'

'Well, I would say that about £500,000 is owed by them and the other £250,000 is owed by smaller traders, people who have their own shops here and there.'

'Fine. Well, on the small-trader side of things, the bank would value them at around 25 per cent, and the larger stores we'd value at around 75 per cent.'

'What is going on here? This is unrealistic. I have got a company that has a net asset value – i.e. when I get all my money in from the people who owe me, and when I flog all my stock and when I pay off all my creditors – of at least a million and a half pounds, yet you, if I'm following you correctly, are valuing it at around half a million quid?'

'Exactly right, Mr Sugar. That's about as much as we would be prepared to lend you and, by the way, we would need a complete fixed and floating charge and debenture over the whole company.'

'What does that mean?'

'That means that, in the highly unlikely event that you *do* go bust, we, the bank, get control of everything.'

'What about all my production-line equipment and my machines and injection-moulding plants?'

'Sorry, Mr Sugar, zero.'

Now *that* was a massive wake-up call. But let me tell you, they were spot on, as I learned in later years, when we got over-enthusiastic about ordering too many components and then decided to cease production of the product they were going to be used on. I attempted to sell those components and discovered they were indeed worth next to nothing, despite the fact that the week before we may have taken delivery of 10,000 chips that cost £5 each. And, when it came to replenishing the plant in my factories and trying to sell some of the older equipment – again, it was worth zero. In fact, there were times we had to *pay* to have it taken away. And as far as the small traders were concerned, spot on again. They were constantly going bust, not paying their bills, sending stuff back – that was the type of thing I encountered. As for the large retailers – fair dos, they paid.

So was the bank right? Absolutely right. Let's look at what they were going to earn from lending me £500,000. Assuming the interest rate was between 5 and 10 per cent at the time, their earnings from me for that year would have been anything from £25,000 to £50,000 – all risked on this young man, Alan Sugar. I wouldn't work for 5 or 10 per cent, to be honest with you.

I do hope, Young-Person-Reading-This-Book, that you are not totally demoralised and I haven't shot you down in flames, because all I'm really doing is giving you a reality check.

I feel passionately about this point, about instilling enterprise and entrepreneurial spirit into young people. I find it rather rewarding; so much so that I decided to change the format of *The Apprentice* in 2011. In the first six series it was all about someone getting a job with me, but in the latest series the person who wins will end up going into business with me on a fifty-fifty basis – and they will have the luxury of me injecting £250,000 in cash and value.

I insisted that this seventh series reflected what I've been harping on about. Each and every task was tuned to demonstrate how you could start off on a Monday morning with £250 and come back at the end of the week with, say, £1,000. There it was in full Technicolor, and I do hope that it helped many young people understand that that's how you start a business.

Most of those tasks clearly demonstrated how to do this with no bank loans, no venture capitalists and no need for big factories. You can start something and immediately make some money and become self-sufficient. And that should be a great buzz for any young enterprising person. The winner, Tom Pellereau, has started a business with me, and I have to say, although it's in its infancy, I'm quite excited. It's very small, but I can see that it has the opportunity of growing, so we'll watch this space to see the outcome. Knowing the way I am, I'm not going to let Tom fail, but he's going to have to do the hard work himself. And hopefully this will turn out to be an example of what can be done – and more importantly what *should* be done – by young people.

I cannot overstate the importance of these small, growing businesses; indeed, here is a fact that a lot of people aren't aware of: the bulk of the economy of this country is made up of small companies that employ anything from two to twenty people. That might shock you. You might think it's the giant organisations like Shell or BP or Marks & Spencer. Wrong. The biggest employers are the small companies and therefore they contribute more in taxes and employment than anyone else.

So my opinion on all of this is that anybody starting up a business should not even *think* of doing so with other people's money. I've said this many times, including in an article for the *Daily Telegraph*, parts of which I'm quoting from again here, but you can read it all in full at the back.

You need to start off with some of your own capital or not bother at all. Now, that may sound very draconian and old-fashioned, and it certainly might not apply in the case of high-technology businesses, where perhaps a group of individuals decide to break off from their current employment and set up in research and development – such people may justifiably need to raise some money to seed their work. However, in what I call straightforward commercial buying and selling (or service businesses or retailing), I don't go along with raising money from a third party to get you going. It is dangerous. I believe in starting small. You can control what's going on and you don't have a third party – namely the lender – overseeing you, pressing for their money back.

Apart from the control issue, you need to remember that banks are not cheap; they'll charge you to breathe, with arrangement fees and other costs. They should only be used to your advantage. Consider the cost of money as if it is another expense you have to bear, no different to any other costs you have. There has to be a reason why you need the money.

So ask yourself why you're going to the bank for money. What do you need it for? I spoke to a person a while ago who ran a dry-cleaning shop. He had obviously bought all his equipment a while back. His day-to-day consumables are just the chemicals he needs to clean the clothes. That, plus his utility bills, rent and salaries are his expenses. He has a cash business and yet he was moaning about the bank not lending to him. When I asked why he needed the money, he said he was in debt.

'Why are you in debt?' I asked. 'You are not a shop that has to buy stock. Are you opening other branches? Do you need the money to buy new plant and equipment?' No, it was simple – he was running at an accumulative loss. It was so basic – his takings were less than his outgoings, and had been for ages. So he wanted the cash to pay his salary and his staff's salaries, as his business could not generate it. Sorry, mate, you are totally unjustified in complaining about the bank. They don't back losers. You are insolvent – simple as that. What he needed to do was refocus and see how to start to make money and not just cover overheads.

It is incredible that the simple basics of business go out of the window with all of these modern-day so-called theories and principles. You don't need spreadsheets and complex business plans; you need a pencil and a plain sheet of paper. Take my example of the dry-cleaner. On a sheet of paper, he should write down his monthly costs of rent, utilities, staff and consumables. From this, he will get a figure and understand that, unless he takes in excess of that figure each month, he will lose money. This is a quick sanity check, a wake-up call that all small businesses should do.

As mundane as it might sound, I did a health check every week when I started. I was conscious of my expenses, including my pay, as well as the cost price of the goods I was selling. As mad as it might sound, I wanted to cover my expenses by Wednesday of every week, so that profit made on Thursday and Friday was going to accumulate to net assets – I needed targets. There were weeks when I didn't make it and I had to find the determination to step up a gear the next week to try to make up the deficit.

I started my business before I had lots of commitments, such as mortgages and children. That doesn't mean that you can't start a business if you have commitments, but it is important to have a roadmap in your mind of how you're going to support your private life before you embark upon business on your own.

Over the years, people have written to me or asked me questions at various Q&As. One of the more frequently asked questions by people starting up in business is 'What do I have to do as far as tax and VAT are concerned?'

It amazes me that this seems to be the biggest worry in their heads. I always tell them that this is the *least* of their problems. Go to your local tax office – you will find them to be very helpful and they'll tell you exactly what you have to do. Obviously you need to ensure you continue to pay some form of National Insurance, but the tax office will explain everything. Trust me, this is a walk in the park. However, here's something you'll need to get used to straight away: whatever job you had in the past and whatever new career you wish to pursue, one of the things you most certainly don't know how to do is bookkeeping – doing the books, checking that tax is paid, doing VAT and all that stuff.

I always suggest to people that they learn how to do all this stuff for themselves, rather than subcontract it out to the wife, husband or friend. The reason I say this is because until you do things yourself, you won't pick up the importance of various aspects of business. I was the chief cook and bottle-washer in my company for a long time, even when I got to the stage of employing fifty or sixty people. I learned a lot sitting on a production line; I learned a lot in the accounts department, understanding about import duties, letters of credit and VAT. I learned about dispatching and transport – I learned about *every* aspect of my business. And it all came in handy for the rest of my business career. You might not recognise it now, but I can assure you that getting your hands dirty and doing things which are mundane or not in your 'area of expertise' does pay off in the end.

For example, when we considered constructing a 400,000 sq ft warehouse, my past experience of humping boxes made it easy for me to understand the request of my warehouse manager for fully automated palletisation and loading bays at certain levels. I'd been there and done it, so I could immediately see his assessment was spot on and I authorised the expenditure immediately.

I'll go back to the point I keep making, and that is: a lot of my advice in this book is bound to be based on my personal experience and I have to be mindful of the fact that not everyone is a manufacturer and, therefore, in areas such as research and development and the like, there *is* a need for some capital up front before you can get any income. Obviously you can't all do as I did – go out on a Monday morning with today's equivalent of £100 in your hand, simply to buy and sell. Nevertheless, I would seriously suggest that anyone wishing to start a service business that relies upon a contract (be it software or the development of some form of technology) doesn't embark upon it until they have some order or contract in place from a potential client. And even *that* is not enough for you to go along and raise some money from a third party because, at the end of the day, that third party is going to say, 'That's all well and good, but it still depends upon you delivering the goods.'

You'll need confidence in your ability to deliver what you have promised before you can even *think* about seeing any income. You also need to realise that during the time it takes to get to the stage of having some kind of deliverable product, you'll need to put food on the table – for you *and* your family, if you have one.

I do worry about technical people. I've come across them so often in my life – clever folk who are good at writing software and have some great technological ideas but sometimes forget about putting food in their mouths! They lose sight of what the objective is. They forget that if they have to work seven days a week, eighteen hours a day and through the nights, they need to charge a lot of money. People who have an affinity for technology ought perhaps to take these words as a warning and maybe partner with someone who's more commercial.

Now, I wouldn't want to put ideas into people's heads that I wouldn't be happy with myself, but if you *can* find a way of conducting a 'dummy run' while you are still employed – in your own time and certainly not screwing your employer – then I'd say it was worth a try before taking the giant leap of going into business on your own account.

Don't forget that you started your business because, I assume, you have some experience or expertise in your field. This is the big point: you mustn't rely upon anyone else. It's going to be *you* who defines the way forward. I am sick and tired of hearing people ask what to do and seeing them go to networking meetings and seminars expecting to glean some gems of wisdom. These events are money-making exercises and benefit one party and one party only: the organiser. They have become an escape for people to justify sitting around wasting a day BSing with each other when they should be working. You will learn nothing other than that there are a load of other people in the same boat as you.

You are the only one who knows what to do with your business. There is no shame in looking at your competitors or reading up on what new trends and ideas are around. By all means spend valuable time at exhibitions. Consider, if you are a shop, for example, that while you have a mass of overheads, any new venture you might wish to diversify into – product- or service-wise – can be done with little or no increment of your existing overhead. Think of expanding your range of products or services. Look at the climate and see what new services are required these days. Just as one example, if you are in the recruitment industry, health and safety is now a big thing with firms. Trust me, you don't have to be a rocket scientist to gen up on it. Instead of wasting your time at networking seminars, you may as well sit in your own premises and research it, and then perhaps add the provision of H&S people to companies as one of your offerings.

In my early days, I used my suppliers to finance my stock. As I've said, the bank would not touch me with a bargepole. First of all, you need to build up trust with your suppliers. Treat them as if you have a tax bill or electricity bill. They must be paid on time. There is nothing wrong in establishing extended terms, such as between thirty and sixty or even ninety days. The suppliers will go along with it if you build a history of trust with them. But never buy more than you would normally buy just for the sake of it. You have to pay, and you can only pay if you sell and, by that, I mean make a profit, not just turnover. A retail business sells for cash and, if you have suppliers who offer you terms, you can use this cash flow to stock up with a more diverse range. That's business.

Just as you shouldn't rely on the banks, don't think the government is there to make everything easy for you. One section of a speech I made in the House of Lords on 24 March 2011 (my birthday message!) serves to summarise what I have been saying. You can read the full speech in the appendices.

When I was employed as an adviser to Her Majesty's government last year, I had occasion to visit many small-to-medium-sized enterprises across the country, and I spoke to several thousand business-people. The question most frequently asked of me was 'What can the government do to help my business?'

And my reply, my Lords, was not one which was perceived as helpful. I told them, 'Do not rely upon any government to assist you in running your business. You are people who have chosen to go into business – which is very enterprising, and I'm pleased about that – but do not expect to get any advice from the government on what new products you should make, what ideas you should pursue, what services your business should provide, or how to market your products and generate income – because that's what you're *supposed to do.*

More recently, I remind people: 'Who is there in government who is able to dish out such advice? Just step back and look at them.'

Take, with the greatest of respect, the current Business Secretary

[Vince Cable]. He's never been in business! He's never run a business! He's been an adviser or a politician all his life. He has never touched the coalface. I mean, frankly, what does he know? [. . .]

In my capacity as a business adviser to the last government, I visited many Business Link Centres, which I understand are government funded. The cost of running these organisations was something in the region of £250 million per year. To be perfectly frank, apart from meeting a nice bunch of people, there was no real business advice dished out other than simple stuff you could pick up and learn for yourself by going on the internet.

I would urge the government to redeploy money spent on these types of initiatives in other directions. As an example, there are so many empty premises around the country – large factories and warehouses that can be converted and made into 'incubator factories'. These could contain a core factory and silo workshops on the periphery. The core factory would be accessible to the individual businesses, like satellites around a nucleus.

The government should come clean in their message to help small-to-medium-sized enterprises. You cannot, on the one hand, tell the banks, 'You've been naughty for being irresponsible,' and on the other hand say, 'Go and be irresponsible again and help lost-cause businesses with no asset backing.'

Give SMEs the facts of life. By all means be bold, be adventurous, but be realistic. Don't expect anybody in Whitehall to give you any hints and tips on how to do it because, basically, that's the blind leading the blind. You are the businesspeople, you are the ones with the ideas, and you are the ones who are going to drive your businesses forward. But, regrettably, like everything else in life, there are no free lunches.

All the government can do is provide a good business environment – assistance from HMRC, for example; Export Credit Guarantees if you are successful enough to find export customers; tax breaks for entrepreneurs who sell their businesses; and tax deductions for investment in R&D.

But here's the final point. In taking advantage of all these wonderful tax incentives announced in yesterday's budget, might I just bring everybody down to earth again and say, 'To benefit from them, you have to make a profit.'

And how to do that, my Lords, is something on which this government is not capable of advising.

By now you might be wondering why you spent your money on buying this book, or you might be thinking of using it to prop up a wonky table. Well, I'm sorry, but I warned you that I'm going to tell it as it is. There *are* no free lunches out there and, when you look at the successful businesspeople in this country and the rest of the world, you'll find that most of them did it themselves, out of sheer determination and hard work.

Stick to that and, trust me, you will be satisfied and happy with yourself.

12

Doom on the Pitch

Why football is almost bankrupt, and my unwitting part in its downfall.

It's an astonishing fact that every single person involved in the management of English football is kind of resigned to the fact that it's doomed! They know it makes no commercial sense, they know they are all running at a loss but, come Saturday, they bury their heads in the sand because the game is on.

And I have to admit that I was there for the start of this decline and, unwittingly, even played a part in it.

I look back and wonder whatever possessed me to get involved with football. Naïvety in the beginning, I guess. My beloved Tottenham Hotspur Football Club, which my whole family had been fans of all their lives, fell upon hard times in 1991. There were rumours of them going bust. I thought about the fortune I'd made in the electronics industry and, on a whim, made a fateful phone call to Terry Venables, who, it was rumoured in the papers, was going to put forward a consortium to buy the club.

I'll make a long story short here. After a few twists and turns, Venables and I bought the club from its previous owner. Well, the fact is: I bought the club; the money he put in turned out to be mostly borrowed.

After a year or so, I had a big fall-out with Venables and ended up chucking him out. Again, there were loads of twists and turns and plenty of legal argy-bargy, which I won't go into, as it has already been well documented. Anyway, there was I, in charge of a football club.

I spent ten years trying to do my best at Spurs, but I found it an impossible task. There was pressure on me from the media and the fans to ensure the team was performing and winning things. I was getting all the stick, while the players and the managers, bless 'em, were the innocent parties. It doesn't make much sense, does it? But that was the harsh reality.

It goes to show how the media and the managers of football clubs can turn the fans against the chairmen – or against anybody, in fact. It's similar to the way that politicians in recent years have used the banks as a scapegoat for the poor economy of the country.

The wonderful game of football. Well, it is a wonderful game, and I have to admit that I'm still a big fan and it takes up a lot of my time during the season – watching the games, following the back pages and going to White Hart Lane. Even my wife Ann, who looked at me as if I was nuts when I told her that I was buying a football club, has now become a fan. She can rattle off more names of players from other teams than I can – and she certainly does understand the offside rule.

It *is* a wonderful game and, for the general public, it's something that they look forward to every weekend. It provides so many talking points – their team's performance, their chances of winning a trophy, new players and transfers, referees' decisions. Football's a big topic of conversation. There are millions and millions of football fans in our country, every one of them thinking that they are a football manager, every one of them with an opinion – including me.

England has the most successful league in the world, the Premier League. Successful because it generates the most amount of money. Therefore, the clubs that are members of the Premier League can afford to bring in the biggest names as far as players are concerned.

At our arch-rival's, Arsenal, for example, one of the things you can do on a Saturday there is play 'spot the Englishman'. Their team is made up almost entirely of foreign players. Nowadays, Tottenham has its fair share of foreigners, as indeed do many other Premiership clubs.

Now, you would expect that the richest league in the world, employing the most famous footballers on the planet, would be profitable and prosperous, right? Wrong. In the Premier League in 2011, the cumulative debt of the clubs amounted to over £3 billion – an amazing fact. How did they get themselves into this situation? And how long can they carry on like this?

I was so intrigued, I called up the BBC and told them that I wanted to do a documentary on the finances of football. This was broadcast in May 2011. I sent a few researchers out to pull together some numbers and I arranged to speak to a bunch of people in the football world. Some quite amazing revelations came out of it.

During the period of time I was involved in football, I actually witnessed this transition, and it was one of the most extraordinary phenomena I've seen. It kind of matches the meteoric rise of countries such as Taiwan and Korea – whom I also saw grow during my business lifespan, from under-privileged countries into great industrial empires. But unlike the successes of Taiwan and Korea, for whom I have great admiration, the Premier League has gone the other way. Yes, they've got the revenues, but no, they haven't kept them. The clubs are mostly in debt.

Soon after I got rid of Venables, there was a lot of pressure put on me to do something about the playing performance of the club. I consider myself a quick learner, and my solution to the problem may have made me guilty of kick-starting the modern revolution of importing foreign players. Using a rather logical approach, I went out and bought one of the world's best strikers, Jürgen Klinsmann. And my manager at the time, Ossie Ardiles, recommended the purchase of a couple of Romanians: Gheorghe Popescu, one of the greatest defenders in the world, and midfielder Ilie Dumitrescu.

The fans were delighted. The country was delighted. The media was finally on my side. The back-page headlines raved about 'The Famous Five' – referring to the new forward line at Spurs: Klinsmann, Dumitrescu, Sheringham, Anderton and Barmby. This euphoria only lasted about a month, because the team was losing. And there started the treadmill for me – constantly spending loads of money trying to get results.

In amongst all this, I was attending Premier League meetings, and it is a fact cast in concrete that, in 1992, I was instrumental in convincing the chairmen there to take on board a new television company by the name of Sky. They were all very sceptical, but most of them were also fed up with the appalling manner in which the previous TV company, ITV, was not fairly and equally dishing out the cash they were paying to the league – there was just an elite group of clubs receiving the money. I won't bore you with the details but, after many twists and turns at that meeting, I helped pull off the deal with one of my famous statements to the then chief executive of Sky, Sam Chisholm: 'Go and blow them out of the water, Sam, and offer them a load of money.'

Well, he did. And that load of money amounted to around £50 million per season. Just to put things into context, we'd previously been getting in the region of £5 million to £10 million and, as I said, this was shared by just an elite few. Now, not only had the sum of money gone up tenfold, but the good news was that *all* clubs were going to share in the prosperity; not just Manchester United, Liverpool and Arsenal.

You would have thought all the chairmen would have been over the moon, because even in those days some of the clubs had debts. Their stadiums needed refurbishing and their facilities were run down. And you would have thought that this windfall would be deployed in the obvious way – but not at all. All the money came in one door and went out the other. In later years I famously named this phenomenon 'the prune juice effect'. You know what happens if you drink too much prune juice!

I also came up with a description for some of the mercenary players that the clubs were buying. 'Carlos Kickaball' was the branding I gave them.

Whatever happened to the days when the local boys in the catchment area of Tottenham or West Ham, or even Arsenal, were the mainstays of the team? Things started going downhill when that tradition died. No longer were clubs nurturing kids from their communities, building them up on YTS programmes, with aspirations of them one day playing for the club they lived near. All of that rapidly went out of the window.

The TV deal with Sky was renegotiated in 1997, and it jumped from £50 million per season to – wait for it – £210 million per season. In 2001 it jumped to £520 million per season, and the latest deal for 2010–13 is an amazing £1.17 billion per season, payable to the Premier League for television rights alone.

Now, you would think that with all that money pouring in over the last eighteen to twenty years, these clubs would be prosperous. But instead, they're all skint, with the exception of a couple.

Around 1998, I remember sitting in a Premier League meeting telling the chairmen, 'We've had six years of receiving these massive amounts of money, and look at you, look at all of us. How much have you got left? Nothing. The money has gone to players and agents.'

I put forward a suggestion for the next deal, which was to be renegotiated in 2001 – that whatever we got, the Premier League should keep half of it and release the other half to us irresponsible bunch of idiots. I said that it made no difference how much we received; we'd proved, year in, year out, that we couldn't keep a penny of it. So if we held back half the money and put it into some fund somewhere, in which all of us had an equal share, we could draw down on it as and when we needed – say for a new stand for the stadium, a new roof, a new pitch, a training ground or youth facilities – but *not* for spending on players and their agents.

Well, you would have thought I was doing a stand-up comedy routine. There were actual shrieks of laughter, in particular from Ken Bates, the then Chelsea chairman, who told me to shut up and sit down, in a manner that only Ken can do.

There was only one other person, David Dein of Arsenal, who showed the slightest bit of support for my idea. He could see that what I was saying was right, but the rest of them could not.

I often wonder how an average working bloke can take his two kids to the game on a Saturday – it's got to cost a fortune. By the time he's had a couple of drinks and a bite to eat with the kids, he can rack up, in some cases, £150. Let's face it, for £150 you can get yourself a reasonably good vacuum cleaner or microwave oven. If you don't go for four weeks, you could get yourself a new washing machine or dishwasher.

With these outrageous prices at the turnstiles, people often think that the clubs must be making a fortune on gate money. But in actual fact, turnstile receipts pale into insignificance when you compare them to the £40 million a year *minimum* that each club receives from the TV rights.

People used to say to me when I was at Tottenham, 'If you don't get your chequebook out, a group of us are going to start a campaign to boycott the club's shops and stop buying the shirts.'

My reply to them was 'You can stop buying the shirts, as far as I'm concerned.'

In Tottenham's case, the profits made on shirts didn't add up to a row of beans either. It's a fallacy that gate receipts and merchandise make up a large proportion of a club's revenue. It doesn't. It's the TV money and nothing else, and the revelations I found when I did my BBC documentary are mind-boggling.

I came across football clubs where 92 per cent of their income went on their wage bill alone. Now, you don't have to be an economist to work out that that cannot be right. What other business in the world can spend 92 per cent of its income on paying its employees? Even small businesses like hairdressers – where their income is mainly due to the skill of their staff – can't work at that kind of level.

I found out that a club like Wigan, in season 2008–9, had a turnover of £43 million – £38 million of it being TV money. Their wage bill was £40 million – 92 per cent of turnover. They lost £4 million a year and they accrued debts of £72 million. And this is a club that has an average attendance of only 18,000 and successfully maintained its place in the Premier League that season.

Take West Ham. An average attendance of 33,000, a turnover of £76.8 million, wages of £70 million – again, a 91 per cent ratio of turnover to wages. They're losing £16 million a year and have a debt of £110 million. In fact, that season, across the Premiership overall, wages went up by £132 million and cumulative profit dropped by £79 million. How can this be? How can this wonderful game ever survive? In Germany, the Bundesliga averages about 51 per cent of turnover to wages ratio. Compare this to the Premier League, where the average is about 70 per cent.

And do these high wages in the Premier League make the players loyal? Not at all. There are a few exceptions, of course, but in general the players are mercenaries – particularly the foreign ones, and especially the six-foot, fourteen-stone ones, who go down faster than a vol-au-vent at a wedding reception. These players go where the money is – simple as that. And who's responsible for that? The scumbag agents. Again, I don't want to categorise them all as scumbags; there are a few good ones, but I'd go so far as to say that you don't need more than one hand to count them.

Here's another earth-shattering statistic: in season 2008–9, the total transfer fees paid by all the clubs was £220 million and, wait for it, £80 million of that went to pay *agents* – that's over 30 per cent! Now how can *that* be?

In the real-estate market, there are agents who put properties my way. They charge 1 per cent – it's a known fact. Even the estate agent that sells your house charges you a maximum of maybe 2.5 or 3 per cent. How can anybody justify being paid 30 per cent for introducing you to a player you most probably knew about anyway?

Did Peter Ridsdale, when he was in charge of Leeds United, need to employ an agent to inform him about Rio Ferdinand, who was playing at West Ham? No. But, nevertheless, that record-breaking transfer was conducted via an agent who got paid a bloody fortune.

Agents are dealing with kids as young as thirteen. The agents influence the parents and get them into this greed culture. They cause the biggest trouble for the football clubs. They're not happy unless they're stimulating a deal. Whilst there are rules that say that people cannot 'tap up' players – a football term meaning to lure a player away from his club – the fact is that agents do this all the time.

In 2010 there was the fiasco of Wayne Rooney. Was he staying? Was he going? Who knew? What was it all about? Was it one big blag to make Manchester United give him a bigger salary?

But who am I to talk? I lost all business sense when I was involved in football. Yes, I bought Tottenham for £8 million and got £50 million back when I sold it ten years later, but it was still one of the worst things I've ever done in my life. In spending those years giving my all to try to help Spurs, I took my eye off the ball as far as my core business, electronics, was concerned. And in that ten-year window of the 'dot com' boom – mobile phones and all that stuff – we got left behind. The lesson I learned there was: stick to what you know, keep your nose out of other businesses and do what you're best at. Instead, while I was at Tottenham, all my principles went out of the window. I made irresponsible purchases because I was under pressure to perform. I'll put my hand up and say I was the biggest idiot going – I let agents manipulate things.

In my football documentary, I interviewed Alan Shearer. To be fair, when I asked him about his transfer for £15 million to Newcastle, he said, 'I wasn't worth £15 million. Where did that figure come from?' Supply and demand. But his take on the 2011 £50 million record transfer of Fernando Torres to Russian-owned Chelsea was 'Now that's just unbelievable!' By January of 2011, the half-season point, £200 million had been spent on player transfers alone.

However, Shearer then took the side of the players. 'It's not down to us. We're a commodity. We go out and do our jobs; it's not our fault that people want to pay a lot of money for us, and want to pay us a lot of money.'

'Don't you have a conscience, Alan?' I asked.

'Well, personally,' he said, 'I do, but what's the point in me saying, "No, no, please, don't pay me too much; I'll take less than that" when everybody else doesn't?' I suppose that's a fair point. He went on to explain to me that, as a kid in football, he'd been part of a YTS programme where he'd clean the boots of the senior pros. He learned his trade by doing all sorts of menial tasks, like cleaning out the dressing rooms.

I got a laugh out of him by saying, 'Of course, the youngsters these days can't do that, because they might scratch their Rolexes.'

I remember being at a Premier League meeting. We used to sit round the table in alphabetical order of clubs, so I sat next to Terry Brown of West Ham. We used to look in amazement at the chairman of Leeds United, Peter Ridsdale, who went on an unprecedented spending spree. Terry, an accountant by profession, and I, a businessman, could not work out what was going on. It didn't make any sense whatsoever. It didn't matter whether Leeds won the Champions League, the Premier League, the FA Cup and the Carling Cup. There was still no way they could get enough income to cover their costs. It was a disaster waiting to happen, and that great institution, Leeds United Football Club, finally went into receivership.

And where is Mr Ridsdale now? Oh, he went to Cardiff City, and then to Plymouth Argyle, and now he's off running Preston. Amazing. He claimed that his passion was Leeds. That if you cut him, he bleeds Leeds; if you broke him in two, 'Leeds United' would be printed right through him, like a stick of rock. Maybe he just wanted another shot at football glory.

In recent times, Portsmouth, a small club, tried to become big. They had about three or four owners and got themselves into terrible debt until, eventually, they had to go into administration.

In the documentary, I visited Richard Scudamore, head of the Premier League, and I put this to him: 'Why is it that when a football club goes into administration on Wednesday, they're out there playing again on Saturday? Can you understand why the fans don't give a damn about a properly financially run football club when they can still see their team turning out on a Saturday? When Woolworths went into administration, they shut the bloody doors! You couldn't go in and buy your pick-and-mix any more. It was gone, finished, bust, removed from the face of the earth. But when Leeds United and Portsmouth went into administration – hang on, they're still there! And to add insult to injury, when any other commercial administration or bankruptcy takes place, a receiver or liquidator is appointed who takes any remaining assets, divvies them up and pays out fairly to all the creditors, including Her Majesty's Revenue and Customs. But no – not in football – no, no, no, no.

In football, if there are any dreg ends left over as far as cash is concerned, guess who gets it all? The players! Unbelievable. And what was Scudamore's response? He said he has a duty to the *communities* to which those football clubs belong to make sure their club is still playing.

I put it to him that this was totally unacceptable and suggested that what this industry needs is for one of these clubs to *actually* go into extinction, because it won't be until then that the fans start to realise that they have to stop shouting and screaming at the management of the football clubs to buy more and more players. They need an example; they need a big bankruptcy. Alternatively, never mind deducting the club twelve points for going into administration, they should be slung to the bottom of the leagues – into the Northern Premier League, the Southern League or the Isthmian League – and have to start again from scratch.

Scudamore said that was not really possible. 'Those leagues are part of the Football League and we are the Premier League, and we can't intervene, and blah, blah, blah.' He came up with a load of waffle as far as that proposition was concerned, so I put another to him.

'I want you to imagine that my name is Sheik Al Gorbachev and I've come over to England with my billions. I've bought ten acres of land, I've built a 70,000-seater, state-of-the-art stadium, and I've also spent £250 million buying up some of the best players in the world. Can I come and play in the Premier League please?'

His answer to me was 'No, certainly not.'

'So, where can I play then?'

'Well, you'll have to go down to the bottom and work your way up.'

'Exactly! So when Portsmouth and Leeds go bust, they are also new companies. Why don't they go down to the bottom and work their way up?'

'It's not the same thing, Alan. It's not the same thing really. You're not comparing apples with apples.'

'And whilst on the subject, tell me something else, Richard. How come, when these so-called foreign investors come into this country, you see them standing there on the pitch with the manager, holding scarves above their heads, the great white knights, claiming they've just bought the club – for example, the Glazers at

Manchester United or Hicks and Gillett at Liverpool – and it transpires afterwards that they *borrowed* the lion's share of the money from the bank during the mad banking boom. They then formed other companies, so that the original football club became a subsidiary and was responsible for – wait for it – paying the interest and all the finance charges back to the banks they borrowed from. It was rumoured that, in the case of Manchester United, there was up to £70 million of interest charges payable, just to service the debt that the new so-called owners had incurred. Now, whilst I'm not crying in my beer for Manchester United, the fact of the matter is that that money could have been well used in other areas: building the team, youth development, stadium improvement, whatever. But no, it goes to pay for the ego of the foreigners who have come in and borrowed money in order to buy the clubs.'

Richard's reply to that was that they now have new rules at the Premier League whereby anybody wishing to acquire a football club has to prove they have the money.

I'm afraid that's closing the stable door after the horse has bolted. The fiasco at Liverpool, where the new American owners were put under pressure by the bank RBS, nearly put the club into extinction, and it certainly affected the playing performance on the pitch. They struggled in that particular season, but made a recovery in the end, once they took on Kenny Dalglish.

Now, to be fair, when Roman Abramovich stuck his hand in his pocket and bought himself a new toy – Chelsea Football Club – he didn't hurt anybody. And he still continues to shell out. As I've mentioned, in 2011, he broke the all-time transfer record by paying £50 million for a player. But is that fair also?

I go back to where I started on this issue of football. It's the national sport, which was originally founded on the basis that people would go and support their local football club and watch home-grown players display their talents and skills. How is that the case now? Think of clubs like Wigan, Wolves and Stoke, who don't have the massive financial backing or, more to the point, the fan base and stadium size to support them – what chance do they ever have of offering their fans the dream, when the season starts in August, that they might just win the league? Well, Wolves *did* win the league a few times in the fifties, but I'm afraid to say that the chance of that happening again, in the current financial climate in football, is highly unlikely. And how long will the fans be prepared to put up with that?

13

Fantasy Football

**Giving certain footballers some stick, and why I'm fed up
with bad behaviour in the game.**

In recent years, the term 'fantasy football' has been used a lot. I
don't play the game, but I do have my own fantasies when it comes
to football.

Firstly, there was one Tottenham manager who hung me out to
dry in front of the media – George Graham. Every two weeks he was
telling the media he needed another three players. I still have nightmares about those times. I hate myself for putting up with all that
nonsense. Why I never opened my mouth and fought back, I'll never
know. But, you see, it wasn't the done thing: the chairman must stay
silent; the mouthpiece is the manager. If I ever had my time again,
never mind winning the Premier League or the FA Cup, I would get
some satisfaction from speaking up and not being the bloody wimp
I turned into during the ten-year period I owned Spurs.

And yet some would say that I was the *only* one who would
speak out. The more I spoke, the more stick I got in the newspapers, the more screaming and shouting and booing I got from
the fans. So you can understand why the rest of the chairmen kept
their mouths shut back then, and still do today.

What I *should* have done was call a press conference and say,
'Hold on a minute, have I missed the plot somehow? This is the
great George Graham – God's gift to football. He's been here for

about four months, he's bought six players and he keeps telling me he wants another three players. Well, in fact, gentlemen of the press, this man has spent more money in his short period of time at this football club than he has ever spent at any club in the whole of his career, and we *still* are not performing! Now, is that my fault, or is it perhaps that he ain't that good? What do you think?'

I'd also love to be a presenter on Sky Sports. I'd love to be that bloke who stands there after the game interviewing the players.

First, I'd speak to someone from the winning team. 'Well, Billy, that was a good game, wasn't it?' Billy would be sweating, swigging on his bottle of water and coming out with the usual load of incoherent rubbish.

'So, Billy, tell me, how did you see the game?'

'Yeah, it was good.' Swig, swig. 'It was a great game. Yeah, great game.'

'Yes, Billy, it was a good game, we know that. Have you got anything more to say? I mean, what did you think about the build-up to the first goal?'

'Yeah, well, you know, Tommo's flicked the ball over to Danno, Danno's slipped it across to Willo, and Willo's stuck it in.'

'Yes, we know that too, Billy, because all the viewers and I have just been watching the match, so have you got anything else you can add, other than that?'

'No, not really . . . Just a good game, a good game.'

'Billy, do you think you deserved Man of the Match?'

'Er, well, it's great, you know, but it's a team game – we all did our bit.'

'Well, actually, Billy, Willo scored the three goals, not you or the other boys – so why are you standing here?'

'Yeah, well, Willo will be all right about that – he knows it's a team game.'

'If it's a team game, will you be sharing the champagne with them all?'

'Oh yeah, cheers.' Swig, swig.

Then I would interview a player from the losing team. 'So what went wrong there, John?'

'It's obvious really, isn't it – the chairman needs to get his chequebook out. You can see we need to get a load of players in – it's as simple as that. I mean, the players we have aren't good enough.'

'I see, John, I see. So tell me, John, would you like to be specific as to which *particular* players out of the eleven on the pitch were no good?'

'Well, I can't say that, it's not for me to say . . .'

'But you just *have*, John. You just said you haven't got good enough players, so which ones? *Who* was no good – the centre backs, the goalie, the strikers? Come on John, name them. You named the *chairman* as the villain here – saying he ought to get his chequebook out – so let's have some other names. Come to think of it, are *you* a better player than the others, John, or do you think maybe *you* should be replaced? What do you reckon, John?'

I'd love to have that conversation. It's my little football fantasy. But, of course, it will never happen.

Fantasies aside, there have been times when I actually *could* have spoken out, but didn't. One speech I wish I'd made was to the agent of that great player Darren Anderton, England's blue-eyed boy. He was always injured and hardly ever played for Tottenham, but he'd somehow magically find his fitness when it was time for an England call-up. Can you imagine how frustrated I was, paying this geezer £20,000 a week at the time (which sounds a pittance for footballers in this day and age) – a guy who could never play for us, but got fit when it came to playing for England? And imagine how I felt when I heard that Glenn Hoddle, who became the England manager at one point, had decided to take Darren Anderton under his wing, as far as medical care was concerned, because, to use Glenn's words, 'Your people are making Darren run!'

'Oh, I'm so sorry, poor diddums. He's got to run? Ain't he a bleedin' footballer?'

And what was Hoddle's solution? Our physiotherapist at Tottenham at the time, Tony Leneghan, told me that Darren was under the care of a certain Eileen Drewery. Now, in my naïve mind, I thought that she might be some orthopaedic doctor or a specialist in sports injuries. No – Eileen Drewery turned out to be a faith healer! Darren Anderton would lie on a bed somewhere and she would hover her hands over his body and ask him to have positive thoughts.

'Tony, you're having a laugh, son, surely. This must be a wind-up.'

'No, I swear to you, Mr Chairman. That is exactly who she is and what she does. Glenn's all into this faith-healing stuff and positive thinking.'

I know *now* what I should have said to his agent, who kept telling me that Darren was not happy and that he wanted more money. 'Not happy?' I should have said. 'I'm paying him £20,000 a bleedin' week and some faith healer is waving her hands over him while he's lying on a bed thinking of England. And *he's* not happy? Well, *I'm* not bleedin' happy either, so you can go and piss off.'

But did I do that? No. What a bloody idiot.

Another thing I have trouble coming to terms with is the fact that the football industry is known to have a few dodgy characters in it, but this is all accepted.

There have long been rumours of bungs and all that type of stuff, though I do believe this has largely disappeared these days (or at least become a little bit more sophisticated and gone beyond the brown-envelope-halfway-up-the-motorway days, perhaps to Swiss bank accounts). However, even when some of these people are revealed as scoundrels, do the fans care? 'Nah, never mind. He's a good bloke; he's a great fellow; he's a top manager.' Unbelievable. In any other industry, these people would be flung out; they'd be unemployable.

And what about the behaviour of the players? The England captain, John Terry, was stripped of his title because of allegations of an adulterous affair with the ex-girlfriend of one of his team-mates. This was a bit of window dressing for when the World Cup was on. When the dust had settled, he was given the captaincy back. This is the captain of the English football team, and football is England's national sport. He is out there for young people to look up to and aspire to be. And who are they looking up to? A man who has repeatedly cheated on his partner. He's also been involved in fisticuffs in the past, was fined by Chelsea for drunkenly abusing some American tourists the day after 9/11, and reportedly took £10,000 for giving a private tour of Chelsea's training ground (he said the money was going to charity). This is the *England captain*! But do we care? 'No, he's a good bloke; he's a great defender.' Incredible.

There are double standards in the game, as we saw when Sky got all high and mighty on the moral kick and sacked Andy Gray and Richard Keys for making comments about a female lines-person. But it's okay for the England captain to get up to all his shenanigans – that's fine, we'll have him on one of the football chat shows and it will drag in more viewers. The Andy Gray incident is reminiscent of the time Sky dismissed Rodney Marsh for making a lead-balloon joke in relation to the tsunami in Thailand a few years back, making a play on words with Newcastle's nickname, the Toon Army. My personal theory is that both Marsh and Gray were getting a bit too big for their boots, reckoning that they were the organ grinders rather than the monkeys, and maybe, just maybe, Sky's moral stance was a good excuse to chuck them out. I have no evidence of this; it's just my opinion, and I might be wrong. If so, I might owe Sky an apology.

And as for the great national team, can we find a British manager to manage England? No – only foreigners. How can that be? If I had told my father, God rest his soul, that the England manager was going to be an Italian or a Swede, he'd have said I'd gone nuts. But that's the situation we have now – a manager who can barely speak English running the England football team. Isn't it supposed to be about man management? If you can't speak English, how are you going to get your point over to the players? I saw an unbelievable statement a while back in one of the newspapers, where Fabio Capello said, 'I only need to know a hundred words of English to communicate with the players.' I think that says it all. Most probably ninety of those words are expletives.

Mind you, when you see the England team line up for a match and the camera pans down the line while the national anthem is playing, you always see that Rooney is not singing. I would like to ask him why.

I almost expect the answer would be 'Well, you see, like, wack, I don't know the words, but I was humming the tune.'

Another fantasy of mine would be to manage the team. I remember someone saying to me, when we were doing badly at Spurs, 'Why don't you go down to the dressing room and give the players what for?'

Of course, that was completely out of the question, but my fantasy would be to chuck the manager out and tell the players, on the basis of simple logic, that because I got all the stick from the media and the fans, I might as well make it worthwhile and become the manager. Why not? At least getting all that stick would make sense.

Here's the first team talk. 'Now, I know what you're thinking – what does he know about football? What has he ever won? Well, it's true, I have not travelled on the coach for six hours on a winter's day, and neither have I played football, up to my knees in muck and bullets, but here is the clue, lads – I pay your bleedin' wages and I am your boss. So let's get some facts on the table. Each and every one of you has been playing football since you were thirteen or fourteen years old – that's all you have ever done. So what can I, or for that matter the bleedin' Special One, José Mourinho, teach you about kicking a ball? I'd like to see what the Special One can do without a chequebook down at Leyton Orient. If you can't kick or cross a ball by now, you shouldn't be here.

'Now, you'll see I have a load of coaches here who'll make you train and keep you fit and do all that set-piece stuff they do. What *I'm* going to do is kick your bloody arses out if you don't get fit and perform. Never mind 4-4-2 or a Christmas-tree formation, it'll be P45 and piss off. And if you don't think I have the balls to do it, just try me out. If any of you bleedin' prima donnas don't like it, you have the chance to go now. There is the door – put in a transfer request and I will get you away, because you're *not* as good as you think you are. There's a bunch of kids out there in the youth team and reserves who would bite my hand off if I gave them a chance.'

Then, on match day, this would be my final talk in the away dressing room at Old Trafford.

'Okay, let's take a look at you. All your heads are down – you've already decided, without kicking a ball, that you've lost. You have a tosser chairman, who is now the manager, who knows sod all about football, and you're doomed, right? Well, *you* are the tossers. Man U have eleven men, like we do – the reason you think their eleven men are better than you is because you read it on the back pages of the papers and saw how much someone paid for them. And you've also read what every sports hack in the media has said – Spurs will never win here today. So I tell you what; how about I go and see Sir Alex and say, "Here are the three points – nice to see you," and you lot refund me your wages this week?

'Now get out there and show your designer girlfriends and

wives that you are real men. It's eleven against eleven – simple as that – but until you believe in yourself and not the bullshit in the papers, you have no chance. If you want to, you can put your iPod earphones in so you don't hear the crowd, although what that has to do with it, I don't know. Just use your imaginations and pretend they are cheering for you.

'If we lose, I'll be giving an interview to the TV people after the game's over. And it won't be all that crap about "We'll go away and regroup and collect our thoughts and pull ourselves together and get ready for next week." No, none of that nonsense. I will be saying, for example, that you, Danno, were terrible and I don't know why I pay you fifty grand per week for a pathetic performance like that. And you, Willo, you looked like you were out there having a stroll in the park – the bloke who walks my dog could have done a better job. I will name names and place the blame on *you*, because, sunshines, I am not on the bloody pitch – *you* are. I'm not going to take any stick any more, but you are going to get your fair share. It's shit or bust, lads. If I am going to get the stick, then I will do it in style.

'Now, I'm going to put up the team sheet in ten minutes. If anyone doesn't like what I've said, speak up, because, as you know, I've brought another six players along in case we need them.'

In the post-match interview, when asked if the £25 million we got for the sale of a centre forward would be spent on new players, I would say, 'Well, actually, no. I'm going to buy a twin-jet-engine Bell Ranger helicopter and build a helipad at the ground, so that I can get home quickly to watch *Strictly Come Dancing* and *The X Factor*. Also, we don't have a shirt sponsor for next season, so I am going to put a picture of me on the front of the shirts with my two hands up and a facial expression that says, "Well, what can I do?"'

Can you imagine the headlines in the daily rags, and all the money they'd be paying the players for their exclusive stories? Yes,

I know they earn £60,000 to £100,000 a week, but old habits die hard – they'll still take £500 for their story.

I know I'm a bit nuts, but I really would do that if I had my time again, if only to go out in style.

It is a fascinating phenomenon that winning and losing is all about the players' frame of mind. How many times have we seen a team suddenly spark into life when a new manager is appointed? Take, for example, Liverpool – one of the most famous clubs in the world. When Roy Hodgson was appointed as Liverpool manager in season 2010–11, I knew deep down that it wouldn't work – the reason being that the players knew he'd never won anything. And because of that, he didn't have the dressing room on his side. Sure enough, that great club slipped down the table – but then they appointed Liverpool legend Kenny Dalglish, and all of a sudden the same players started to perform! Now, don't tell me that Kenny taught them anything new or that he's some tactical genius. Okay, he knows the game, but so does Roy. It's all in the players' heads. One day Sir Alex Ferguson is going to retire, and we wait with bated breath to see who will take over. I am willing to bet that, when that day comes, the results will not be as consistent.

So often you see players' heads go down when the team lets in a couple of early goals. Instead of the players stepping up their game, you can see by their body language that they're resigned to defeat. Then suddenly they get a goal back, followed by an equaliser. The whole spirit of the team changes within minutes, and it's clear to anyone – even a non-football expert – that they will go on to win the game.

With all the money that has been poured into the game and the enormous changes to the face of football, you would think that those who govern the game would also evolve and change with the times. Unfortunately not. The game is run by a bunch of old stick-in-the-mud characters who came out of the ark and who argue against any logical changes to improve the sport. It took them years to implement the current back-pass rule, and I would like to have been a fly on the wall the day they decided, back in the fifties, to allow floodlit football at night. Can you imagine what went on there?

Nowadays, the loss of a game, or even a goal, can mean the difference between staying in the Premier League or dropping down, winning it or coming second – and that translates into big-time money either way. The consequences of a referee's decision can have an impact on tens of millions of pounds for an individual club.

About fifteen years ago, when I was on the board of the Premier League, I was asked to evaluate a goal-line technology device which would establish beyond any shadow of a doubt whether the ball crossed the line or not. I went with one of my technology guys from Amstrad to suss it out, and reported back that it worked. However, it was never adopted, the reason being that FIFA and UEFA, the bodies that govern the game, wouldn't allow it. These idiots have resisted it for ages – it seems to be a pet niggle for them. They refuse to accept it, despite being harassed by everyone at the top level in football. They say that the cost of implementing it in all members' grounds throughout the world would be prohibitive, and so, for example, a small team in Africa could not afford it.

Well, neither can they afford floodlights, is what I say. They say that the lower level games played over at Hackney Marshes, for example, would not be able to deploy it. So what?! It should be used in top-flight football and at the World Cup, the European Championships and the Champions League – where the clubs and the organisers can afford it.

Another argument is that the game will slow down and lose its flow. That is total rubbish. As we all know from watching on TV, we can see a replay within seconds – as could a fourth official on a TV monitor in the stands. All they need is two buttons, one red and one green, that illuminate a corresponding green or red light for the referee to see. We also know that by the time the players have finished running after the referee and remonstrating with him, the decision could have been confirmed five times over, so the 'slowing down the game' excuse is nonsense.

The fifteen-year-old technology was quite sophisticated; however, these days, there would be no need even for that – let's face it, you can buy a webcam in Argos for fifty quid. Okay, perhaps use a better quality device, but you get my drift. Maybe have four of them embedded in the goal posts, all focused on the goal line and connected by wi-fi to some monitors in the stand. I would say £3,000 for the lot. And if you're worried about wi-fi, they could easily be hard-wired under the pitch and the cables run into the stand. There really is no excuse at all.

As it happens, Spurs seem to have been particularly unlucky with goal-line decisions. There is a famous example when we were disallowed a blatant goal at Manchester United, although the ball was *eighteen inches* over the line. Even Sir Alex admitted it after the game.

Towards the end of the 2010–11 season, Spurs were chasing Manchester City for fourth place in the Premier League in order to qualify for the Champions League the following season. So, quite apart from the prestige, coming fourth rather than fifth meant about £40 million to the club in cash terms. In a crucial game against Chelsea, Spurs took the lead, but then Chelsea were awarded a goal when the ball did not go over the line. On the instant replay on TV, it was there for all to see. After the game, all the commentators confirmed it was not a goal, as indeed did the managers of both teams. To add insult to injury, later in the game, another goal was awarded to Chelsea that was blatantly offside – again, both managers and the commentators agreed it was not a goal. The end result was that Spurs lost 2–1, my point being that had they *won*, they would have got three points and, had the rest of the season played out a certain way, they could have overtaken Man City and taken fourth place. Or, to put it another way, it could have earned Spurs £40 million.

Let's analyse it another way. Chelsea were chasing Manchester United to win the Premier League. If Chelsea had ended up narrowly winning it, then the two goals they got against Spurs which should *not* have been awarded would have cost Man United the glory of being Premier League champions – as well as a load of money.

In the end, it turned out that the three points wouldn't have helped Spurs and didn't help Chelsea, but they *could* have, and that's my point.

There's only one way to deal with these lily-livered leaders of the game, and that is legal action. I was once told, after Spurs were handed a draconian punishment by the Football Association, that there was nothing I could do about it. I won't bore you with the whole story, but I got the decision reversed after a long legal battle. This amazed my Premier League chairmen colleagues, many of whom had been in the game a long time. They told me I'd broken the mould and smashed the FA; I'd done what no other person had ever been able to do.

I was also the first to have giant screens in the stadium showing the game *live*. This was rejected by the FA and some referees, until I told them all to get stuffed or have a legal fight about it. They backed down. Funny that – many stadiums have them now.

Going back to the Chelsea game, if those three points would have meant fourth place and a Champions League spot, then if I had been in charge of Spurs, I would have taken legal action against FIFA and cited that brain surgeon Sepp Blatter, who won't move football into the twenty-first century in the way that cricket, tennis and rugby have been. Imagine a writ arriving on his desk – to him personally – for forty million quid! Most probably, it would have no standing in law, but it would make some very big, innovative waves and might get others to follow. I would definitely do it!

And while on the subject of Sepp Blatter, what a bloody farce it is that all the senior members of FIFA were attacking each other over alleged bribery claims. Rumours have been running wild for years that the whole of FIFA is corrupt, but nothing ever seems to be done about it.

When you consider the astronomical amounts of money being offered to football by sports companies or beer companies, you can see that there is temptation there. What makes me laugh is that FIFA judge themselves – they hold disciplinary meetings or investigations against their own members – and all that seems to happen is they find ways either to justify someone's actions or suspend them. Now, in any other walk of life – if this were a government department, for example, or a large company which suspected that fraud had been going on – naturally they would call in the police to investigate. Not in football. Instead, they deal with it themselves. It's kind of like, 'Okay, we've caught you bang to rights. Tough luck – you've been rumbled for nicking a few million quid, so clear off. You're off the committee.'

Let us also consider the choice of where the World Cup is to be hosted. There is a charade that is played out, with the countries putting forward their bids to put on the event, delegations of FIFA committee members that go to each country to appraise the facilities and see if they're up to scratch, all the schmoozing and entertainment that goes on to try to convince them to choose that particular country. What a bloody joke. I remember commenting on this fiasco when FIFA was checking out England's facilities. Suddenly, Sky News interrupted its broadcast to show a procession of limousines driving into Wembley. It was as if there was a royal wedding or a visit from the President of the United States. Who bloody cares about seeing a load of black limos pouring into Wembley? To add to the joke, Britain hauled out its dignitaries, including famous sports personalities such as David Beckham. We spent an absolute fortune on our World Cup 2018 bid; indeed, there was a committee set up by the FA just to handle this.

The FA chairman at the time, Lord Triesman, happened to make a private comment that four members of FIFA wanted a bung to vote for England. Unfortunately, the person he spoke to recorded the conversation and went on to sell the story to a newspaper. Subsequently, Lord Triesman resigned as FA chairman. There were endless apologies made by the FA and the government about these nasty allegations, and for a while Lord Triesman was branded as the man who lost England the right to host the World Cup by insulting FIFA's 'honourable' selection procedure. When I spoke to Lord Triesman, he told me that he stands by his suggestion that corruption is rife in the selection process of choosing the venue for the World Cup. He told me that he was going in front of a committee that was investigating England's failed 2018 bid, and he said he was going to name names. He was true to his word, and this opened another can of worms, resulting in FIFA starting its own investigations.

In the meantime, there has been a battle for the presidency of FIFA. Sepp Blatter has held the position since 1998, but when a new challenger emerged, Mohamed Bin Hammam, his chances were dented by accusations of corruption – allegations were made that he and FIFA vice-president Jack Warner had tried to bribe members of the Caribbean Football Union – one has to question by whom. However, the fiasco went on, and Sepp Blatter too was accused of corruption. In a last-minute announcement in May 2011, just before Bin Hammam was due to go before the ethics committee, he withdrew his application to become president. At a hearing on 29 May it was decided to suspend Bin Hammam and Jack Warner, and that further investigations would take place to see if they were guilty of the alleged bribery. But, surprise, surprise, Sepp Blatter was exonerated by FIFA's ethics committee and allowed to put himself forward for re-election, and on 1 June he duly won his one-horse race.

To tie up the loose ends, at a press conference held on 29 May, it was disclosed by FIFA that, on the basis of a 200-page dossier the FA had handed them covering its investigations of Triesman's claims, the four members he'd accused of corruption had been completely cleared.

Then Jack Warner resigned on 20 June. FIFA said, 'As a consequence of Mr Warner's self-determined resignation, all ethics committee procedures against him have been closed and the presumption of innocence is maintained.' And Warner said, 'This is giving the impression that FIFA is sanitising itself. I've been hung out to dry continually and I'm not prepared to take that.'

On 23 July, after a two-day ethics committee hearing which he did not attend, Bin Hammam was found guilty of paying or offering bribes and banned from football activity for life. He still maintains his innocence and apparently intends to appeal the decision.

So what the hell is going on? Never has there been a truer endorsement of the saying 'There's no smoke without fire.' The problem is that FIFA is like the mafia – it is not a government-controlled organisation, and it's hard to see who has the jurisdiction to shut it down and reorganise it.

If the football associations of, say, England, Germany, Spain, Italy, France, Brazil, Portugal and a few others all got together and put forward a vote of no confidence and set up another association to control the game, this would send shockwaves to FIFA. Let's face it, they have plenty of time to revolt during the four-year period between World Cups. A lot can be done in four years and, as far as the European Championships are concerned, the leading countries in it can set up their own championship, without either FIFA or UEFA – but they don't have the balls to stand up to these governing bodies, so it's never likely to happen.

I do believe the answer lies with governments, not just in

England, but across Europe; they should poke their noses into the game. After all, governments control the media, telecoms, environmental issues and financial services, so why not football?

I know I probably sound like some clever clogs trying to be smart, but my wife and friends will tell you that long before the 2018 World Cup vote, I said it would be Russia. My logic was that all this tendering and visiting is just a charade – let's face it, it's the World Cup, and it's right that it should move around the world. In the past, places like South Korea (who co-hosted it with Japan) have been selected as they became emerging powerhouse nations. Africa was a continent that made sense, as indeed was America, when it was held there. So consider what other continent was left. Well, ever since the World Cup started in 1930, Russia has been ruled out from hosting it, as it had always been a communist state, cut off from the world. But in the last twenty years or so it has become a big commercial power, with massive oil resources, trading with the world and producing several billionaires. So to me it was an absolute no-brainer that Russia would win the vote and, more to the point, that the Middle East had to be another territory that would get it one day. And so it transpired that the 2022 World Cup was awarded to Qatar. This, if you think about it, is just common sense – so why the fashion parade? Why didn't FIFA simply say that it needs to be seen to be fair to emerging territories?

14

You Are Just a Number

**The changing face of finance, our debt culture, and how
even I don't get loyalty from my bank these days.**

Remember when you used to go into your bank and see the same
face behind the counter every time you handed over your paying-
in book or withdrew some cash? You might have even known the
bank manager. Nowadays they try to stop you from coming into
the bank at all – they'd much rather you got on the phone or used
the internet.

I have observed that while banks want to divert you away from
simple contact with a bank teller, they have a dilemma inasmuch
as they'd love to close branches (to save costs on rent and staff),
yet they also want to sit you down and try to talk you into buying
other services, such as insurance and mortgage protection.

You used to pay your utility bills – gas, electricity and water –
by cheque. Those days are gone – now you pay for almost everything by standing order or direct debit. There are some people,
particularly of the older generation, who just can't get their heads
around that. They don't like the idea of their electricity company
just taking money out of their bank accounts. I do sympathise a
little with them, but that's the way it is and, of course, when you
reflect, it's a very efficient way of doing things. Why bother writing
out a cheque every three months, then putting it in an envelope,

buying a stamp and going to a post box, when you can sign up for it to be paid automatically by standing order?

I'm sure most of you have been through the hassle of having to change your bank account or deciding that you no longer want to deal with a particular vendor, or wanting to stop a payment, or making claims against charges you don't think should have been made. You know how difficult it is to do that on the telephone, via that other phenomenon of modern-day life – the call centre.

You phone up your bank and after the third ring some automated voice answers inviting you to press various buttons until – if you're lucky enough – you get through to a human being who will take you through a whole list of security questions to make sure they're actually talking to the right person. And woe betide you if you've forgotten the telephone password you set up five years ago – you've had it. What they do then is put a block on your account, at which point *nothing* gets paid, because they think you're some fraudster. So before you *dare* pick up the phone, you need to have every single detail in front of you, including your blood group, a sample of your DNA and a record of the last time you had constipation. It's like an obstacle course.

I get very frustrated when they throw a new question into the equation, but what frustrates me even more is that when you finally get through and deal with the matter you phoned up about, the person on the other end of the phone goes into a sales spiel for some other product they want to sell you. And if it's not that, they ask you to take part in a survey on how well you've just been treated and what you think of the service.

What happened to the old days, when I used to phone Mr Brown at the bank and say, 'Can you just transfer fifty quid to John Smith's account please?'

'Sure, Alan, leave it to me.'

Boom – the phone went down – end of call.

For sure, those days have gone. When I was sixteen and I got my first job with the Ministry of Education and Science, I walked into Lloyds Bank in nearby Berkeley Square. I didn't have a bank account and needed one in order to get paid. So I walked from the office in Curzon Street and the first bank I saw happened to be Lloyds. Forty-eight years later, I am still with them. It seems to be one of those things – you tend to stick with your bank, as you do your insurance broker or doctor. Throughout these forty-eight years, they have been my personal bank, as well as the bank through which all my business transactions have been conducted. I was loyal to them and, in the early days, they were loyal and helpful to me. However, since depersonalisation of service came in about fifteen years ago, all that loyalty went out of the window. I am just a number now. Some of the people I speak to there weren't even born when I first opened my account back in 1963.

In the recent banking crisis of 2008, a new wave of executives was put in place at the top level, and their dealings with my companies became very clinical. One such example was brought about by the fact that, during the banking crisis, Lloyds had taken over HBOS. HBOS had been quite irresponsible in their lending; particularly in lending to some fly-by-night real-estate clients. HBOS lent them money against very little collateral on over-valued assets, sometimes agreeing to 100 per cent financing – meaning that the fly-by-nights put in nothing themselves. *My* company had taken some financing from HBOS to buy a very large building for £112 million. We had put up £23 million and HBOS lent us the rest.

After Lloyds took over HBOS, the real-estate values in the market started to drop, and the new wave of management came to me, saying that their new valuation of the property they had lent against was, as they put it, 'under water'. In other words, they decided the value of the building had dropped to a level at which they would never have lent the amount still outstanding to them. Suddenly they had changed their methods of doing business, using some new post-crisis criterion, not the old irresponsible one.

I called a meeting with the most senior people at Lloyds to try to sort this matter out. Present at that meeting were about six so-called specialists from the bank, my son, Daniel, and me.

I started off by telling them that I had been with the bank for forty-eight years and, as their records would show, I had never let them down. I pointed out that they had written off hundreds of millions of pounds in bad debt on irresponsible loans they had made to fly-by-nights, but that I was not one of them – I took my debts seriously. I was not going to fold the single-purpose company down, of which the building was the only asset, then hand them the keys and say goodbye (like the fly-by-nights did), lumbering them with the problem. No, I told them, I would honour my commitment, but they would need to come up with something from their side and stop talking nonsense about loan-to-value and all that rubbish.

They gave me some lip service about how valuable a customer I was to them, but this was all double-barrelled bullshit. They ended by making the most ridiculous proposal, which only an idiot would accept. I turned to Daniel and shrugged my shoulders – never mind the forty-eight years of never letting them down; they applied the same principles to me and my companies as they did to others. My history with the bank meant jack shit.

I guess I shouldn't have been surprised. Maybe the world has passed me by, and some of my own standards are now perhaps old-fashioned, some might even say naïve. I have grasped it now and realise not to expect any favours or special treatment because of my long-term custom. Sad, but that's the way the world has changed.

Fortunately, my main company (which owned the single-purpose one) has many other assets, and I decided that Lloyds could get stuffed – when the loan became due for repayment, I would simply repay it and then tell them to sod off.

Now, when it comes to the utility companies, you need a degree in economics. They bombard you with so many different offers – on-peak, off-peak, high-user, phone after six, twenty selected callers, night-owl rate, winter tariff . . .

And don't you think it's a bit of a con when you get persuaded by a utility company to swap your gas or electricity supply over to them – having shown you, by looking at your old bills, how they'll save you loads of money – and then a few months later they're writing to tell you they're very sorry but their charges have got to go up?

Now, if you're one of those pedantic people who have the patience for this sort of thing, you *could* play the game: 'Yes, I'm dealing with the London Electricity Board at the moment, but after three months I'm going to swap to Scottish Power, and six months later I'm moving over to British Gas, because they can sell me electricity cheaper than the others.' Yes, if you are a complete nutter and can be bothered to scrutinise the bills and make sure all these changeovers are done correctly, I guess you *could* play the game, but who does?

What's even more annoying is that sometimes the so-called helpline for information on how to use their products or services is an 0845 number, so you're actually *paying* to phone their call centre – maybe in Bangalore – to ask how to use something you've bought from them. Bloody cheek!

Unsolicited telephone calls are another pain in the arse. If a company gets your details – because you were foolish enough to give them your home or mobile phone number when you filled out a form online – you get people calling you all the time to make you new offers. It completely gets on my nerves. I'm much more careful now whenever I buy something online – I always make sure that those boxes are unticked. Funny, isn't it, how they always seem to be pre-ticked for you, so that the default option is: 'We will send you new offers . . . We will contact you . . . We will give your name to other people so that they know what type of products you buy . . .'

No, thank you very much! Watch out and untick those boxes because otherwise you'll be bombarded; your email inbox will be filled up. And even after opting out, some of these vendors take no notice and continue to inundate you with offers. It's fortunate that I have an IT manager in my company and I can just get him to block them, but I have no idea what the ordinary man in the street does with his Hotmail account. I guess the geeks out there will say that it's possible to do it with spam filters and all that stuff, but the average person probably gets fed up having to deal with it.

So never give out your phone number or email address unless it's a mandatory thing. Always check those boxes and either tick or untick them, and read the words next to them very carefully, as these companies are extremely slippery. You might be ticking a box to say that you *do* want something when your intention was to say that you *don't* want it. I say this because it's happened to me, and I'm supposed to be relatively bright.

We've become a nation of subscribers. It's all monthly subscriptions – fifty quid a month for your Sky TV, thirty quid a month for unlimited texts on your mobile, twenty quid a month for your internet, as well as other bits and pieces. I suppose, from a young person's point of view, they like to know where they stand. When you add it all up, it shows you, in simple terms, what you need to earn each month before you put a piece of food in your mouth. Add that to your standing orders for gas and electricity, water rates and your mortgage, and I suppose it's a clinical way of having a fixed sum in your head of what your burning cost is.

But have you ever tried to work out the rates for mobile phones? Again, you need a degree in mathematics to do it. In fact, it doesn't surprise me that there are now consultants who advise companies on the best tariffs available in the marketplace. These experts spend their time advising their clients to churn off this company and churn on to that one.

At least the legislators have made sure you can keep the same phone number and transfer it from one network to another – which is a great thing, because it wasn't like that in the beginning. Also, the legislators have made sure that the mobile phone operators let you know how much calls and texts are costing you, particularly when you're abroad. What a bunch of monkeys they used to be – talk about making hay while the sun shines. Mobile phone costs abroad used to be outrageous; at one stage, you were actually paying to *receive* calls. I hear that there are moves for these costs to be reduced by having an international roaming agreement between the various mobile companies, in order to sort this out before various governments get involved and start punishing them.

I remember the story of this poor girl who loved *The Apprentice*. She was away on business at some seminar in Monaco, and she used her mobile dongle in her laptop to watch *The Apprentice* on iPlayer, as she was such a dedicated fan. She got a bill for £870. Now, I know I'm good, but I'm not worth that much!

Then there are the credit card companies, soliciting people left, right and centre. What you've got to remember, folks, is that they want you to *owe* them money, because apart from the 2–3 per cent they might charge a retailer when you buy something from them, they make their money by you *not* paying off the whole lot each month. And we're talking outrageous amounts of interest here – I've seen up to 29 per cent in the past. And some of the retailers are getting as bad as the credit card companies, offering their own store cards and hoping and praying that you don't pay immediately and choose to pay the minimum amount.

Regrettably, this has created a debt culture, where people have accumulated multiple credit cards, maxed them out and are now simply focused on paying back the minimum amount every month. If you speak to the credit card companies, and they're honest, they will tell you that they make a fortune. They know that they're going to get knocked occasionally, and that's all taken into account. They know, for example, that some people simply won't pay or will become personally bankrupt, but it's all part of an actuarial calculation carried out by some very clever mathematicians. Even if they pitch their interest rates high, as long as they make it clear in their adverts (or on the forms you sign) when they suck you in, they are not breaking the law.

This has spawned another little industry – more so-called experts who help you close out your debts. What a lot of rubbish. It's out of the frying pan into the fire. Trust me, these people are no saints, and they are not your saviours – there is no free lunch here. What they do is take over all the debts and tell you that you've now got just one debt to pay, instead of perhaps six. But they're in it for the money – your money. They're not doing it out of the kindness of their hearts.

Another thing that is becoming dangerous in the UK are these pre-payday cheque-cashing companies, where you ask them to give you a loan against your salary, which is coming, say, in two weeks' time. The interest rates are ridiculous and, again, people get stuck on a treadmill, where they have to pay back outrageous amounts of money for a piddling £100–200 advance against their salary. I seriously think that the government's regulators need to have another look at all of these so-called financial services, such as credit cards and money-lending. It is a scandalous situation and, with the greatest respect to some of the people these companies prey on, they are not the most gifted academically. They get sucked in by smooth-talking salesmen, and in many cases they don't understand what they're letting themselves in for until it's too late.

All this is part of the changing face of finance. I would say that this practice of seducing people into debt never existed thirty or forty years ago. Certainly the banks and the people in them were far more honest, far more down to earth and far more helpful towards people. They would simply say to them, 'No, you can't have any money, and here's the reason why . . .'

15

Blood on the Tennis Court

**The dangers of playing mixed doubles with my wife,
and my McEnroe moments.**

Over the years, I think I've tried everything to keep fit. I've certainly spent a lot of time playing tennis – indeed, I have a tennis court at home. However, forty-odd years of pounding away on the tennis court has taken its toll on my groin and back. In fact, I haven't played on my own court for at least five years. These days, I can only play on clay or soft-surface courts and, instead of the usual two hours of singles I used to play every day, I now have to restrict myself to a maximum of twice a week to get the right balance. Otherwise, if I overdo it, the only part of my body that's not hurting is my hair.

Sometimes it seems that everything I do, I take to the extreme. People ask me how I can play in the baking midday sun in Spain or in Florida, with temperatures in the nineties. I guess the adrenalin works in me to mentally block out the heat that most people can't put up with. Actually, one of the reasons I tend to play at that time is because, in the holiday-type resorts I end up at in Spain or America, all the conventional early-morning slots are taken. The courts only become available around eleven thirty, when, as they say, only mad dogs and Englishmen go out in the midday sun.

Like all tennis enthusiasts, I must have tried out every single new racquet that has been launched over the last forty years. We all tend to fall for it when we see Borg, Connors or McEnroe playing with a certain racquet – and, more recently, the likes of Federer and Nadal. Of course, the reality is that a top player could beat me with a racquet he picked up in a toy shop.

The sports business is a massive industry. Companies such as Nike and Adidas spend a fortune advertising their brands using famous sports personalities. The whole concept of selling a bit of sports kit – be it shoes, racquets, shorts or a shirt – is based on the buyer having visions of themselves being as good as the famous person seen wearing or using the item in real life. It creates a kind of snobbishness where, if you're not seen wearing the right kit, you think that, not only will you look a mug in the way you are dressed, you'll also be a mug in the way you play.

Another massive industry is sports drinks and power bars. These are highly priced items that, to be fair, do contain ingredients that replace the electrolytes and carbs you lose when you engage in heavy physical exercise. However, the truth is that water and some chocolate or fruit will do the same in most cases.

In Spain, for example, when I play tennis in the summer, I take loads of water and some sachets of sugar from the coffee shop in the clubhouse. After an hour or so, I might be seen opening a sachet and swigging it down with some water. I've often been asked by onlookers, 'What are you taking, Alan?', expecting me to tell them about some special concoction. You can imagine their surprise when I show them that it's just some sugar from the coffee shop.

It makes me laugh when I go to my friend Stuart's shop in Florida. Stuart is a character you could write a whole book about. I've been going to his shop for about twenty-seven years and he's found himself a niche in the market. He's known as one of the cheapest vendors of tennis racquets in south Florida but, more importantly, he strings more racquets than anyone else in the whole of Florida.

In fact, he is a man after my own heart, and his story is quite interesting. As a kid, he did not excel at school academically, but he was sports mad; tennis mad, in fact. He realised that he was not professional standard, so he decided to open his own sports shop. He packed up all his personal belongings in a large holdall, left his hometown of Baltimore in Maryland, jumped in his old Datsun car and drove to Florida with a few hundred dollars to his name. To cut a long story, he convinced one of his family members to give him a loan so he could take a shop, and the rest is history. To use his words, 'I look back sometimes and pinch myself that I came here with a single bag and a few hundred dollars. Now I have one of the most popular tennis shops in Florida and live in a great house in one of the most exclusive parts of Boca Raton.'

As I say, Stuart is real character, so you can imagine how surprised Ann and I were one day to see him in his own TV advert. Back then, in the early eighties, local cable TV companies offered local shops the opportunity to be on their network for a very low cost, say $100 for five slots. What made Ann and I laugh was the fact that Stuart had organised the filming, using one of his staff and a cheap camcorder. He did all the talking himself, while his staff stood behind him like tailors' dummies. But the funniest thing was that Stuart's grandmother was in the adverts – she even said a few words, which was hilarious, as she had that typical New York-style drawl of an old Jewish lady. I remember going into the shop a few days later and telling Stuart that I'd seen his advert. I offered him a new idea for a script, if he should ever make another one. I suggested his grandmother should say, in the same drawl, 'Everybody who buys a new racquet or a tennis outfit can come out back and have a free bowl of my special matzo-ball soup.'

Being in Stuart's shop is an experience in itself. I've never come across another person who can take part in seven conversations at the same time. It's obviously something he's become skilled at, and he must be a bit of a control freak. While his staff are assisting customers, he's listening to every one of their conversations, and will suddenly break away from his own customer and interrupt a conversation where someone's asking about a pair of tennis shoes, then on to another person who's asking how tight his strings should be or what size grip he should get.

The reality, of course, is that we're *all* amateurs, and we're all bloody useless – it doesn't make any difference whatsoever what type of shoes or racquet we have – but if you listened to some of the conversations in his shop, you'd hear fifty-year-old women asking him whether this would give them a serve similar to Rafa Nadal's, as they'd noticed he tends to play with this particular racquet and seems to crack his arm backwards . . . And Stuart, bless him, has the patience to talk to these people.

I'm gonna take a flying guess now and say that, over the past forty years, I must have bought forty or fifty racquets from Stuart. Why so many? Well, I was known for smashing them. Admittedly, it has been a long time now since I last flung a racquet on the floor in anger, but these new carbon-framed racquets don't stand the Sugar rage test. I remember once in Florida, I got so angry with myself that I threw the racquet on the floor and it broke in half, bounced up and landed upright, with half of the main frame bent over.

On one occasion, I had reason to meet the owner of Head tennis racquets. In fact, I bought an aeroplane off him and, while chatting with him, I told him about my reputation for going through racquets like matchsticks. So part of the deal was that he would throw in six racquets with the plane. To my horror, I noticed that the ones he supplied were made in Taiwan, while my original Head racquet was made in Austria. They looked identical, but did they play the same? I guess so, but I thought that they couldn't be as good, and, psychologically, that changes your game. Another load of rubbish. As I've said, any top player could beat me with a cricket bat.

Now, my wife Ann also plays tennis, and she enjoys it a lot. She plays doubles. Many years ago, I used to play doubles with her. She has the honour of having given me my first sports injury. This was at a time when I'd taken up flying – which she told me was a dangerous hobby – but, actually, playing with her was arguably more dangerous. She swung the racquet back, smashing me straight in the mouth and bursting my lip. I think that was one of the last occasions we played together!

I find doubles boring – it's not energetic enough, and you don't feel in control of your side of the court, which I guess must mean that *I am* a bit of a control freak. Doubles players will tell you that it's a special talent – particularly at the net – and I agree with them, but I never really got into playing doubles. On the odd occasion when I do, I tend to flunk pretty badly.

The toll of playing tennis all my adult life caused me to tear my groin. I saw a load of doctors, who told me that it would repair itself and get better, but it was so bad that there was a period of about two or three years when I simply couldn't play properly. In fact, I was taking painkillers just to be able to play at all, which was bad news. At the time, I was still associated with Tottenham Hotspur Football Club, and all the physios we had there were also giving me their tuppence-ha'pennyworth of advice.

I was sent to see Mr Gilmore, a surgeon in Harley Street. He had allegedly patented some new operation, known in the sporting industry as 'Gilmore's groin', and had apparently performed a successful procedure on Darren Anderton (aka Sicknote). I should have known better when the Spurs doctor, Mark Curtin, sent me to Gilmore, bearing in mind that Sicknote never seemed to be cured. Anyway, I underwent a serious operation in Queen Elizabeth Hospital to repair my groin so I could get back to playing. I'd only had one other operation in my adult life (when my shoulders had calcified up and I had to have them cleaned out), so I'd been through the anaesthetic procedure before and I was very nervous. I don't like the idea of being put to sleep and being totally out of control. It was the last resort, as far as I was concerned, and anyone who knows me will know that I must have been in excruciating pain to actually agree to have this groin operation.

Surprisingly enough, unlike the shoulder operation, where it took me at least six or seven hours to come round properly from the anaesthetic, this operation went quite quickly. I went along to Gilmore and he had all his patients lined up like in a cattle market. The whole floor of that hospital was full of footballers and other sportsmen – and me! It transpires that this guy whips them in and out like a production line, and I was the eleven o'clock slot. I didn't know what to expect after such an invasive piece of surgery, and the scar was at least six inches long, down in the groin area.

The most horrifying part of it was that people warned me that I might have problems doing a wee afterwards. Now, that kind of thing really preys on your mind. Even if you don't want to do a wee, you start drinking loads of water, just to prove you can – and I couldn't! I'd heard all sorts of stories of people who had had hernia operations and groin operations and then had to have catheters fitted. So there was I, in Queen Elizabeth Hospital, standing at the loo for hours, trying to get a bit of pressure up, constantly gulping down more and more water until, eventually, about six hours on, the rivers started to flow. I was more relieved about that than worrying whether the operation had been successful. Trust me, you don't want to be in that position. Any bloke reading this book will understand what I am saying.

Mr Gilmore came in a few hours later, telling me what a glowing success the procedure had been. Everything was going to be all right. He was going to introduce me to the physio soon, and tomorrow they'd give me a physio regime to get on with, and then they'd kick me out.

Me being me, I stuck to the physio regime meticulously. The operation was in March and I knew I was due to go to Florida in April, where I hoped I could start playing again. When I looked at footballers who'd had this operation, they seemed to get back to training after about four weeks. Well, I did start to play again in April, but things weren't right and, to make a long story short, I struggled for another two years with excruciating pain – the operation hadn't worked at all.

Again, I did the rounds of the doctors, but they all pointed me back to Mr Gilmore. 'He's your man,' they said so, reluctantly I went back to him. This time, I told him, in a joking way (as he appreciated my sense of humour), that he might get done under the Sale of Goods Act, and I'd thought of a good idea: I would write him a cheque, deliberately making the words differ from the figures, so the cheque would bounce, in anticipation of him phoning me up, saying, 'Your cheque has come back,' to which I'd reply, 'Yeah – so's my bleedin' groin!'

Anyway, I had the second operation and I'm pleased to say there were no wee-wee problems second time round. Mr Gilmore told me that the operation was another glowing success and that he'd found out what had gone wrong the previous time – the stitches were perhaps a little too tight, plus he'd removed a foreign body.

I said to him, 'Well, who put the bloody foreign body in there in the first place?', at which he just laughed and told me to take some Panadol if I was in pain and to 'Have a nice day'. Well, I'm pleased to say the operation did work, and I got back to playing tennis.

That era was one of my ballooning periods and I'd stuck on about two stone so, once I got back to playing again, the weight fell off. But all this highlighted the fact that I couldn't play as hard as I used to, and that's when I rekindled my passion for cycling.

16

Always Wear a Helmet

My passion for cycling, a near-death experience, and why French drivers wind me up.

As a kid, I used to build my own bikes and cycle all over the place. When I was in Florida about five or six years ago, I popped into a bike shop and started speaking to them about these new carbon-fibre-framed machines. Now, Stuart, the tennis shop man, was also into cycling, and he decided to become my adviser on the best and latest bike to buy. We went to the bike shop and he kind of took over. According to Stuart, everything the salesman was saying was no good, and he was trying to palm me off with some kind of tutt. Instead, Stuart insisted I should buy a Pinarello bike, made by the famous Italian firm. To be fair to Stuart, he knew what he was talking about. As I started to suss out afterwards, some of these other bikes, particularly the American brands – made in Taiwan – have massive margins for the dealers, while real branded bikes like Pinarello don't have such a fat margin. So you can understand why they try to palm you off with a load of tutt.

I started riding regularly up the Florida coast on this bike, sometimes with Stuart, but mostly on my own. At first, I achieved what I thought was a fantastic twenty miles – nowadays, I do a sixty-mile ride every other day! I've got a great sixty-mile ride out in Essex. Funnily enough, though, what people find more amazing is that I am able to dismantle the bike, fix flat tyres, change tubes, adjust the gears and all that stuff. In truth, it all came back to me from when I was a kid.

My wife Ann would say, 'What? You fixed a puncture? How did you know how to do that?'

I'd look at her with a bemused expression, as if to say, 'What's the big deal?' It shows you that you never forget how to do some things.

Typically, I threw myself into cycling full blast, getting into the sixty-mile rides within a couple of years. Then Ann was telling me, 'You look too skinny. You look too withered. You've lost too much weight. Stop it!'

Bloody hell, no one had ever said that to me before! And it was endorsed by a few of my pals as well. Anyway, that didn't last too long. I worked out that I was burning off too many calories and therefore reverted to eating a bit more.

As you may have seen on the TV show I did with Piers Morgan, when he came to visit me in Florida, I make my own power drink for when I go on long rides. This is the recipe:

The Alan Sugar Power Drink

Ingredients
Two bananas
A handful of blueberries
Some orange juice
Some cranberry juice
An eighth of a teaspoon of table salt

Method
The whole lot goes into a blender, resulting in
this reddish-brown goo.

I tend to swig it at ten-mile intervals. It's better than all that over-priced commercial stuff on the market.

Some of my friends, also in their sixties, who suffer various aches and pains from the sports that they've done over the years, wanted to join in and come riding too, so I took them along to the bike shop. I think I've flogged four bikes for Leo, the owner, who now thinks the sun shines out of my backside.

The biggest problem in trying to get some of my pals to learn to ride a bike was what we call the clip-in pedals. The theory behind the clip-in pedals is that you get an additional 30 per cent of power when you bring your foot up. The problem with them is knowing when to *unclip*, so you don't fall off!

On one occasion, while on a ride up the coastal road in Florida, I was demonstrating how to clip in and out to one of my friends. I took my eye off the road for no more than a split second, the front wheel of my bike went down into a slit where the grass joined the concrete and I went flying. We were doing around twenty miles an hour at the time. It is absolutely frightening how quickly it can all happen; literally, in a split second. After flying through the air, I smashed down and gashed my arms and legs. The fellow I was supposedly teaching bumped into me and also fell off. But there's an important moral to this story. I finally got up and collected my thoughts, blood pouring from my knees and arms. As I checked the bike for damage, my son-in-law, who was with us on the ride, said, 'Look at your helmet – it's split in half!'

I'd obviously hit my head on the ground so hard that the helmet split in two, so *never, ever* ride a bike without a helmet – that would be my message. If I hadn't been wearing a helmet that day, I don't even want to *think* of what I'd have done to myself. Anyway, being the nutcase that I am, I put the chain back on the bike, straightened up the saddle (which had bent in the fall), straightened up my friend's saddle and decided not to ask the wife to bring out the car. Instead, we cycled back seventeen miles.

When I got home, my young grandson opened the door and got the biggest shock of his life – all the congealed blood on my arms and legs had picked up the black tar and dirt from the road. I must have looked a right state but, fortunately, no bones were broken. The helmet had saved my head, and all I had were loads of deep grazes. Young Joe, my grandson, had the job of helping me put the dressings on my arms and knees each evening, before I got ready to go out. He took great pride in that, popping into my bedroom at six-thirty every night, ready to do his job.

The scars are still there on my arms and legs. They serve as a reminder of one thing – never take your eyes off the road. In many cases, the problem's not you; it's others. Never pull up beside a car in America (on the right-hand side) because they could turn right immediately. Never pull up beside a large lorry; always stick behind it at the lights because they can't see you when they're turning left or right. Always assume that every motorist on the road is a lunatic and that he's going to brake at any moment. Always assume, if you're on a winding road, that there's a big lorry coming round the corner towards you. Look at the potholes and drains in the roads and go around them. These are the things that I've taught myself to think about when riding. In pilot's terms, we call it situation awareness.

So I think I've become a bit of an expert now. I'm very cautious, but I'm also a bit unlucky. Recently, I must have broken the record for the amount of punctures you can have in one ride – five! It started off with two. Fortunately, I had two spare tubes, the tyre levers and some gas cylinders to re-inflate the tyres. But when the third puncture came, it was a case of having to call the wife out to pick me up and bring me home. When I got home I repaired the tyre again and replenished the little bag on the back with two more tubes and two more gas cylinders – and off I went. I couldn't believe it when the newly repaired tyres went too – one after eight miles, and another after a further six miles. I think there was a message there that day, so when I changed the last one, fifteen miles out, I decided that enough was enough; I was going home. The guy in the bike shop could not believe it, as I'd only replenished the tubes and gas cylinders the day before. He was wondering whether I'd gone into the wholesale business or something.

I now have three Pinarello bikes and, of course, they are the best ones. Why have I got the best ones? Well, I suppose I'm a good old mug-punter consumer. Do they make me go any faster? No. Do the young boys always fly past me? Yes. But I guess I can afford to have them, so I've got them. And why three bikes? I don't know. You can only ride one at a time.

News got around very quickly in Britain that I was a bit of a biker. In fact, Jonathan Ross, when I was on one of his shows, showed a picture of me in cycling gear. This prompted the whole of the cycling publishing industry to contact me for interviews, and I've done quite a few rides with journalists out in Essex. The importer of Pinarello in England, a company named Yellow, is of course pleased to have me as a so-called celebrity riding its bikes, and continually informs me of all new models that are coming out. I have to say, I do find it rather interesting reading the bike magazines. I've become a bit of a bike geek and even visited the bike exhibition in Earl's Court for the first time. When I went on the Pinarello stand, I forgot for a moment that all the young kids there would know me from *The Apprentice*, so the place was suddenly jam-packed with people taking photographs.

I take my bikes with me on my plane. It's one of the advantages of owning your own aeroplane, I suppose – you can shove them in the hold at the back. They've been all over the world: Florida, Spain, Italy, France . . . Everywhere I go, they go.

One of the best areas for riding is the South of France, and I look forward to that every year. Last year I set myself a task, together with my son-in-law, that we would cycle from San Remo to St Tropez. This coincided with the time that I first went on Twitter, and it was rather an exciting event. I took pictures of signs and landmarks in every town we went through. For example, at San

Remo, there's a 'Welcome to San Remo' sign. When we got to Monaco, there was the famous casino and harbour. And at the border of France and Italy I took a picture of the sign there too. This was all prompted by the fact that no one believed I was doing it!

At Nice, there is a famous statue. In Cannes, I took a picture by the red carpet at the film festival. And finally, when we got to St Tropez, I took a picture of the port there and a close-up of my Garmin GPS, as evidence that we had done 111 miles in seven hours (and that I'd burnt off 7,100 calories).

It was a great event, and there was a real sense of achievement. I think the people on Twitter really enjoyed it – and fortunately I didn't get any punctures. We stopped for lunch just outside Cannes. The average temperature during the course of that day must have been about ninety degrees, and we each must have downed at least fifteen litres of water on the journey. When I finally got back to the boat we were chartering, my legs were covered in black grime and grit that had stuck to the suntan lotion I'd put on. The boat had left San Remo at the same time we left on our bikes, and of course it got there before us because it went as the crow flies. When the crew stopped for lunch at some point, they sounded the horn as they saw us go by – shades of the Tour de France, I don't think.

I also do a lot of riding in Spain, near my house in Marbella. There's a small town there called Istán, which is roughly a ten-mile ride, up a mountain. It takes me about forty minutes to get up it, and about twenty to come down. I normally go up and down twice. It's funny to see the faces of people who are cycling up while I am coming down, who then see me cycling up again as they are coming down. They do a double-take, as if to say, 'Am I seeing things?'

Where I stop in Istán, there's always a bunch of old, retired Spanish gentlemen sitting around at a certain spot where there are some benches overlooking the great views of the sea. They have got to recognise me on my daily rides so, from time to time, in my very poor, broken Spanish, I have a chat with them, mainly about football. I like to start an argument – usually about Real Madrid and Barcelona – and then leave once it starts to brew.

I was looking to find a new route in Spain, so I thought I'd try riding up to Ronda, which is a much larger town than Istán. One rainy day I drove up there in the car to suss it out. I noted that from a certain point it was forty-five kilometres, which I thought must be a cinch, as that's about thirty miles – so there and back would be sixty miles, the same as my normal UK and Florida rides.

Was I wrong! After I set out one morning, my first mistake was not to take the bike by car to the point where I'd seen the sign saying 'Ronda 45 km'. Instead, I rode to that point, which was about ten miles. Then I started the climb. It hadn't looked so much of a climb when I'd gone in the car – I could have sworn it was part climb, part flat – but to cut a long story, I got to about twenty-seven kilometres, after *constant* climbing, and found a café frequented by motorbike riders. I had knocked myself out to such an extent that, for the first time in my life, I felt a bit giddy and my face went a pasty white. I went into the café and ordered myself two Cokes and a large slice of chocolate cake. I wolfed the lot down and, after about twenty minutes, the colour came back to my face. I decided to go back home. I'd learned a couple of lessons there – I hadn't eaten before I set out and I had the wrong type of chain on this particular bike.

But here is the funny bit. On the way down, at speeds of up to 40mph, I didn't have to pedal once for at least forty-five minutes. However, when I got to the bottom and tried to pedal, my knees had frozen up because of the cold wind blowing on them on the ride down! What a bloody state. It took me five minutes or so to unfreeze my knees and get going to pedal the ten miles from the bottom of the run back to my house.

Lesson learned there, but I'm determined it's not going to beat me. I will try again, but will be well prepared next time.

One of the things I've noticed out on the roads is how drivers treat cyclists. Many of them are very good, though sometimes they're a bit too good, in that they hoot when they overtake you, which gives you a bit of a shock. Then there are others who are total raving lunatics and who just flash past, sometimes so close that their wing mirrors can send you flying. I have often pulled up beside a car at the lights in Florida and asked the person what the hell they think they're doing! They're completely oblivious to the fact that they nearly knocked me off my bike, and they look at me as if *I'm* mad. There are specific bike lanes there, into which they're not supposed to encroach, but that doesn't stop them.

A couple of things wind me up tremendously in France. Again, it's a great cycling country, and they too provide bike lanes, but in the summer the tourists tend to go walking, holding hands, sometimes with a row of kids beside them. You come up behind a family walking along four abreast in the cycling lane, and if you ring the bell, they look at you in disgust, as if it's *your* fault, as if *you're* the one in the wrong. They are totally unapologetic. They act as if you've endangered them, when in fact *they're* walking on a licensed cycle path. It's not as if there's nowhere else for them to walk – there's a perfectly adequate pavement there.

And then there are the French drivers, who, when you dare to ride in the road, start gesturing at you to get on to the cycle path. Fortunately, being in my sixties, I've mellowed a little, so I hold back from making nasty gestures which will be seen in the bully's wing mirror. I'm sure in my younger days I would have ended up having a fist fight with some of these idiots but, to be perfectly honest, there are also idiot cyclists, particularly in central London. I never cycle in central London. Thanks to Mayor Boris Johnson and his bike-hire scheme, cycling is a popular thing to do in the City and, to be fair, those types of cyclists are fine. But you get this other wave of nutters on their streamlined racing bikes who weave in and out of the traffic causing cars to brake sharply, jumping the lights, riding up the pavement. They are lunatics, and they should be banned.

I remember a debate in the House of Lords where this topic came up. The minister in the new coalition government dodged the issue of problem cyclists by saying that licensing people on bikes was something that they couldn't do for some logistical reason. I suggested, in one Question Time, that as a cyclist I would be the first to admit that some cyclists are dangerous – affecting pedestrians and causing accidents – and that the law should be changed so they could be nicked, just like motorists, for jumping the lights or driving without due care and attention.

There's a definite need for a change in the law and, until there is, I can understand why some drivers treat all cyclists with contempt. It is most probably those who have experienced the idiots who ride around in London. Consider that an old fart like me, on the flat, in a no-wind situation, can get up to 25mph on these bikes, and some of the youngsters get up to nearly 30mph – that's as fast as *cars* are allowed to drive in a built-up area. I do believe there needs to be some change in the law, and I would be the first to back it.

Having said all that, it's not surprising that cycling in London is becoming more and more popular these days, because, let's face it, driving in London is a nightmare. On top of that, petrol is now over £6 a gallon, and then there's the congestion charge. If you don't drive, you've got high prices on the trains and tube, not to mention the danger of catching colds and flu when you're pressed up against your fellow passengers in the morning.

And so I see more and more people cycling to work, and that's got to be good news because it's healthy. Perhaps the new generation are going to be a bunch of healthy people, and London might become like Amsterdam, where bikes have always been the preferred mode of transport. Mind you, I do wonder sometimes, watching the streamlined bikes that come past, what do the riders do when they get to the office? They must be sweating. Do they stink a bit – particularly in the summer? Do they have a shower? Do they have a change of clothes in the office or what? Well, that's another issue, I guess.

I've been trying to encourage my two sons, Simon and Daniel, to take up cycling, but they say no, it's not for them, though I think Daniel might be warming to the idea these days. Instead, they do what I used to do years ago – go to the bloody gym.

I have to say that when I tried the gym, even the one I have at home, it is so bloody boring! You really have to have a certain mentality to get up in the morning and go and run on a running machine for an hour, looking at a blank wall or a television that's on in the distance. I honestly don't know how people do it – it is the most boring thing I can imagine.

Another problem with the gym, as I see it – and I might be sounding a bit of a hypochondriac now – is that the people there are always moaning about their back aching or some other ailment and always seem to have coughs and colds. If you go to the gym in winter in particular, it seems as if all the other people there are coughing and sneezing, not to mention putting their hands on their noses and mouths and then touching the bars on the rowing machine or the cross-trainer.

I keep telling the boys, 'Haven't you learned yet? You go there to keep fit and you're forever getting sore throats, infections, coughs and colds.'

Some gyms will tell you that they've got attendants there who are constantly wiping down the equipment to make sure you won't pick up any infections. I say that's a load of rubbish. I remember talking to Tottenham's doctor, Mark Curtin, and complaining to him about the high absenteeism in the first team squad. We were playing Leeds one freezing February day and a load of the players weren't available because they had the flu or a virus. After the game, the players were coming out of the ground and walking to the coach – in just short-sleeved T-shirts!

I said to Dr Curtin, 'There you are, that's it! See? No wonder they've got coughs and colds all the time. Look at them! They've just come out of a steaming-hot shower, they're wearing T-shirts and they're walking across the car park in freezing-cold weather.'

Now, Dr Curtin is a very nice, polite man. He said to me, 'Well, Alan, no, not really. Let me explain to you – you don't get colds and flu from *being* cold. You might get hypothermia and, in extreme cases – when you walk out of a very hot environment and breathe in some cold air – you might get a situation where it affects the lungs a little, but you do not get viruses and coughs and colds by being cold. You get them by catching them from other people, by touching your nose or your mouth after having touched something that's been in contact with a person who's infected. Alternatively, you might be sitting in a plane or a train and someone nearby is sneezing and coughing. You don't see the microscopic globules flying through the air from someone's sneeze or cough, but you breathe the germs in, and that's how you get a virus.'

'So, Doc, all those years my mum used to say to me, "Wrap up and keep warm, otherwise you'll get a cold" – that was a load of rubbish then, was it?'

'I'm afraid so, Alan. That was the old days. That's what people used to think back then. You dress up warm for comfort – I mean, let's face it, you don't want to be freezing and shivering – but I have to tell you, that's got nothing at all to do with getting colds and viruses.'

Well, there's a bit of trivia that might have enlightened you. I've signed on to that now, and I've got loads of this alcohol rub lying around everywhere I go: in my cars, in my plane, at the office, at home – particularly in the winter, when everybody around is coughing and sneezing, I'm constantly putting this alcoholic goo on my hands. I have become a bit of a Howard Hughes!

17

Don't Twiddle the Knobs!

Why I love flying, but hate flying bores, and what to look out for when buying a jet.

When the kids were young, about thirty-six years ago, I used to take them out on a Sunday to give Ann a bit of a rest. One of our regular stopping places was Stapleford Aerodrome, where I'd let them watch the small planes take off and land. I've always found flying and aeroplanes a fascinating subject. I can remember, as a young lad, my brother-in-law Harold encouraging me to make model aeroplanes that actually flew. He'd help me construct them out of balsa wood and a kind of tissue paper which you glued on. The aeroplanes flew under the power of a big elastic band, which was twisted by winding up the propeller.

One day, around 1975, I decided to enquire in the clubhouse at Stapleford about what one has to do to become a pilot. They gave me a brief explanation and I thought that it might be a good idea, a bit of a challenge. When I told Ann, she went nuts, telling me that I was mad, that it was dangerous and all that stuff. But despite that, I said that I'd have a go.

'I'm going to be flying with instructors, so it shouldn't be that dangerous,' I told her.

My first flying instructor was a young man by the name of Ralph. His aspiration was that, after he'd built up a certain amount of hours flying, he was going to become a commercial pilot. That didn't mean anything to me at the time, but I know now that most people who want to go on to become commercial pilots start out by getting their private pilot's licence, then become flying instructors and build up hours while they're instructing students. This allows them to go on to take more complex examinations before they become a commercial pilot.

My first experience was in a Piper Cherokee single-engine plane. Ralph's first job was to try to show me how to steer it. It's quite funny that, instinctively, you hold the control column and turn it as if were the steering wheel of a car – and I still see people do that now. However, you actually steer a plane with your *feet*, using the rudders (which in many cases also operate the nose-wheel steering). I did fifty hours of lessons and also had to take some written examinations, which, from what I recall, were not as complex in those days as they are now. There was one paper you had to sit which incorporated every aspect of flying: meteorology, aircraft operation, navigation, and all that stuff, whereas today there are, I think, seven separate exams that have to be taken.

Eventually, I went on my first solo flight, and was told to land at Biggin Hill initially. I was to go in and see the bloke in the tower and get him to sign a piece of paper to say I'd actually got there, then I was to take off again and land at Ipswich airport, where I had to do the same, then find my way back to Stapleford. All of this had to be done by dead reckoning – map reading – there was none of the fancy GPS systems we have these days. And you weren't even allowed to use what's known as a VOR (a navigational aid); you had to look out of the window and spot things on the ground to make sure that you were in the right place.

I ended up taking my general flying test, which included some rather hairy acrobatics known as spinning. These days, it's no longer on the curriculum; I guess because it was too bloody dangerous! You fly along straight and then you pull back on the power, stick the nose right up in the air and, as the aeroplane stalls and starts to fall, you kick over the rudder and the plane goes into a spin – a bit like a falling sycamore seed that looks as if it's helicoptering down. Then you have to recover. The truth of the matter is that the Piper Cherokee is a very hard plane to get into trouble with – you'd have to be a real dummy. A further truth is that if you just sit there while it's spinning and let go, it might even sort itself out. However, during the test, *you* have to demonstrate how you would recover.

One of the things about flying is that it's no good for the macho or cocky person who treats safety rules and regulations with contempt, the kind of person who likes to show that they're the big I Am. People who don't care what the weather conditions are like and break all the rules are usually the ones who end up killing themselves. I am not one of those people, but I do recall, during those early days of flying, sitting in the clubhouse hearing lots of people bragging about their risk-taking – how they ignored this rule and didn't bother with that. As a young man, it is easy to be persuaded or tempted into doing things you shouldn't do. Fortunately, I resisted those temptations, and these days I tell young students I see in the flying club to keep away from certain people and to stick to the rules, stick to the facts and not to cut any corners. I tell them not to listen to anybody who says they do, because flying is a serious matter.

The first aeroplane I bought was a Grumman AA5, which was quite similar to the Piper Cherokee – a simple aeroplane. I did a lot of flying around in that plane, and took the kids up occasionally. I also did the usual private pilot thing of flying over to Le Touquet for lunch and coming back again.

Even in those days, in relative terms, flying was an expensive hobby, and only people who had a few quid could afford to do it. There were always lots of people hanging around the clubhouse who loved the idea of flying, but could not afford the hourly rates the club charged for hiring a plane. These people would always be eager to come along if ever there was a flight to be had, if they were fortunate enough to be asked. I won't mention their names, because it would embarrass them – well, at least it would embarrass one of them, as the other one's dead (not from flying, I would add). But it did kind of aggravate you a bit when you saw them schmoozing around and hinting that they wanted to fly.

Now, the worst type of co-pilot, in my opinion, is the one I call the knob-twiddler. It really winds me up. When you're pilot in command on an aeroplane, you have to have total control, unless of course you ask your co-pilot to do something. Some of these hangers-on not only ponced flights off me, but also tried to take over the cockpit controls, touching knobs, tuning radios, adjusting throttles and all that stuff. One day, on a flight back from Birmingham, one of them was interfering so much that I called Luton to tell them I was en route from Birmingham to Stapleford, but I wished to divert to their airfield.

'What are you doing?' the co-pilot asked me.

'I'll tell you what I'm doing,' I said calmly. 'I'm going to land there, you're going to get out, and then I'm going to fly off to Stapleford, because you can't stop touching the bloody controls and interfering.'

'Oh, don't be so silly, Alan. Sorry, sorry, I won't touch anything any more. I promise I won't touch a thing. Now, don't be daft.'

I kept him worrying for a little while by pulling back the throttle and starting a descent, but then I realised I was really being a fool for bothering to land at Luton when I had no reason to. That story quickly flew around the club, and I never had any more interference from the ponces.

On one of my round trips to Le Touquet, with my friend Graham and his wife-to-be, we were over the Channel on the way back when I detected a bit of a problem with the engine power. Not to get too technical, the RPM needle was wavering a little bit, which it shouldn't; it's normally in a constant position. I didn't take too much notice of it at the time, as I was more focused on crossing the Channel and getting back over dry land. You don't want to be ditching a plane over the sea, I can assure you. Although we are trained to do it, I wouldn't want to try. Anyway, we landed at Southend and cleared customs, which you had to do in those days (before we were full members of the European Community).

Before taking off again from Southend Airport, I decided to give the engine a good test, opening it up to full power and making sure that all the temperatures and pressures were okay. All appeared to be perfect, so I decided to fly back to Stapleford. But shortly after take-off, the engine really started running rough. I'd turned on course towards Stapleford, but coming up in the distance was the town of Brentwood, a built-up area. By now the engine was back-firing and stuttering badly. I had to make a decision there and then – do I try to struggle on and pass over Brentwood in the hope of getting to Stapleford and landing, or do I ditch it immediately? It seemed that, with every minute that went by, we were losing more and more power, so I took the decision to shut the throttle down and make a landing in some farmer's field. As soon as I pulled the throttle back, the propeller stopped dead, which it doesn't normally do – the engine had completely seized! So that was it: I was committed to a forced landing. Thankfully, we're trained to do that, and as long as you've got lots of open green fields around, you shouldn't have a problem. You just choose one of them and glide the plane down. I landed it perfectly on this field, with no problem at all. Graham wasn't worried, as he was also a fully qualified pilot, but I think his girlfriend was a bit concerned, to say the least!

There's a funny ending to this story. Having got a taxi home from the farmer's field, I called the boss of Stapleford Aerodrome and told him what had happened to my plane and that I needed him to send out his crew to recover it from the field. They were going to load it on to some sort of flatbed lorry, bring it back and fix it.

Now, remember, I had made a textbook landing and the plane was not damaged at all, apart from the original engine problem, of course. Stapleford's owner sent out a bunch of monkeys with their flatbed lorry, which had a small crane on it. When trying to jack the plane up on to the lorry, one of the ropes broke and the plane crashed down on the lorry smashing its whole tailplane. So after I had landed the plane perfectly, these idiots smashed it up trying to get it on the lorry.

But it gets worse. When they finally brought it back to Stapleford, the owner obviously agreed to pay for the damage his people had caused to the fuselage. No problem. Then they took the engine out of the plane and found that one of the cylinders had completely broken up and disintegrated. The whole engine would need to go away for repair, which would take about five weeks.

When the engine finally came back, they refitted it on the aeroplane. Next thing you knew, the idiots had started it up – but they'd forgotten to put a new oil filter in. They'd left the old one in, which was full of fragments of broken metal from when the engine had conked out. Once they started it up, all this crap went straight back into the engine and damaged it again, so the whole lot had to come out and be sent away once more.

But wait for it, because the story hasn't ended yet. I decided, having experienced an engine failure in a single-engine aeroplane, that I would upgrade to a twin-engine plane, on the basis that, if one engine fails, you can still fly the plane on the other engine. Given that we were doing lots of journeys over the water, I thought it would be a better idea, and it certainly would keep Ann happy. Unfortunately, she'd got the news about my engine failure and had realised that, had it happened a little earlier, we'd have ended up in the drink. So I bought a new twin-engine aeroplane in part-exchange for the old plane. The dealer, quite rightly, wanted to check-fly the old plane to make sure that it had been repaired properly. Coincidentally, the dealer, a gentleman by the name of John

Fricker, had a son who was one of the engineers from Stapleford Flying Club and had worked on repairing my old plane.

I took Fricker Senior out to the plane and we taxied along ready for take-off. I couldn't help but notice that the RPM reading was much lower than one would normally expect. I didn't actually mention it and thought perhaps he wouldn't notice. He did, of course, so we taxied back to the hangar to investigate what was wrong. It turned out that Fricker Junior had forgotten to connect a cable which stops the carburettor icing up in cold, humid conditions using what we call 'carburettor heat', which has the side effect of a drop in RPM when deployed. He had left it permanently activated by not connecting the cable – this despite him handing the plane over to me as 'back in service'! Needless to say, the servicing of my aeroplanes was never again done by this lot.

I'm going to fast-track the flying story a bit now – because it's probably becoming a bit boring to those of you who are non-technical – and just tell you that I didn't really like flying the twin. It was too burdensome and didn't have the flying-by-the-seat-of-your-pants feeling you get from flying a single-engine aeroplane. Instead, I bought another plane, a Piper Arrow, which was quite leading-edge technology back in the late seventies and early eighties.

By that time, I was concentrating much more on my business. Amstrad became a public company in 1980, and the chief of the merchant bank which was sponsoring the flotation of Amstrad happened to notice that there was an aeroplane on the company balance sheet. He told me that, as I was a young man and my business seemed to revolve around me, it wouldn't be a very good idea to let the stock market know that I was a private pilot with a single-engine aeroplane, as they would start to worry about what would happen to the company if Alan Sugar went down in the drink!

And so it was at that point that I lost a bit of interest in flying and gave it up for quite a while. Twenty years later, I came back to it.

Now, it's funny – they say you never forget how to ride a bike. Well, you never forget how to fly a plane either. In particular, you never forget that instinctive knowledge of how to flare out the plane just at the point of landing; it's a bit like smooth clutch control on a car.

When I went back to reinstate my licence in 2003, I had to get about seven or eight hours of flying under my belt. And due to civil aviation rules, they made me sit some new exams, particularly to pass the instrument and meteorological conditions licence. So it was back to bookwork again, to the fascination of Ann, who couldn't believe that I was going to get stuck into textbooks and all that stuff. Again, it was a bit of a challenge, but it's not as if the previous stuff you learned gets lost for ever; you just need your memory jogged. However, bear in mind that, in 2003, I was fifty-six years old, so remembering a bunch of numbers and rules and regulations was not as easy as it had been when I was a younger man of thirty. And that's what it's all about – loads of different technical expressions and details, and various computations of numbers and figures, all of which make you very, very confused. And, I might add, the minute you pass the exam, you tend to forget the whole bloody lot. Only the boffs and the real fanatics remember it.

Why did I go back to flying again? Well, the simple reason is that, during that twenty-year void, I actually became the owner of lots of private planes. At one stage, I even had a company which chartered the planes and, me being me, I would dive right into the detail. Normally, a millionaire who wants his own private plane to fly him all over the world simply entrusts it to a company who will provide him with the service, the pilots and all the other stuff – but not me! I wanted to know the ins and outs of a duck's arse, mainly because I knew that some of these companies tend to rip off the owners. And then there's the guilt of owning an asset which

I'm not going to use day in, day out. Rather than have the plane sitting there at Stansted Airport doing nothing, I wanted to make sure it would be usefully employed by chartering it out, to have some income from it in order for me to justify ownership. My target was that all my personal flying in that plane would actually cost nothing, with the income from the charter business covering the cost of maintaining the aircraft, insurance and all the other aspects.

Being the type I am, not only did I manage to achieve that, but I also managed to make a profit out of it. This tempted me into buying two other jets for the sole purpose of chartering them out, and it became a business. When I used to go on these flights, I would sit in the jump seat of the plane, watching the pilots control them. Not only did I pick up lots of experience again, albeit in a much higher class of aircraft, but also the flying bug came back to me!

One such aircraft operator is a nice chap by the name of George Galanopoulos. He owns a company called LEA, which is actually stationed at Stapleford. George had started off as a private pilot and became a commercial pilot, but he was rather enterprising and decided to start his own air charter company based around some propeller-driven, twin-engine planes (Piper Seneca and Beechcraft King Air). I used to use George occasionally to fly me to Europe, as it was very convenient just to step out of my house in Chigwell, drive ten minutes down the road, jump in a King Air and be in Paris or Frankfurt in an hour or so.

I remember when I first decided I would buy a jet. It was a Cessna Citation 2 and, again, me being me, I looked into every aspect of it, including getting a personalised registration on the aircraft. I got G–SPUR, as I was chairman of Spurs at the time. I gave George the opportunity of operating the plane for me, on the basis that he would drum up some charter business, so that *my* flying would be free of charge or billed to me at cost only.

Sometimes I think back to some of the heated discussions that

George and I had over the years. I remember telling him I had his card marked and that he wasn't going to rip me off, and that he'd have to learn about the harsh facts and realities of life. As ever, I wanted to know every single detail of everything, and to this day George will tell you that he has never come across another aeroplane owner who knows more about the planes than the company that operates them! Nevertheless, he learned and I learned, and I was loyal to him when I bought my next two jets, allowing him to operate those also. And from then on, he was able to grow his business.

I believe that, if you asked him, George would say that I was of great assistance to him and, in fact, having three aeroplanes available to him for charter coincided nicely with the mad boom-economy that was going on, with all these poseurs and banking tossers who were flying all over the place at the drop of a hat. God forbid they would travel by EasyJet or a British Airways economy flight – they would find some reason to justify chartering a plane to go to a very important meeting in Geneva. Load of bollocks in most cases.

George eventually took on a few other owners who wanted to buy similar planes to mine. He'd learned the costs of operating the planes through the experience he'd gained from mine, so was able to advise other owners how he would operate their planes, albeit, I'm pretty sure, under more beneficial terms than he was getting out of me.

When I deal with him these days, I remind him, 'George, you're not dealing with some multi-millionaire who's clueless about operating a plane, but who just has a death wish to have one – in other words, some wally you can rip off left, right and centre. You're dealing with *me*!'

To which he usually replies, 'I know!'

But good luck to him, because it was interesting to see how a young, enterprising man and his partner, Patrick, built up a very successful operation. Today, I think he operates fifteen large jets.

He is moaning, as usual, because the economy is poor, but I don't think we need to cry too much for him.

And that brings me on to aircraft salesmen. This is nothing at all to do with George; I'm talking about salesmen employed by aircraft companies such as Cessna and Embraer. They are a special breed of people.

If you're envisaging a shady second-hand-car salesman like Del Boy – with a sheepskin coat and gold bracelets and medallions – that's nothing compared with this lot. They even *look* like a completely different breed – normally you will see them beautifully suited and booted, looking very respectable. But they have a little bit of a problem with the facts they quote about their aeroplanes. When they tell you that the plane can make it non-stop from London to New York, they fail to mention that that's only achievable if there's a 500mph tailwind and each passenger weighs three stone!

When they show you the price of the aeroplane, they forget to mention that you're just buying the bare bones of it, with no frills onboard. Their game is to lure you into agreeing to have all the extras, and you get a shock after you've signed the contract, when you realise you're not just paying what you thought you were for the basic plane. Instead, you can end up paying 50 per cent more if you've been sucked into agreeing to the luxurious carpets, leather and wood, onboard electronic gadgets that you'll never use, satellite telephones, internet connections, and so on. Well, I caught on to that very, very quickly. I am the aeroplane salesman's worst nightmare.

I bought an Embraer Legacy back in 2007 – a great plane, a thirteen-seater – and used it quite a lot to fly to America and all over Europe. One of the problems with the plane was that it didn't have the capability to fly non-stop to New York but, on a good day it could just about make the airport at Bangor, Maine, which is further up the north-east coast of America. The advantage of landing there first was that you could deal with all the customs and immigration, then fly off freely to any other airport in the USA.

Then, Embraer announced a new aeroplane known as the Legacy 650. This, they claimed, *would* make New York non-stop 95 per cent of the time. More importantly, it would make Dubai to London, a new route that had become popular with private fliers, without the need to stop and refuel. So I decided to buy one of these new planes.

If you could have been a fly on the wall, you would have killed yourself laughing. I know George would have, because he heard all about it afterwards and cracked up.

I met the salesman from Embraer, Simon, to go through all the technical details of the plane's purchase and to define the interior. At the meeting, which was in Miami, Simon was all suited and booted, along with his Brazilian colleague.

I got straight to the point. 'Simon, watch my lips. I am not having any other tutt on this aeroplane – I don't want it. I want the basic price – $26 million – that's it. I'm not having anything else on this plane – do you get it?'

Despite this, he kept mentioning other things we might like. Ann was with me and her eyes would light up. I knew she was thinking, 'Well, that's rather a good idea. Why don't you have one of those?'

I kept repeating, 'No, not interested, don't want it! Stick to the basic stuff.'

Now, this aeroplane has mains electricity in it, just like you have at home (220 volts or 110 volts), with electric sockets you can plug things into. As you know, these days you can go into Asda and buy a little microwave oven for £49. Well, wait for it, the microwave oven certified for use on an aeroplane (which has to be built in) is something like $42,000. Yes, forty-two thousand dollars! Well, that's the price that they want to charge, but fortunately the microwave came as standard in this particular deal, so that was okay. However, the oven (which heats up the food normally packed by the flight caterers in those metal trays) *was* an extra, and having been adamant about having no extras, I made a little error in not having one of these ovens because, when the plane was delivered, the operator told me that it was going to be rather difficult for the charter market, as people expect to have hot food.

They were right – it was a cock-up, and I decided to fit one afterwards. Now, if I tell you that the cost of this little oven, which is no more than thirteen inches square, was five times more than the first house I bought when I got married, you will understand how ridiculous some of the aeroplane accessory prices are. It is an absolute, total con, because – think about it – what stops me going into Asda or Comet, buying a small oven and simply plugging it into the electric socket on the plane? Well, apparently there are some Civil Aviation Authority rules and regulations that prohibit this.

The same can be said for an electric kettle. I won't even bother to tell you how much the certified electric kettle is for this aeroplane. I know you're not feeling sorry for me over this – if I can afford a $26 million aeroplane, why am I moaning about all these bits and pieces? Well, it's the principle, I guess. Having been in the electronics industry and being a rather technical person, it annoys me immensely to see how some of these companies, who spend a bit of money getting these accessories certified, charge an arm and a leg for them.

And then, of course, there's the carpet. No, not normal carpet – this is special, certified carpet! No one has ever been able to explain to me what's so special about it, but apparently it's got something to do with the fact that it doesn't burn like ordinary carpet. And the leather that goes on the chairs is also certified leather – another total rip-off. Are there special cows groomed for aviation?

Back at the meeting, the smoothie Simon started to show me the various veneers that were available for the wood finishing inside the aeroplane. I told them to forget that too. I wanted a new style of interior – piano black, the kind of ebony look that you'd see on a grand piano. His eyes started to roll like a slot machine. 'Oh, that's going to cost a fortune.'

'No it's not, sunshine,' I told him. 'In my business, I've dealt with wood, and it's not going to cost any more than veneer. In fact, it should cost less than veneer because it's simply spray-painted and lacquered – so put that in your pipe and smoke it. Get back to the ranch at Embraer and tell them I'm not paying any more for it. In fact, you can give them the good news that I won't be asking for a reduction.'

There's a funny ending to this story. Having finally kitted out the plane beautifully in black and grey, Embraer have now adopted this finish as one of their own; they show it in their catalogue as one of the options they offer their customers. It does look good, if I say so myself.

People who know I'm a pilot often ask me whether I fly the Legacy myself. The answer is no. I'm not allowed by law to fly the Legacy, although, technically, I could do it, as it's quite simple to fly. Again, I don't want to bore you with all the rules and regulations, but the aeroplane is British registered, and in order to fly a British-registered aeroplane you need a British Instrument Rating, which is something akin to a university degree, and at my age I'm not going to put myself through some very complicated examinations.

In the United States, however, this qualification is much easier to obtain, so I decided to get an American Instrument Rating back in 2005, and at the same time get rated on a multi-engine aeroplane. And so, technically, if my Legacy was an American-registered plane, all I would need to do is to take ten or twelve hours of simulator training and I'd be certified to fly it as number-two pilot.

If you think that the general bureaucracy in the world has gone mad, you haven't lived. The bureaucracy involved in flying is a nightmare. My American licence was granted to me on the basis that I already had an English licence, so when I decided to take up flying in America, I had to write to the British Civil Aviation Authority to tell them to write to the American Federal Aviation Authority advising them that I existed as a pilot. In the middle of all this, unfortunately, there was 9/11, and from that moment on the FAA became very, very hot as far as foreign pilots were concerned. I had to get certified by some American government department, where I had to give my fingerprints, passport details, photographs, the flight school I trained at and all that stuff, in order for me to embark upon the instrument rating.

Digressing for a moment, I have not flown on a commercial airline for over fifteen years, so I have totally lost touch with what it's like at airports these days. Obviously all countries are hot on security since 9/11 but, having listened to some people who travel regularly, it sounds like a nightmare to me, with long queues at passport control accompanied by some rather stupid questions and random searches. I say 'random' because from what I can understand, security is not 'profiled', in order to avoid upsetting certain minorities. This means that customs officials will routinely confiscate a bottle of barley water from a little old lady, as it may be bomb-making fluid, or they'll do pat-downs and body searches on a blond, blue-eyed family on their way to Majorca. All this when common sense would tell you that there have never been any instances of these sorts of people perpetrating terror attacks. I do sympathise with the authorities on this, because if they were only seen checking people of the same ethnicity as past terrorists, there would be hell to pay with human rights claims. It is a problem, but I guess I'd better leave it there, otherwise I will get into trouble.

*

Going back to my own flying, recently, I decided that I wanted to remove the limitation on my American licence whereby it's valid only as long as my UK licence is valid and instead try to get a stand-alone American licence.

Well, you would have thought I was putting myself up for election as the next president of the United States. I was told that I'd have to re-sit all the examinations and undergo another flight test. I protested to the authorities that this was ridiculous, that I already had 950 flying hours and you'd normally ask this of someone who'd had just 50 hours. It fell on deaf ears, and if you know anything about America, you'll know you cannot buck the system. But me being me, I wasn't going to give up the idea of getting this licence. I was determined to do it all again from scratch. I bought a load of books containing all the rules and regulations and some software that simulated the written examination. I spent about three weeks going through all these bloody rules and regs – map reading, weather conditions, meteorology, aircraft operating instruments – all the same stuff I did back in 1975. In fact, I asked my two grandsons, one nine and one seven, to help me with my revision. I gave them a book and told them to ask me the multiple-choice questions. They were enjoying the fact that they were acting as teacher to their sixty-four-year-old grandfather and, when I got one wrong, they went into hysterics. In the end, they were quite impressed, because I didn't get many wrong – I'd learned by heart virtually all the 758 questions and answers published by the FAA.

Afterwards, I turned the tables on my grandsons and told them that this proves how important it is to learn, and how they must concentrate at school. At this point, they closed the book, gave it back to me and asked Ann if there was any cake or sweets.

Now, the FAA has a certain affiliation with some British flight institutions, which enabled me to sit this exam at Farnborough Airport. I was put in a room and dealt with by a very polite lady, who was there to invigilate while I took the exam. I say very polite because she didn't go so far as to body-search me, but she did make it perfectly clear that she wanted to see that I wasn't about to cheat by bringing hidden bits of paper or calculators or anything like that into the exam room. I needed to get 70 per cent to pass. I managed to get 85 per cent, so that part of the job was done.

When I got to America, I got hold of the flight examiner, a Mr Brooks, and told him that I'd listened to all his advice. I'd managed to get the letter from the British CAA showing that I was indeed a pilot sent to the American FAA. I gave him my passport and I gave him my pass certificate. He then sat down and started reading through my log book. He decided he wanted evidence that I'd done certain exercises. Despite me telling him again that I had done 950 hours of flying, he wanted me to show him where I had flown on my own, across country, more than 200 miles.

'What do you mean by *on my own*?' I said. 'What about if my wife was onboard?'

'No, I mean on your own – no one else in the aeroplane.'

'What, not even a passenger? Not even my grandson?'

'No, you, on your own.'

Well, the truth of the matter is that I very seldom fly somewhere completely alone, so I had to search my memory to remember which flights I'd made on my own, and whether any of them were over a 200-mile or more stretch.

Then he threw in a third element and said, 'Oh, by the way, that 200-mile journey – you have to have landed at least three times.'

At this point, I was about to knock his block off, but I thought, 'I've come so far that I'd best play along with this charade,' so I informed him of various journeys I had made. On one in particular – flying to East Midlands Airport, when I went there on behalf of the government to speak to some people in Nottingham – I knew for a fact I'd flown on my own. That was roughly a 200-mile round trip, albeit it I hadn't landed at any other airport.

Mr Brooks could see I was getting rather aerated, so he conceded that this was in order. But then he threw yet another spanner in the works and wanted to see the night flights I'd done, again on my own. I was honest with him and told him that the last time I'd flown at night was back in the eighties. I showed him my certified log book. The CAA had accepted the fact that the original log book had been stolen when my house was broken into – the thieves had nicked my flight bag. He was not convinced and told me that he would have to stand up in court, under oath, and say that he had certified that I'd done everything. Therefore, the flight test that day was going to be postponed until I'd gone off and done a 200-mile night flight and got it certified by an independent flying instructor. How I never clocked him one, I don't know, but I reminded myself again, 'You've come this far; bite your tongue and get on with it.'

That night, I flew to Venice (on the west coast of Florida) and back again with an instructor and got him to sign it off. I called the examiner to say that I was ready to take the test. Again, I was expecting that he would take me out for a quick flip, use his common sense, bearing in mind *I had 950 hours' flying experience*, and get it over with quickly. No such luck. He wanted me to do the full monty. He warned me that I was not allowed to use GPS and he wanted to see me prepare a manual flight plan, using a map, show reporting points along the way and calculate the times I was going to arrive at certain places. He also wanted me to do something known as 'weight and balance', to make sure that the plane was within its limitations. All this shit I'd forgotten thirty-odd years ago.

'Come on, Brooks, this is ridiculous!' I said.

'No, no, those are the rules, those are the regulations. That's what you've got to do.'

And so I had to sit down the night before and try to remember how to do all of this rubbish. I meticulously plotted a route to Sarasota and got on the net to remind myself how to do the weight and balance thing. I thought I would wind him up on the morning of the test by saying to him that I didn't know how much he weighed, so I was going to put 300lbs in (about 21 stone) and this would put the plane out of weight and balance. He didn't get my English humour.

We did the flight test. It all went perfectly well – loads of stalls, loads of steep turns, forced landings, emergency landings, short-field landings – and eventually he signed me off.

By now you might be asking yourself: what is he doing all this for? Good question. I guess it's because it's there – it gives me a sense of achievement. It's not as if I'm in an aeroplane every day; I just love the thought of being able to control a brilliant piece of engineering and all of the technical stuff that goes with it. I can honestly say that my latest plane, a Cirrus SR22, has got more avionics and gadgets on it than some jumbo jets.

I tend to go flying at weekends – I go up in the air, fly around in circles for an hour and come back. I don't go anywhere in particular. Ironically, most ordinary people are a bit nervous of flying, particularly of taking off and landing, but we saddos with our 'touch-and-gos' (when we come in to land then take straight off again) do the very thing that normal people hate! And what else do we all do? We sit in the clubhouse and talk a load of rubbish to each other about technical issues, experiences, rules and regs – all pretty sad stuff. But as I say to Ann, 'You could have been a golf widow. Some blokes go out and walk around a golf course for five hours. I just pop out for a couple of hours and do a bit of flying, so actually you're quids in.'

She's been up with me for a few flights, although she doesn't like it at all. Being in a small plane is kind of alien to her, and of course it's a bit bumpy; it's a bit like riding a roller coaster. On occasion, in America, we fly across to the west coast of Florida to Naples, and the only bit she likes about that is the shopping.

We are a special breed of human being, private pilots. No one else can understand why we do it, no one else can understand how we can sit and talk about the same old nonsense over and over again; about how our flight instruments were not reading that well today, or whether the radio is working properly, or whether the HSI has broken, or the fuel gauge is under-reading or over-reading. It's very difficult for non-fliers to grasp.

However, I'm not as bad as some of them. Recently, one of my friends in America, who also owns a Cirrus (and very kindly allows me to use it when I want to), asked me whether I wanted to go to Lakeland, where there was a big flight exhibition on that weekend. I thought it sounded quite a good idea. I hadn't been to many flight exhibitions, so I decided to go. Naïvely, I didn't realise that at this airfield there were going to be a lot of aerobatic displays, with the equivalent of our Red Arrows and a load of old American military planes flying around, looping the loop and all that stuff. I say 'naïvely' because, when we landed there, the marshal on the ground said, 'You were lucky – you're the last plane to get in.'

'What do you mean by that?' I asked. 'Get in?'

He replied, 'They've closed the airspace now, because it's twelve o'clock and the air show is just about to start. You can't get out again till six o'clock.'

'What?! You mean I'm stuck here for six hours with all these bloody fanatics sitting in their deckchairs?'

It was a baking-hot day and immediately this horrible realisation came over me that I was trapped. I felt a bit sorry for my friend because it kind of looked as if he'd sucked me into it. It wasn't his fault at all; it was my fault for not realising that all the saddos of the flying world were congregating there. There were stands displaying some of the new aeroplanes available in the market, as well as a load of big marquees full of vendors selling bits and pieces that go inside aeroplanes – everything from oil filters, to pressure gauges, to maps and GPS devices. The place was full of geeks enthusiastically milling around.

I suffered six hours of torture! The heat and the crowds got so bad that my friend and I found ourselves going into the booths of certain vendors just to find a chair to sit on, even though it meant talking a lot of bullshit about the possibility of us buying something. Eventually we were allowed to leave, and at least we had one stroke of luck because, having been one of the last planes in, we were parked in a position where we would be one of the first to get off. And credit to the organisers, they arranged for planes to take off two at a time in parallel. There were 600-odd planes there, and we must have been about the fortieth plane to leave. If we'd been parked where the 600th plane was, we would have had to wait another two and a half hours for our slot.

So, a saddo I might be, talking to some of my mates at the flying club on a Saturday, but at least when I've had enough I can get up and go. And I ain't *so* sad that I'd put myself through six hours of torture ever again. I mean, let's face it, once you've seen two jets flying through the air, looping the loop, how many more bloody times do you want to see the same thing? Once is enough, maybe twice, but twenty times? And five different aeroplanes all doing the same thing? And this load of brain-deads are sitting there in their deckchairs with their binoculars, looking at all this as if it's the eighth wonder of the world.

So it turns out I might not be *such* a saddo, but one thing about our fraternity is that we're all sticklers for making sure our planes are totally up to date, and by that I mean loaded with the latest software and equipment, with all the maintenance and oil changes done exactly on time. In fact, I am so pathetic that I end up changing the software even if the plane hasn't flown. It kind of preys on your mind if something on your aeroplane is not exactly perfect – you end up not being happy until you fix it. And many of my pals back at Stapleford are exactly the same.

Remember me telling you about knob-twiddlers? Well, my new friend in America is one of those. There is nothing worse than some busybody touching the knobs and reminding you to do this or do that when you already know exactly what you have to do. In fact, it's quite off-putting because one thing you *must* do when you're flying is be totally focused and have a roadmap in your head of what you are going to do and when. Because the plane actually belonged to my knob-twiddling American friend, I can't categorise him as one of the ponces I referred to earlier. However, I did tell him that if I was to be the pilot in command, then would he kindly mind not touching anything unless we were about to die!

The thing is, to another qualified pilot sitting next to you, it may *look like* you've forgotten to do something, but things go wrong when people can't help themselves and they go and do it for you! I have been chastising one of my pals at Stapleford, Bob Smith, about this for many years, and I have to say that he now sits with his arms folded and doesn't touch my aeroplane while we're going along, unless I ask him to.

I'm training my friend in America to do exactly the same. In fact, I've told him about Bob and I wind him up by calling him Bob when he goes into fiddling mode.

I do make sure that I practise what I preach if I'm ever sitting in the number-two seat. I never touch anything unless I'm asked to do so. I mean, can you imagine driving your car and you're going down the road and someone's saying to you, 'There's a zebra crossing coming up there – are you going to stop, because there are two people waiting? There's a 30mph speed limit ahead, so start slowing down now.' Or, worse still, can you imagine them reaching over and switching on the indicators for you? You can see how that would get on your bloody nerves. Well, it's the same thing in an aeroplane, only ten times worse.

In fact, the last thing you want is someone rabbiting to you when you are supposed to be concentrating – it makes you forget to do things. In your mind, you have to have a picture of the airport you're about to land at. When you've got two of your mates, who are also pilots, bellowing in your ear, 'Just over there, turn left, turn right. Yeah, you're going to go down there . . . no, you're going to move over there . . . you've got to go crosswind; you're going downwind . . .', you get confused, and it's happened to me on a few occasions.

I sometimes think – out of spitefulness or mischievousness – that when I'm in the number-two seat flying with these guys, I should start pestering *them* and getting them in a fluster, just to show them what it's like. But I guess it's safety first, in my mind, so I sit there nice and quietly and don't do anything.

But God forbid if you *do* get something a bit wrong – for example, not putting the flaps up quickly enough or misunderstanding the landing pattern at an airport (as you may well do if you get distracted by these other pilots fiddling around and driving you nuts) – well, then the post mortem as to what went wrong is worthy of the sinking of the *Titanic*.

18

Paperclips and Nuclear Missiles

**Casting a businesslike eye on government, and some suggestions
for better ways they could spend our money.**

There is no way I could ever be a politician, let alone prime
minister. That's not to say that, at times, when faced with the latest
government fiasco, I haven't thought for a moment that I *could* do
a better job. I expect most of us have!

I've also been asked by people whether I would, for example,
stand as mayor of London; indeed, there was once a large front-
page headline in the *Evening Standard* saying, 'You're hired! Sir
Alan is people's choice as Mayor.' I killed that off quickly by telling

people that I couldn't possibly put myself forward for such a position. For a start, there would be too much of a conflict of interest, considering I'm in the real-estate business and am always asking for planning consent from the various councils in London. Can you imagine if one of my companies got planning consent and I was the mayor? There wouldn't be enough trees on the planet to produce the newspapers criticising me.

I did get an insight into how the government and the civil service operate during my short secondment as an adviser to Her Majesty's government, when I specialised in the Department of Business Innovation and Skills. First of all, I was amazed at the number of people employed in that department, and I was a little confused as to what each and every one of them was supposed to be doing. I wasn't there long enough to delve into detail and work that out, nor was it my remit. Nevertheless, I saw enough to realise that, as far as governmental matters are concerned, I would have no idea how to organise anything; I wouldn't know where to start! It needs a special breed of person who's spent all their life in government and politics. And I guess it goes along with my philosophy that in business, and elsewhere in life, you won't succeed unless you have a lot of experience.

But there are times when you would think that common sense would prevail, for example, with the recent cuts the government has been talking about. In my view, they're jumping from the frying pan into the fire. Most of the cost of the government comes from paying for the civil service. If they have to scrap hundreds of thousands of these jobs, yes, a number of people will be off the government payroll, but they will no doubt receive large redundancy packages in many cases and start to claim unemployment benefits. It will be interesting to watch this space and see how, on the one hand, the government will boast how well they are doing implementing the cuts and how much they've saved, while on the other hand, there'll be complete silence about how unemployment benefit payments have shot up. As for the redundancy payments, they will most probably be covered by some small print in the budget as 'extraordinary non-recurring costs'.

One of the things that fascinates me the most is the government procurement policy. The government is the largest spender, the biggest punter – if you like – for most businesses. Everything from paperclips to, let's say, nuclear missiles. I have seen some of the people in charge of procurement and, just as I would be no good as a politician, they are no good at commercial procurement. In fact, most of them are clueless.

I have mentioned in my speeches a couple of times in the House of Lords that the government needs to look at things in a fresh way. You cannot expect to cut costs by being efficient in procurement if you do not use professional people who have done it as their day job all their lives. But in trying to recruit those people, you also have to understand that they're not going to come and work for civil service pay.

And there's the dilemma. Let's say, for example, that the government is spending £600 billion a year on procurement. If they bring in a team of professionals, they may have to pay the top people, say, £3 million or £4 million a year, and in turn they may have to employ a group of a hundred specialists underneath them who get paid anything from £100,000 to £250,000 a year. And let's say that the cost of that new team comes to £70 million. However, instead of spending £600 billion per year, the professionals have procured the same amount of stuff for £400 billion. Now, anyone with any commercial sense would say, 'That's got to be the right thing to do.' But the big problem, of course, is the media – can you imagine the headlines in the *Daily Mail*? Joe Bloggs, effectively a civil servant, is being paid £4 million a year of tax-payers' money to head up government procurement, when poor people in Middlesbrough are struggling on the breadline.

I say the government has got to have to balls to stand up and say that one thing has got nothing to do with another. If they are tasked with cutting costs, they have to employ the right people. It's the simple principle that, if you pay peanuts, you get monkeys. People like Sir Terry Leahy and Sir Stuart Rose were, of course, paid well by the companies they ran and were incentivised with bonuses. Why should people with knowledge of procurement and infrastructure waste their time being paid a pittance? The government needs to wake up and realise this, and have the balls to explain it as simply as I have to the voting public. And while they are at it, if I were prime minister, instead of grovelling trying to justify it, I would add, 'Not only are they being paid £4 million per year, but if they save us another £50 billion, I am going to award them a bonus of another million.'

In August 2010, shortly after the coalition government was elected, it seconded the services of Sir Philip Green for a couple of months to do an efficiency review on government spending. His report included some rather shocking details. For example, there was clearly no co-ordination across all government procurement – there were examples of people buying photocopying paper for, say, £73 a box, while other departments were paying £8 a box for the same stuff. So, obviously, people at various levels were getting legged-over. This is another problem: give a person a budget to spend, and they will spend it. If you give them the spending power they don't have on their own salaries, they will go on a spending spree.

Now, to be fair, large expenditure in government is all dished out by way of a tendering process, so there's no question of anything dodgy going on. It's very open; it's very transparent, and there aren't any bribes or anything like that these days. But it comes to a stage when you have to draw a line – you cannot go out and tender for everything. The problems really occur when autonomy is given to civil servants to spend up to a certain amount – say, £1,000 a month – without having to go through a tendering process or ask for permission. It is here that our tax pounds are being abused. These people are like kids in a sweet shop who can't get rid of their money quickly enough. And as for negotiating on prices, they are totally incapable or cannot be bothered.

As most of us know, budgets are normally cast for a whole financial year, and certain expenditure is allocated to various departments, to be spent in that period. There was always a famous rush in March to make sure the entire budget was spent before 31 March – the end of the financial year – which was ridiculous. To put it in simple terms, if a particular government department had, say, £5 million allocated to them, and throughout the course of the year they'd only spent £4.5 million, there was a last-minute bum-rush to spend the last half a million, simply because they were allowed to.

Now, people like me who run a business, or indeed anyone who runs a home, may have a budget. However, if we haven't used all the money we've allocated to it, we don't go out and spend it just because it's been budgeted for. So why should those in charge of government departments do so? Well, the answer is that if they were awarded £5 million to spend in one particular year and they only spent £4.5 million, they would argue that, when they went to cast their budget for the following year, they would not be able to get an increase. Even worse, they might be pushed down to £4.5 million. This means that, instead of getting a pat on the back for saving money, they get a hard time when trying to get the next year's budget allocated.

I can see a small dose of inefficiency in the House of Lords, where antiquated systems still continue. As a simple example, every single word that is spoken in the House of Lords is recorded daily in writing and a Hansard report is printed and sent to every single member of the House of Lords. Imagine how much it costs to print it overnight, collate it and then distribute it by a courier or postal service? Now, if I had my way, they'd just pay for every member of the House of Lords to have a computer – it would be much cheaper. I mean, let's face it, most of them do anyway, and all one would need to do is email the information each day. Why do they need to use all this paper? I would guess they could save a few million pounds a year, when you consider the people that must be involved in the process. That is just one simple, logical thing that any commercial person could spot within five minutes.

Shortly after the 2010 general election, a lot of people asked my opinion on the new coalition government. I gave them a stock answer: that you can't really form an opinion in a month, or even a year. I guess you have to wait for a couple of years before you can justifiably compliment or criticise. But one can't help but comment on a few of the fiascos that went on during and after that general election.

I remember telling Gordon Brown that he should not agree to do live television debates in the American way, where the opposing parties slag each other off. Unfortunately, however, BSkyB stimulated the idea by asking David Cameron whether he'd be prepared to do a live debate, and he answered in a positive manner, which kind of forced Gordon to agree. And then the thing began to escalate. It would be unfair for BSkyB to broadcast the debate exclusively, so the other TV channels would also be allowed to show it. And here's where the big mistake came. Initially, everybody thought it was just going to be Brown and Cameron having a fighting match, but the Liberal Democrat Party kicked up a fuss and said that they should be involved. And so we ended up with this kind of *Britain's Got Talent* reality show, where the three party leaders battled it out on television – one night on ITV, another night on BBC, another night on Sky.

Now, I'd like you to imagine you are Nick Clegg, the Lib Dem leader, and bear in mind the following: deep down in your heart (and in the heart of every Lib Dem member), you know you don't have a hope in hell of ever winning a general election. It's either going to be Conservative or Labour, and that's how it's been for the past ninety years. So, with that in mind, and with a little bit of mischievousness in your head, you can freely enter into those TV debates and make all sorts of claims and promises about what your party would do if you were in power, knowing full well you've got more chance of being struck by lightning.

The net effect, of course, was that Mr Clegg came out smelling of roses. He was saying what everybody wanted to hear, knowing that there was no chance he'd have to keep his promises! It was a kind of spoiling tactic, and spoil things it did, because, as I told Gordon, 'Allowing Clegg in the middle on these shows is going to mess things up.'

And if I'd had a dialogue with Cameron, I would have said the same to him. 'You're best off not doing it, and then the pair of you can just slug it out in the normal way.' But look what happened – the promises that the Lib Dems made confused the nation to such an extent that the Conservatives got a very small majority of votes over Labour – not enough to allow them to govern the country – and this forced them to form a coalition government with the Lib Dems. A deal was done over the course of a couple of days – or, as I call it, a prenuptial agreement – where I guess the Lib Dems ensured that they would get the backing of the Conservatives on certain things they wanted changing in government if they entered the coalition.

I should imagine that Cameron bent over backwards in the end to do a deal. I mean, if you think about it, what was at stake here was everything that he'd ever worked for – to actually be the prime minister of Great Britain. It must have been a very hard thing to turn down. And if I were negotiating on behalf of the Lib Dems,

I would have sussed that out immediately. He *had* to come to an agreement if he wanted to avoid calling another election. And so the famous deal was done. Suddenly, Nick Clegg was the deputy prime minister and Vince Cable was made Business Secretary. I can't imagine that, in their wildest dreams, did they ever think they would achieve such positions of power. It's a bit like some screaming Tottenham fan mouthing off about how bad every manager has been, how bad the chairman is and shouting, 'What a load of rubbish this team is – it needs a new manager!' Then all of a sudden you say to him, 'Righto, okay – *you* are going to be the manager tomorrow. Here are the keys to the ground. The dressing room's the second on the left. Good luck. Bye!' It's a stupid example, but I imagine that's how Nick Clegg must have felt, having suddenly been invested with so much power. To take the analogy a bit further, it was as if Clegg was the Leyton Orient manager who'd just discovered that he had to manage Barcelona in the Champions League final.

With all this power thrust on them, Clegg and Cable must have been thinking to themselves, 'Oh my God, what have we done? What have I said? What have I promised? I'm gonna look a right mug if we don't manage to come forward with all the things we said we wanted.'

A classic example of this was the increase in students' tuition fees, something which the Lib Dems said they were going to oppose. And shortly after the coalition was in, what happened? The fees went up and there were riots in the street. I don't know whether Cameron was playing a very clever game – only time will tell – but certainly in the early days of the coalition, it appeared to me that he was kind of standing back when it came to these major policy decisions and allowing Clegg and Cable to do a lot of the dirty work. Perhaps Cameron is not stupid – maybe he wants them to fall on their swords; maybe he wants to turn all the Lib Dems away from the coalition. Again, I guess it's a case of watch this space and see what pans out. The Lib Dem drive on the Alternative Voting system was passed in the House of Commons and the House of Lords on a fast-track basis to allow it to quickly go to a public vote, and in May 2011 it was completely defeated by a firm 'no' from the public. At the same time, the Lib Dems lost a lot of their seats in the local council elections, reflecting that the public have seen though their promises and BS.

In the meantime, whoever's in power needs to get their act together. Like me, I'm sure that many British people would like to know once and for all how many trillions we spent in getting involved in the wars in Iraq, Afghanistan and, more recently, Libya. I'm going to admit it – perhaps I'm a bit thick – but I don't know what business it is of ours to poke our nose into other countries' affairs. Now, I've expressed this opinion many times on Twitter and a lot of the followers have said to me that they're surprised at my naïvety. They all come back and say one thing: 'It's oil, Lord Sugar! Anywhere there's oil, America and Britain are interested.'

Well, is it oil? I don't know. Or is it what the US and British governments claim – they want to help oppressed people who are being downtrodden by dictators and living a life of terror? Well, that *sounds* a plausible story, but when I watch Comic Relief or Sports Relief once a year on television and see those terrible pictures of starving and dying people in Africa, I can't help thinking that the same governments don't seem to care about *them*. They leave it to the people at Comic Relief, who raise a considerable amount of money from the public; money which, with the greatest respect, is not enough to do more than scratch the surface, so great is the problem. I also wonder with aid money in general how much gets confiscated or nicked by the authorities in those oppressive and often corrupt regimes but, pushing that issue to one side, if we're so concerned with helping people, why is it that the British and American governments get busy in places like Iraq, Afghanistan and Libya, but do almost nothing about the starving and the dying in Africa?

Getting back to my point, perhaps it's a case of charity begins at home. We should look after our own and not worry about what other nations do. Instead of spending billions fighting these wars, all this money we've 'found' from somewhere could be more usefully deployed in our own country. Now, it might be argued that war does generate employment within the country, as it creates a need for weaponry, uniforms, armoured vehicles and things like that. Well, even that argument is flawed because, when you look at it very carefully, a lot of the stuff is purchased from other countries – much of it from America, for example.

Here is a very wacky idea, and I'm sure I will be shot down in flames by various economists, who will explain to me why it won't work. But I'm going to say it anyway, even if I come out looking like a mug. Instead of spending trillions overseas and poking our nose in things that are nothing to do with us, why don't we take those trillions and invest them in my project – NUTS!

Everybody at the age of fifty-five who can prove that they have been employed in Britain for more than twenty years and have paid tax and national insurance will be paid to give up their work to make way for younger people. Instead of redundancy pay, the government will give them a million-pound bond. And with that million-pound bond, which can be used, let's say, over the course of twenty years, there are certain rules that apply:

Rule 1) You can't do any moonlighting or have a job
          on the side.
Rule 2) You have to pay off the mortgage on your house,
          or buy a new house.
Rule 3) You have to buy yourself a new car which is
          assembled in Britain.
Rule 4) You have to go on holiday at least once a year to
          a British resort.

Now, although this may sound a weird and wacky idea, just think about it for a moment. There are approximately fifteen million people over the age of fifty-five, and if every one of them, on becoming fifty-five, had to go out and buy a car, it would mean there would be a demand for millions of cars over a period of time – British-assembled cars. It would mean there'd be a demand for builders and contractors either to refurbish houses or build new ones. There would be a rejuvenation of the British holiday resorts, and there would be spaces made for younger people to get jobs. The money, effectively, would be thrown back into the economy and, instead of spending it on some McDonnell-Douglas missile or fighter plane from America, it's actually being spent to buy consumer products or housing materials – inflating our economy and generating a tremendous amount of employment in all those allied industries.

Now, apart from anybody else who's having a good laugh reading this, thinking what a load of rubbish I'm spouting, of course our friends in Brussels would turn around and say that it's totally illegal. Well, that's back to the government again – it needs to have the balls to tell them to shut up and mind their own business. Yes, my idea might be open to abuse – you'd get the odd scoundrel who'd still do a bit of work on the side, and the government might have to employ a few snoopers (if cheats got caught, they'd lose the million-pound bond). Obviously, people like me, who don't need the government's money or are in a fair old way of business, could turn it down. And so there'd have to be some kind of asset test to see whether you deserve it or not. My idea really applies to the average man in the street – the schoolteacher, the nurse, the shop assistant – all those types of people who have worked hard all their lives.

*

Here's another idea that may seem mad but could end up saving us a lot of money which is currently spent on policing and housing prison inmates. I have this theory which I'm sure will cause a lot of controversy and argument amongst the readers of this book. Some of you might agree with me and others will be violently against it. Now, I'm not saying it's a perfect solution, but I think what I'm about to say is workable in around 90 per cent of cases.

The fact is, 90 per cent of violent crimes and thefts are driven by the desire to get money to buy drugs, and a high percentage of the people in prison are there because of these drug-related crimes. My simple idea is to make the drugs freely available to over-eighteens. If you can picture the small sachets of Sweet'N Low that you see in restaurants to use in your tea and coffee, imagine cocaine or marijuana being supplied in packets like this, purchasable in pharmacies like Boots for, say, £1.99 a packet – the £1.99 including approximately £1 of tax, in the same way that tobacco, alcohol and petrol are taxed. The production of the cocaine would be fully legalised, obviously, and it would be made in factories in the United Kingdom. Marijuana is already grown legally in the United Kingdom, to supply drug companies.

As outrageous as all this may sound, just think about it for a moment. Look at what falls away: the whole spectre of drug barons, drug cartels, drug dealers – they are gone, completely finished overnight. The villains who go out and steal to get money for drugs – that's gone. The drug dealers in the marketplace that prey on people – they're gone. All totally wiped out by legal trading.

Prisons – half empty. Police – freed up from 50 per cent of the rubbish they have to deal with every day and allowed to deal with other matters. The vacant prison cells could be used to give magistrates more scope for putting people away and in the longer term magistrates could tighten up their levels of tolerance, elevating some so-called petty crimes to serious crimes which come with a prison sentence. This, in turn, will mean that young people will realise that pinching the odd Mars bar from Mr Patel's newsagent's is now an imprisonable offence and, therefore, won't do it any more – it will stop.

So there's the positive side of things. Now the negative side. Some people reading this may think I'm totally out of my brain to even consider legalising drugs and having them freely available. Their argument will be that legalising these types of drugs would encourage people who wouldn't normally have used them to do so. I take that as the most valid argument against my idea, to be honest. Other arguments don't stack up, because cigarettes, for example, are known to kill you, yet you can go and buy them. Alcohol is also known to kill, and is addictive, yet you can go and buy that too. Of course, in my idea, the little packets would be plastered with cigarette-type warnings such as 'This is going to kill you,' so you can't say fairer than that.

I guess another argument would be: where does one draw the line? What about crack and heroin, which are arguably more dangerous than cocaine and marijuana? Nevertheless, I do believe there is something there, as outrageous as it may sound. And it's not actually impractical, because the truth of the matter is you don't need to walk more than 500 yards from your home to buy this stuff – we all know it, and the police know it too. *I* say, if people want it, they'll go and find it. And if people could get it for £1.99 rather than £50, would they take more? I don't think so, and that's another angle, because the question arises: would it be cool to use this stuff if everyone could get it? Some young people think it's only cool to do something they know is illegal – the minute it becomes legal, it's no longer cool.

It's only the seed of an idea, and it most probably has some flaws. For example, it could start another form of illicit trade because, as I mentioned earlier, there might be a £1 tax (over 50 per cent), and this would spur on the next wave of villains to think of a coup whereby they purchase loads of the stuff for export.

However, if we adopted this scheme in our country, we would ban the export of these drugs because, if we didn't, we'd effectively be encouraging the breaking of the law in other countries.

It's a crazy idea, I know, but as I say, somewhere within it there's the nucleus of an idea that could work.

In my short time as a government adviser at the Department of Business Innovation and Skills, my two assistants there were bombarded with questions about me, under the Freedom of Information Act. These questions were clearly designed to cause trouble and to waste people's time, and many were obviously coming from – at the time – the Conservative back-benches. And so I thought it was rather opportune when I noticed on Sky News that the new foreign secretary, William Hague, was travelling by private jet to go and investigate the affairs in Libya and northern Africa. The coalition government – in particular the Conservatives – do not stop singing the same old song about the necessity for cuts and savings, 'after the economic mess we were left in by the previous government'. So I decided that *I* would use the Freedom of Information Act to enquire how much this little outing of Mr Hague's cost.

I wrote to the appropriate people at the Foreign and Commonwealth Office and was given a reference number. Under the Freedom of Information Act, there is a statutory date by which they have to reply. Well, of course, there was no reply, and so, having taken advice, I wrote to them again, stating that if I didn't get a reply immediately, I would refer the matter up to higher levels of appeal. Almost magically, just two hours later, an email came back with a full reply on the subject. I do wonder whether they were hoping I might have forgotten and they'd get away with not responding.

It turned out that Mr Hague's little jolly cost £113,000 and, wait for it, he was accompanied by a delegation of other planes, including those of the RAF, which cost another £162,000. Now, apart from the fact that nothing at all has come out of his visits, what the hell is the government doing spending the thick end of over a quarter of a million pounds on sending him out to effectively do nothing? At the same time, we are hearing stories about cuts for pensioners and cuts in hospitals. I know I'm sounding a bit like the *Daily Mail* now, but it infuriates me when you see these two-faced people talking about the need to tighten our belts and cut back, yet in two days they go and blow over a quarter of a million pounds.

And then there's that other brain surgeon George Osborne, who's really landed on his feet. He looks like a rabbit in the headlights when he's up speaking. I don't for one moment think he ever expected to be chancellor, although, as time goes by, I expect he'll become more proficient. In his budget of 2011, he came out with a classic piece of window-dressing. If you're a politician, you know it will go down well if you say, 'We are going to look after the poor and hit the rich.' And one of his little ideas was that he was going to tax private aeroplanes. I say it was window-dressing because there were no details whatsoever on how he was actually going to do it, which clearly demonstrates to me that they hadn't thought it through, but decided it was a wonderful PR stunt to get the ordinary man on their side.

There are a few thousand private jet flights per year in Britain, carrying around 20,000–30,000 passengers, as opposed to the tens of millions of passengers who travel on normal commercial airlines. And so, if you were to apply the same tax per passenger to private flights, the amount of revenue received wouldn't add up to a row of beans – in fact, it wouldn't even pay for William Hague's little jolly. It's a classic political stunt, and I wonder whether it was actually directed at me personally!

It's a bit of a conspiracy theory, but I kicked up so much fuss about William Hague and his private planes that maybe, some-where deep within the bowels of the Conservative Party, they decided they'd come up with something that was going to hit me. I don't really know – it's just a thought.

As yet there are no details of how this new tax is going to be implemented, and I would guess that it will get brushed under the carpet as a PR stunt that had its use and is now over.

I have to admit, I find sitting on the opposition benches in the House of Lords, looking for ways to criticise and whack the gov-ernment, much easier than sitting on the government benches having to defend Labour policies. Perhaps it's what I was destined for!

Then again, I don't want to become as bad as a *Daily Mail* journalist, just picking on things for the sake of it. So whilst I do stand up in the House of Lords and give the coalition a bit of stick, it is fair to say that some of my speeches are balanced. I'm not afraid to admit that the past regimes also made mistakes, and the items I complain about are genuine issues; big, fundamental flaws and molehills I am trying to turn into mountains. And so I'm happy with myself in that sense.

19

'No Comment'

Whacking the press, super-injunctions and how to handle journalists.

Now, I've had a lot of run-ins with the media over the years. Some people say that I shouldn't let them bother me, that I should just treat criticism and slurs as water off a duck's back. However, me being me, I'm afraid I can't resist it. It wasn't until I became relatively famous, back in the eighties – when my rags-to-riches story was picked up by the press – that I realised the power of the media and how important it was to the prosperity of my company. In those days, all the reporting about me was mainly to do with the fortunes of my company. All the positive comments in the media – particularly in sections of the financial press – had an impact on the share price of my company and on the sales of our products. Of course, I had to accept that, once I'd put myself in the public arena, I had to take the rough with the smooth, and it's a fact that the media will build you up as a success story in business, but will also immediately comment when things go wrong. As long as that reporting is factual and accurate, then I say, fair enough, facts are facts. And so I haven't really had any gripes at all with the financial media, because they reported good news about me in the good times and bad news about me in the bad times. That's business.

But it's amazing how influential the press is on the ordinary man in the street. It reminds me of the time when my dear mum, who I used to visit regularly on a Sunday, once said to me, 'I saw in the paper that you're going to start making car-phones, Alan.'

'No, Mum, it's not true,' said I.

'It *is* true,' she said. 'It's in the paper.'

I said, 'Mum, it is *not* true. They're just making it up. They're guessing; it's rubbish. Trust me, I'm your son. I know what we're doing and we're not making car-phones.'

And I remember her turning around and walking off to make some tea, mumbling, 'Well, it was in the paper . . .', as if to say, 'It's still true. I don't care what Alan says.'

That funny little tale demonstrates how some people believe *everything* they read in the papers and how the press can damage people's reputations with inaccurate reporting. Happily, these days, I think the younger generation has come to understand that some of the newspapers are becoming comics and that you have to take what they say with a pinch of salt.

With the advent of the internet and rolling news on television, the younger generation tends not to buy newspapers, and the circulation of some of the big-name newspapers is dropping like a stone. However, some of the tabloids, like the *Sun*, seem to be maintaining their circulation. One might argue that this is because their readership is perhaps not computer-literate and hasn't joined the internet bandwagon. With that in mind, you can also argue that their type of journalism has been tuned to attract that type of person. There's an old saying, 'Never let the truth get in the way of a good story,' and I think that is the case with some of these tabloid newspapers, where the headlines can be terribly misleading. You might also apply another saying here: 'A lie is halfway around the world before the truth has got its boots on.'

Over the years there have been lots of articles written about me, my companies and other things I've been associated with. A lot of it has been very frustrating because, to put it bluntly, it's been a pack of lies, and I've spent hundreds of thousands of pounds fighting newspapers in the courts. The main beneficiary of my winnings has been Great Ormond Street Hospital, whose senior executive sometimes jokes with me that they're hoping one of the newspapers will write some more lies. Over the years, I must have donated a few hundred thousand pounds to Great Ormond Street from damages obtained from newspapers. But does one ever really put right the damage that the newspapers cause? And do you ever get the proper right of reply? The simple answer is no.

Years ago, there were famous cases, like that of Sir Elton John, who once took a newspaper to court and received a settlement of £1 million. However, in the nineties, the Court of Appeal ruled that the damages paid out to people who had been defamed or libelled were outrageous and so, these days, the judges are directed to inform the jury, should they decide to award damages to a plaintiff, to take note of examples of pay-outs to people who have suffered *physical* injuries – for example, a broken leg, or the loss of a limb, or the loss of the sight in one eye – and compare those injuries to the damage inflicted upon someone who has had lies told about them.

In this day and age, even if you're awarded a figure as high as £50,000–£200,000 (which is towards the top end of the market), to achieve that in the courts can cost up to £500,000 in legal fees! And, as the law stands, you are not allowed to recover all your legal fees if you win. Most probably, you will recover only 60–65 per cent, which means that, even if you're awarded £200,000, you'll have actually *lost* some money. Of course, if you lose, it can cost over £1 million as you will have to pay the defendant's costs too.

It is this phenomenon that certain newspapers rely on. They get a bee in their bonnet and pick on people whom they know can ill afford to run a very expensive libel action. Take, for example, politicians. I mean, as bad as they are, the reality is that the majority are *not* wealthy people and they can't afford high-class lawyers to fight newspapers, so most of the time they have to either find a lawyer who will work on a no-win, no-fee basis or swallow it and simply let the newspapers write a load of trash about them.

The same can be said for the royal family, who have to sit around and read some stuff which sails very close to the wind as far as the truth is concerned. The newspapers rely upon one fact: that no senior politician or member of the royal family is likely to turn up in court, in front of the public and the media gallery, and sit through a cross-examination or give evidence. In fact, it can be argued that it's actually good for the circulation of a newspaper if a court case is brought against them because, throughout the course of it, the events that go on in the courtroom are reported in the media, which, as far as they're concerned, makes good reading and can be used to fill their pages every day. Consider that a massive television advertising campaign to try to boost the circulation of a newspaper can cost hundreds of thousands, if not millions, of pounds, then compare that to some outrageous headline on a front page which gets the attention of the public on the newsstands. Even if the whole lot is a pack of lies and the person they're writing about takes them to court, it's actually much cheaper for the newspapers to do this than run a TV campaign.

As a result of the relatively low damages awarded compared to costs, a newspaper can use the court procedures to protect itself and make taking a case all the way to court a high-risk gamble for the person bringing the claim. The defendant, namely the newspaper, can make what's known as a 'Part 36 offer'. This is an estimate of what it thinks it would be ordered to pay, as far as damages are concerned, if it lost. Once the offer is made, it puts the onus on the claimant to decide whether they wish to take the risk of fighting the case right the way through to the bitter end in court, because if the jury ends up offering less than the Part 36 offer, then not only will the claimant be stuffed with their own costs, but they'll also have to pay the newspaper's costs (incurred because it made you the Part 36 offer). That's a risk most claimants can't afford, so they end up having to take the money and don't get their day in court to properly vindicate their reputation. So, bearing in mind that the average awards are £25,000–£50,000, it's cheaper to knowingly defame or libel someone in order to boost your circulation when you know that the worst-case scenario is a £50,000 cost.

There is, of course, the Press Complaints Commission, which is supposed to assist people in bringing claims against publishers. However, I believe it is treated with contempt by the media. Most lawyers will tell you to forget it, as it has no real clout.

There is the lack of a moral anchor within the tabloids. One minute they will praise a celebrity; the next day they're writing horrible things about him or her. The articles are not news stories but op/ed pieces. A storyline is dreamt up in editorial meetings, when the editor says, for example, 'Let's put the boot into Alan Sugar today.'

A journalist might pipe up to protest: 'But I just wrote a glowing report on him yesterday.'

'And now I'm telling you I want you to give him a kicking,' says the editor. And so the journalist will go off and deliver a spiteful piece. No moral anchor.

And it's getting worse because the libel laws are going to change again – to be even more in favour of the publishers! This is because, in some cases – examples of which are currently being debated in the House of Lords – small-time publishers such as scientific journals, which are run on a shoestring, have been fighting for freedom of speech so that they can print articles (for example, accusing giant drug companies of certain malpractices) without the risk of being bullied or destroyed in libel actions by the giant drug companies. Usually, in these cases, the little publisher can ill afford to fight the case and has to back down and retract what it's written. So the law is changing to protect the small publishers' freedom of speech. But on the flip side, this new law will make it easier for the bigger newspapers to libel and defame people who can't afford to fight a court case. These big and powerful companies will be able to get away with murder because they'll know they are dealing, in many cases, with a man of straw. As you can see, this is going to be a rock-and-a-hard-place situation – although the law is to be changed, with the best intentions, to stop small publishers being bullied, you can bet your life the law will be abused by the giant newspaper organisations so that it's even easier for them to tell more lies.

I don't know whether you've ever noticed, when reading a newspaper, that sometimes you see a little postage-stamp-sized apology for publishing something which was incorrect. The wording is normally very garbled and half-hearted. These 'apologies' come about as a result of legal action taken against the newspaper. When the newspaper realises it's been caught bang to rights and has no defence whatsoever, it agrees to issue an apology (and, most probably, pays some moderate damages and legal fees to the person complaining). However, the point is that the apology is *tiny* and bears no resemblance to the size and prominence of the original offending article. Therefore, it's highly unlikely that the same number of readers who saw the original article will see the apology – so the law is an ass in that respect, and always has been. I've always advocated that if someone has plastered me on the front page of a newspaper with some pack of lies, then when they apologise, their apology should be of the same size and prominence and in the same position in the newspaper. However, for some reason or other, the law says not.

A quite topical subject these days is the super-injunction. It seems that, on the back of privacy laws set out in EU legislation, people can now seek protection against the media to prevent them from publishing matters that are considered to be an infringement of their privacy. The newspapers don't like this at all. They claim that if they have a story on, say, some high-profile footballer who has committed adultery, they should be able, under the guise of public interest, to tell the story.

It is hard to take sides on this. On the one hand, if a high-profile person is so stupid as to place themselves in a compromising position, one could argue: why *should* the courts protect them? On the other hand, does being famous mean that you should have less privacy than other people? After all, adultery happens every day, but if you're Fred Bloggs having an affair with the woman next door, it's not newsworthy and you'll never be splashed over the front page of the *Sun*. Can you blame a celebrity wanting to protect his wife and kids from reading about his affair in the tabloids and from having all their friends read it as well? But then, what if, as part of your public profile, you put yourself forward as a devoted husband and people buy into that? Isn't it only right that your hypocrisy is exposed?

People argue that the super-injunction, or gagging order, is a legal loophole for the stinking rich and only available to them, as it costs a lot of money in terms of lawyers and court fees. On the other hand, as I've said, the less well off are not famous and thus are unlikely to be targets of the media. An exception would be most politicians, who do not have money, but are still high-profile due to the nature of their position – most of them would certainly not have the financial clout to obtain an injunction. One also has to consider that's it's not just the rich footballer whose privacy is being invaded – what about the person with whom they had the affair? They usually have no money either.

Of course, it's not all about adultery. What if the super-injunction were used to cover up violence, rape, fraud or other illegal practices in which a high-profile person is implicated? Here is the dilemma. If they are guilty, then I say the media has a right to expose them for sure, but at what point should they be exposed?

When the police are investigating someone but have not charged them? Or should it be when the police have charged them? Or when a full-blown trial has taken place and a jury has concluded that the person is guilty? The latter is not good for the media, as there is no scoop there – any high-profile person in court on charges would be public knowledge.

That's why the newspapers went after Christopher Jefferies – the landlord of murdered Jo Yeates – so heavily, digging into his background as soon as the police arrested him, even though he hadn't been charged with anything. It gave them great front-page headlines. But the *Sun* and the *Mirror* went too far in the words they used to describe him, suggesting he was guilty. As we know, he was released without charge and Jo's neighbour, Vincent Tabak, admitted manslaughter, though the prosecution would not accept the plea and his trial for murder was set for October 2011. In May 2011 the attorney general initiated contempt of court proceedings against the *Sun* and the *Mirror* for their coverage, on the basis that judicial matters remain sub judice. I guess this was based on an opinion that the coverage by these papers might have disadvantaged Christopher Jefferies in the eyes of a jury, or allowed his lawyers to plead an unfair trial due to the fact that the media had already implied that their client was guilty. In July the papers lost their case and the *Mirror* was fined £50,000, the *Sun* £18,000. On the same day a total of eight papers (including the *Mirror* and the *Sun* again) paid out substantial libel damages to Jefferies. Only time will tell if they have learned their lesson.

In recent times, the power of the super-injunction has been undermined by something known as parliamentary privilege. This is a law dating back a few hundred years whereby members of both the House of Commons and the House of Lords can say what they want in the chamber, without any form of redress for libel claims, and are immune from prosecution. This privilege, in my opinion, has been abused. In the House of Lords, Lord Ben Stoneham of

Droxford raised a question on behalf of Lord Oakeshott on 19 May 2011, asking the minister why ex-RBS banking boss Sir Fred Goodwin was being protected by a super-injunction. This was a deliberate and blatant attempt to make a farce of the judge's ruling using parliamentary privilege. Everyone knows that the gallery in the House of Lords is attended by the media, so Lord Oakeshott knew exactly what he was doing. He knew that once Sir Fred's name was mentioned, the super-injunction, which was designed to protect him, was broken. The same happened a few days later, when the Liberal Democrat MP John Hemming named the famous footballer Ryan Giggs, who was also protected by a super-injunction.

My point is simply that the House of Lords and the House of Commons are law-makers – they make the laws and instruct judges to implement them as they see fit. Putting to one side whether or not you agree with a judge's ruling, the fact is that it *is* a ruling, and it should not be broken. The average man in the street or member of the media who breaks a court order would be guilty of contempt of court, which is an imprisonable offence, so how come MPs and some members of the House of Lords do exactly that, in a spiteful, malicious manner, using the loophole of parliamentary privilege? Whereas you might excuse innocent, unqualified people on Twitter, who don't realise the implications of what they are saying, these people know exactly what they're doing. Of course, the media love it.

Parliamentary privilege was introduced for good reason. It dates back to times when the king or queen made the laws and parliamentary protection was needed so that debate could take place in the chamber. However, today's blatant misuse of it could lead to it being abandoned. I think Lord Oakeshott should be investigated by the House of Lords Committee as to his motivation for blowing the story. Oakeshott might not think that Sir Fred Goodwin should have the right to cover up matters relating to his personal life by using the courts; however, that is not Oakeshott's decision or, to put it bluntly, any of his bloody business. The decision, right or wrong, was made by a judge entrusted by the government to implement his ruling and, as such, it must be respected.

They say that as you get older you mellow. Well, I guess I've mellowed a bit, and these days I tend to allow a lot of the comments made about me to pass by. I'm more able to think of the newspaper as tomorrow's chip wrapper, but I've also become very aware of who I'm talking to and I'm very guarded in what I say.

Like all things in life, the more experience you have in doing something, the better you get at it, and I find it fascinating to try to work out what kind of angle a journalist is taking, and therefore what kind of story they are trying to create. It takes you a few minutes to suss out whether the person in front of you is actually hostile or not. In most cases, the journalist seems perfectly nice and pleasant in their manner, but this does not mean they have good intentions. There are a few tricks to handling them that I've managed to pick up over the years, the first being that I will only talk about subjects that I am totally expert in, where I have all the details in my brain or at my fingertips, so to speak.

Also, showing your anger and excitement to a journalist, face to face, is bad news – it makes them feel that they've touched a nerve – so remaining calm and talking slowly about the situation is the way to deal with it.

Another trick, and I have adopted this on many occasions, is to simply refuse to do any interviews or make any comments whatsoever. That, I have to say, is one of the best things you can do – not get sucked into commenting. Another useful tactic is asking journalists to put their questions to you by email, answering them with simple one-line answers – denying or accepting their allegations – and then informing them at the end of your reply that you reserve your rights. What does that mean? Well, it's a warning which the newspaper's legal department will fully understand. It means that you have answered their questions and have told the journalist whether they are right or wrong, and if they go ahead and print an allegation contrary to the facts you've stated, then you have reserved your right to take them to court. Ninety-nine times out of a hundred, this results in the allegations not even being printed.

Another technique I use when giving interviews for television is to always enquire whether it's to be a live interview or recorded. If it's recorded, that means it can be edited, which means that the points you wish to raise might be cut out and the recorded interview skewed to the agenda of the broadcaster. A typical example of this was the clip that was played continuously on *Have I Got News For You*, where I told the BBC reporter he was talking nonsense. Of course, it was heavily edited and did not reflect what I really meant in its true context.

So my first principle is: if there's nothing in it for me, I won't give an interview; I simply turn it down. If I do give an interview, then I don't comment on matters I know nothing about and I don't get sucked into political arguments that will come back to haunt me through comments I might make.

If the interview is live, here's a little trick that always works well. If I'm asked an awkward question, I'll raise my eyebrows in surprise and say, on live TV, 'Now, that's funny, we never rehearsed that question!' It's a bit of a blag on my part, I must admit, because normally you don't rehearse the questions, but it makes the journalist look as if they've totally rehearsed and orchestrated the interview. It puts them on the back foot and catches them off guard. They say, 'We haven't rehearsed anything,' to which I reply, 'Sure we have – you gave me a list of questions you were going to ask me and this wasn't on it. Why have you just thrown that one in?' It completely messes up the flow of things and, in a lot of situations, if it's on a news channel, they'll cut the thing immediately and go straight to another subject.

The bottom line is, I don't do interviews these days unless they are completely neutral or unless, being perfectly honest, there's something in it for me. And the best advice I can give to some rising celebrity or business executive is: don't talk to the newspapers and don't talk to TV news reporters – in fact, don't talk to the media at all. Of course, sometimes you can't avoid it, and one of the uses of a PR company (aside from setting up interviews) is to control the media on behalf of someone like me and put them right – making sure that they're getting the right message across.

I'll share with you one little concept that Nick Hewer and I developed from sheer experience, when he was handling my PR. This is it: when you receive a telephone call from a journalist who's got hold of the scent of something going wrong, and you can tell that that journalist is hostile, you put them on hold. Since you know that the story will eventually get out there, you go to one of your 'friendly' journalists at another newspaper and you give them the story and ask them to spin it in a softer manner. This scuppers the scoundrel who wants to make you look a mug. You keep him dangling on a string for twenty-four hours and then you go back to him and report that his story is old news because it's been in the paper already. There's nothing worse for a journalist than being told he's got an old story. That is the Sugar/Hewer patent – well, it's not really patented, but I have to say that even the firm of lawyers I've used for many years has called upon Nick to use it to assist them with some of their clients. It works nine times out of ten.

Having said all that, because of my involvement in *The Apprentice*, we do have a press conference once a year, to launch the new series, and I do give the occasional interview about the forthcoming series, or on the morning of the final, because I see this as a way of promoting the programme. It's part of my obligation to try to make the series successful. I find it funny that over the course of the past six years or so, while I've been doing *The Apprentice*, I've heard the same old questions asked time and time again. I sometimes say to the journalists, 'Surely you *know* you've asked this question a hundred times – can somebody ask me something new?'

And then there are photographers. To be honest, I feel sorry for those poor sods because I don't show any tolerance for them, and this is something which has built up over the years. In my naïve early days, when I was being covered by the business media, I would agree to have some photographer come and take pictures of me. In those days, they would spend half an hour shooting rolls and rolls of film – different types of lenses, different lighting, close-ups, full-length, jacket on, jacket off. In the end, it got on my bloody nerves. And what got on my nerves even more was to spend an hour with one of these photographers and then, when the article was printed in the newspaper, you saw a library shot that they'd taken from some archive! All this led to me developing a very short fuse with photographers.

In my defence, if I do agree to be photographed, I always make sure everyone involved is warned about what they're up against! The photographer is told to come much earlier and bring an extra person. They can take as much time as they want setting up their lighting and getting everything perfect, using the person they've brought along as a stand-in for me. Then, when everything is set up, I will give them ten minutes maximum. I tell them, very respectfully, that if they're not prepared to work under these conditions, then I have to decline.

And so I've got myself a bit of a reputation amongst the photographers fraternity, but they're all pretty cool with it now, because most of the time they waste is on setting up their lighting and all that stuff, and they know my reputation for impatience.

I wouldn't like to tell you how many times the photographer has asked me to stick my hand out and say, 'You're fired!' These days, I just refuse point blank.

Then you get the slippery photographer's assistant, who comes along with a few props. It's usually some dolly bird in skinny jeans and a blouse, with half her anatomy hanging out, smiling at you and being awfully polite, saying, 'Would you mind just holding this cup, Lord Sugar?' The cup most probably has got something like 'Grumpy Old Man' written on it.

'No, I'm sorry, darling, it's not on.'

'Would you hold this live chick?'

'No, sorry, not on.'

Every trick in the book has been tried, and up until now I have succeeded in avoiding them. You might be saying to yourself, 'What does he expect? He is, like it or not, a high-profile character and he should realise that this is part and parcel of the life he has chosen.' And that *is* fair comment, but I also think it's reasonable for me to try to dodge as much of it as I possibly can.

I remember one day, when I was attending court to give evidence in a particular case. There were loads of photographers hanging around outside, and as I walked along the road towards the courts I could see a bunch of them, hustling for position to take a picture of me. You've all seen those pictures of people entering a courtroom – the photographers try to shoot you with a glum, worried look on your face. I remember asking the junior solicitor who was walking with me to step to one side for a moment, so I could walk up to the photographers alone. As I approached them, I put on a big, beaming smile and stuck my two thumbs up. You could see the disappointment on their faces. I play-acted like this all the way to the courtroom, where photographers are not allowed. When they got back to their offices, their editors must have had a fit. 'This isn't the picture we wanted – we want him miserable, not smiling. What's the matter with you, you idiots!' And, of course, none of the pictures were printed.

All this comes with experience. Basically, newspapers are not run by a bunch of nice people. The journalists themselves are a special breed. I often say that, in many cases, they are pathetic people who love the power of the pen. They are spiteful individuals whose mentality is to pry and dig and give people grief. They've never achieved anything themselves, but they can't wait to attack someone who *is* trying to achieve something. That's why you very rarely see any positive stories in the newspapers.

Over the years, I've been asked by certain newspapers to write for them. Indeed, when Piers Morgan was editor of the *Daily Mirror*, I did a regular weekly column for him – giving business advice – which was quite successful. I've written articles for *The Sunday Times*'s business section, the *Daily Telegraph* and the *Sun*. I quite enjoy doing it.

On one particular occasion, brought about by my new popularity as the host of *The Apprentice*, I was approached by the then editor of the *Sun*, Rebekah Wade (now Rebekah Brooks) to write a regular column for them. I explained to her that I needed to be inspired in order to write a regular column, and coming up with something different every week would be difficult. It would prey on my mind – a bit like doing homework – and I didn't want to be boxed into a corner, having to report with my copy on a certain date so, respectfully, I said no.

'I won't do a regular column,' I added, 'but what I *will* do is, when I get an idea I'll give it to you first.' And we worked together for a bit on this basis, where I would write some articles that were topical and of interest to me.

On one such occasion, I informed her that I was about to get a scoop because Prime Minister Gordon Brown had agreed to let me interview him. And not only could I do an article for them, but they could also publish exclusive clips of the interview on their website. This was an amazing coup. I went ahead and interviewed Gordon (you can see those interviews if you want by going to my YouTube site at www.youtube.com/amshold).

To make a long story short, having done the interview with

Gordon and had it cut up into nice little five-minute chunks, the *Sun* completely and utterly messed it up by editing it. I went nuts, and Ms Wade didn't like the way I lost my rag with her people, so she slagged me off in some emails and we fell out.

That was not the end of the story, however. A few months later, in January 2009, I was at my home in Florida, around the same time that Israel had invaded Gaza in response to continual rocket attacks. I was minding my own business when I got an email from the deputy editor of the *Sun* at the time, Dominic Mohan. He told me they'd received information that, in revenge for Israel's invasion of Gaza, some fundamentalist group had drawn up a hit list of people to be attacked – and I was on that list. He asked me whether I was going to increase my security and all that stuff.

I said to him, 'You're talking total nonsense. Nobody has contacted me. I don't have any security and I'm certainly not going to get any security. And, by the way, I'm in America; I'm not even at home.'

He told me that the police had been informed and they were active on the matter. I denied any knowledge of it whatsoever and suggested to him that he did not repeat this stuff in the newspaper. Despite me telling him this, the *Sun* went ahead and published it, and, although there were other names allegedly on the list, it was I who was the front-page headline on next day's paper. There was a picture of me, accompanied by the story that I was under threat from terrorists, with quotes from the *Sun*'s terror expert, Glen Jenvey, saying that I was at risk and should expect to be the subject of a hate campaign. Later investigation revealed that a person under the name of Abu Islam had posted my name on the Ummah website, and that this was the source of the suggestion that I was on some hit list. As the trail was uncovered by Bloggerheads website, it became apparent that Abu Islam was none other than Glen Jenvey! Well, it wasn't hard to work out who had initially fed the story to the *Sun*. Nevertheless, Dominic Mohan's email to me said he was justified in publishing the story based on the expert testimony of Glen Jenvey. The whole lot was a total pack of lies, and I was furious. At the time I thought this was a deliberate and spiteful move by Rebekah Wade to pay me back for the Gordon Brown incident, but maybe that is unfair.

I put my lawyers on the case, and I also took the step of not just suing the newspaper, but suing Rebekah Wade personally – joining her in on the action, which is something I wouldn't normally do.

On 18 August that year, Jenvey gave an interview in which he claimed that he had now converted to Islam and was determined to go public with a confession that he had knowingly and wilfully named me as a terror target. BBC Radio Five ran the interview on 13 September, outlining Jenvey as a fake, and two days later, the *Sun* printed Jenvey's confession that he'd made up all the allegations. The *Sun* issued an apology on 23 September to the Ummah website but, despite me asking for an apology, they never printed one. Jenvey was arrested by the police in December, but I don't think anything ever happened from a criminal point of view. In fact, I believe that the police dropped the whole incident.

Here is a classic example of how a newspaper can deliberately tell a pack of lies that could, in certain circumstances, have endangered someone's life. I mean, who knows what nutters there are out there who might believe the newspaper and decide to inflict damage on me or my family? As it happened, on 7 January, I received an unsolicited telephone call from the police telling me that they had seen the article in the newspaper and that the special terror division of the police had looked into it. They were pleased to tell me, from the intelligence they had, that there seemed to be no truth in it whatsoever. They said that they knew that I wasn't at home, as they'd been to my house, and they were going to send a few patrol cars past my house over the course of the next few days. I mean, that is fantastic service from the police, and I didn't ask for it, but it goes to show you how a spiteful little rumour can have ramifications.

They are nasty, nasty people at the *Sun*, and since then I have severed my relationship with them. As for the legal side, they caved in. I guess that Rebekah Wade was scared of turning up in court, because she was instrumental in making sure the case was settled. They ended up paying £25,000 damages and £125,623 in legal costs, but it wasn't the money; it was the principle of the thing.

More recently, we've seen further evidence of News International's skulduggery with the phone-hacking scandal. This was where *News of the World* journalists, or private investigators on their behalf, managed to hack into certain high-profile individuals' mobile phone voicemails – and at last the police are doing something about it, because it's criminal. As we know, in 2007, the royal editor Clive Goodman admitted hacking into the phone messages of members of the royal household, as well as those of Elle McPherson. He was imprisoned, as was a private investigator the paper used, Glenn Mulcaire. But the story didn't just go away and, earlier in 2011, two more *News of the World* journalists were arrested.

Until now, the bosses always seem to have got away with it by saying that they knew nothing about it, which never seems believable and is hard for anyone to imagine. Consider, if you were the editor of a newspaper and one of your journalists brought you a story, surely you would ask the journalist how he came about that information. The editor, at the end of the day, is supposed to oversee what is printed in his or her newspaper. Then when it transpired that the *News of the World* had hacked into the phone of missing schoolgirl Milly Dowler, who was later found dead, the country went mad. It was the final straw and heads started to roll.

Andy Coulson, until recently the spin doctor for Prime Minister David Cameron, was editor of the *News of the World* between 2003 and 2007. He was arrested by the police to possibly face charges of phone hacking and illegal payments to police officers in the Met while running the paper. And Clive Goodman was arrested again, this time in connection with payments to the police. Then, on 17 July, Rebekah Brooks, the CEO of News International, who had edited the *News of the World* between 2000 and 2003 before moving to the *Sun*, was arrested. Les Hinton, who was seen as Rupert Murdoch's right-hand man, resigned from his position within News Corporation, as he had been CEO of News International when all this hacking was alleged to have gone on.

I wonder how long the journalists or the private dicks who have been implicated will protect the new or old bosses of News International, if they have been. Perhaps we may see some plea-bargaining, if they agree to spill the beans and confess to the police more details of what the bosses may or may not have known.

I have never in all my life experienced a fiasco like this. It seems the fallout from the Milly Dowler issue has spread to the police and their alleged mishandling of the information they had on phone hacking, so much so that Sir Paul Stephenson, the Metropolitan police commissioner, resigned, as did the assistant commissioner, John Yates.

David Cameron was also under fire for his social association with Andy Coulson and Rebekah Wade, and the Murdoch empire. It opened a whole can of worms, as it seemed to reveal how politicians allegedly woo the media for support and how the media itself dictates to politicians. Well, what's new about that? It's been going on for ages!

Whilst the whole Milly Dowler affair was despicable and illegal, and there are no words to express the shock we all felt at seeing how low the papers will stoop to get stories, one does have to step back a moment and look at the carnage this revelation has caused – and wonder if it is being turned into a fight between politicians the police and the media. The planned takeover of BSkyB by News Corporation was cancelled due to the pressure brought on the

Murdoch empire. The police seemed to have the bit between the teeth and, at the time of writing this book, their enquiries are forecast to take years. I somehow think that this won't get brushed under the carpet. And as this book goes to press, more and more dominos are falling, and only the future will show how it is all going to pan out. I have given up being surprised at the almost daily events occurring, so it won't shock me if it even brings the government down.

The focus to date on phone hacking has been mainly on the *News of the World*. To be fair, I guess they were maybe just the ones that got caught getting up to this type of stuff. I am convinced that phone hacking ran rife in the newspaper industry and, to be honest, I am amazed that there have been no more whistleblowers implicating other publications. Maybe it's a case of wait and see.

With the recent revelations about the *News of the World*, the pressure was so great that the owners had to throw in the towel and shut down the newspaper, which had been in existence for 168 years. The harsh reality hit home when public opinion turned on them, forcing advertisers to run a mile. It's a simple rule of business: no income means you have to cut and run. But a lesson has been well and truly learned.

Maybe the newspaper industry has finally had its comeuppance. It has run riot over the years, with only a ridiculous and powerless self-regulating Press Complaints Commission to try to control it. Is it decent to pretend you are a constituent of Vince Cable, MP and Business Secretary and, while talking to him, secretly record him saying what he's intending to do about the planned BSkyB takeover by News Corporation? Is that the right way to get stories? It is certainly not *morally* correct. The fact that Vince Cable was stupid to talk in the way he did is another story, but he was convinced he was talking to normal people, not journalists trying to trap him.

The *Telegraph* broke the whole MPs' expenses scandal and it was the biggest story for years. It was important that the public knew how tax-payers' money was being abused and the result of the exposé has been the cleaning up of MPs' and politicians' expenses. So I guess you've got to say, 'Well done, *Daily Telegraph*!' because there's an example of a newspaper doing some good. But, and here is the big but, where did they get the information to enable them to break the story? How did they get the details which were confidential and government property? It was certainly leaked but did they pay for it, and if they did, is that morally correct? As I see it, if they did pay, they bought stolen property. A Freedom of Information request had already been made in regard to the expenses documentation – could the information have been obtained legally that way? And so, notwithstanding the need to disclose this abuse of public money, is it right that we accept that information obtained by illegal means is okay in this case but not okay in the case of hacking a phone? How would we feel if the expenses scandal had been revealed by phone hacking?

Personally, I think the whole News International and News Corporation fiasco and the Murdoch bashing has gone too far. I agree that the *News of the World* was a very rotten apple in a very large basket of other assets owned by News Corporation, but to try and say that the whole of News Corporation is corrupt and criminal is ridiculous. However, it suits the politicians to imply so. Frankly, they need to look at themselves. Using the same philosophy, both the House of Commons and the House of Lords have seen some of their members sent to jail for fiddling expenses, which of course is criminal. Does that mean that David Cameron and Ed Miliband or Lord Strathclyde, or indeed me as a member of the House of Lords, are criminals? No, of course not. There are rotten apples everywhere.

And to suddenly complain that the media manipulates the public either for or against politicians or political parties is a total joke, because what's good for the goose is good for the gander.

Politicians use the media as much as possible to sway public opinion. They have always done so and always will.

On this subject, those MPs and peers who went to prison should have, but the double standards that exist in deciding *which* of the MPs is going to be punished for what they did with their expenses do confuse me. Take, for example, the current Culture Secretary, Jeremy Hunt. When the whole expenses scandal blew up, it was disclosed that Hunt had to refund some money, and he claimed that he hadn't understood the rules. Bad enough he did that the once, but it was disclosed that he also had to refund a further sum of money because he'd claimed some expenses for a property which he allowed his local party agent to use free of charge – again, he claimed he hadn't understood the rules.

The way I see it, you can't have it both ways. As a senior politician in a very important position – overseeing things such as the BBC and the media and all that stuff – surely you've got to be a very, very clever man? For this reason, I can't understand why David Cameron didn't fire Hunt, because if, as he claims, he didn't understand the rules due to naïvety or stupidity, then he shouldn't be in the position of Culture Secretary! If you can't understand those simple rules, how the hell are you supposed to understand the multitude of complex rules governing the media and television?

It seems to me that it simply suits the agenda of certain politicians to demonstrate that they are going to wield the stick and show the public that people will be punished for their wrongdoings, but only when it's convenient for them.

There must now be a formal watchdog to look over the news industry, just as there is for the broadcast industry, and they need to write the rules of decent behaviour. Yes, they should safeguard the newspapers' right to publish what they want and expose stories that are of public interest, but at the same time they should ensure that no illegal methods have been used to drum up these stories.

It is also my opinion that the laws need to change in this country, to make the editors of the newspapers criminally responsible. For example, if a newspaper prints lies and has been found guilty of doing so on more than one occasion, the editor should, by law, lose his or her right to be employed as an editor. Nothing is going to change in our country, as far as the media is concerned, until one of the big head honchos gets it in the neck. It looks like the police are finally getting the bit between their teeth and following this stuff through. I, for one, would be a great advocate of passing a new law through the House of Lords, making editors criminally responsible for their actions. It is the only way to clean up this mess.

I do want to point out that some newspapers don't get involved in any of this nonsense – the *Financial Times*, for example. It prints the facts, and there are some very interesting and balanced articles in there, aside from the financial news.

Now, my wife and some of my children often ask me why I'm continually arguing with the media. Well, that's because of my make-up. Other high-profile colleagues and friends do warn me that it's not a clever thing to repeatedly have a go at them. In fact, Piers Morgan told me that my continual hammering of the *Daily Mail* is not wise. However, I explained to him (and to Jonathan Ross, at one stage) that the *Mail* should know by now to leave me alone or I will whack them, no matter what it costs. And here's the big point – you don't need to be frightened of the media if you have no skeletons in your cupboard, because, trust me, if there were any skeletons in my cupboard, throughout the course of my life in business, football and *The Apprentice*, you can be sure they would have been plastered all over the newspapers. The fact is, none exist; I have got nothing to hide. So when I put my head on the pillow at night, I don't have to worry about what a newspaper might write – because there's nothing to write about.

So it has become my hobby now to whack them whenever I can on Twitter and at my seminars, or if I do live interviews on TV. Sadly, if I try it in programmes that are pre-recorded, the broadcaster normally cuts it, as there seems to be an unwritten law amongst the media that you don't allow people to slag off the competition – a sort of honour amongst thieves. To be fair, the one exception was Piers Morgan when he was editor of the *Daily Mirror* – to his credit, he did allow me to give Jeff Powell, the sports writer of the *Daily Mail*, a real dressing-down after he had lost a libel court case where I sued the paper and him.

This leads me on to that squirt Quentin Letts, who spends his whole life slagging off politicians, criticising them in a sarcastic manner. When he picked on me, I wasn't going to stand for his nonsense. I decided I *wouldn't* sue the radio station on which he defamed me, but that I would sue him personally. This caused a massive kerfuffle – all his colleagues and fellow hacks got together, saying how disgusting it was that the multi-millionaire ogre was attacking poor old Quentin, who might lose his house if he had to defend a court case. Well, exactly! That's the point – I didn't want him to have the protection of the radio station. It was the only way to give him a slapping. Stupidly, he started to report all the legal communication that was going on between my lawyers and him in his column in the *Daily Mail*. On one occasion, he disclosed part of a letter where I'd instructed my lawyers to write to him saying in effect, 'Okay, we accept that you are a man of straw – not a wealthy person – and on that basis we are quite happy for you to just apologise and pay, say, £500 to Great Ormond Street Hospital. We'll then call the matter settled.'

What did Letts do? In his *Daily Mail* column, he started back-tracking on his slurs, claiming, 'I did not for a moment suggest Sugar was not bright enough to be a peer. I'd flay myself with birch twigs if he thought I did.' And as for my suggestion that he pay £500 to Great Ormond Street, he responded with a grand gesture, '£500? Pah. Let that be £1,000.'

The problem was, I got my PR company to contact him and ask whether he'd actually *sent* the money to Great Ormond Street. He told them to bugger off and mind their own business. So I took the trouble of contacting Great Ormond Street myself, to see whether they'd received £1,000 from Quentin Letts. They hadn't.

I will leave you to draw your own conclusions on this horrible little man. Maybe he *did* pay £1,000 to some charity, but didn't like being told that it had to be Great Ormond Street.

20

Tweets and Twits

**The many uses of Twitter, and why it's necessary to squash
Piers Morgan.**

Some people are quite surprised by the fact that I can be bothered
to be on Twitter – @Lord_Sugar – and have a Facebook page. I have
to admit that, for the first couple of years after all these new social
networking sites came out, I took no notice of them. I wouldn't go
so far as to say that I pooh-poohed them – as many people did,
saying they were rubbish and for kids only. I was very neutral
because I admired the entrepreneurs who had thought up the con-
cepts initially. The sites became money-making machines, and
ordinary university graduates who created them became billionaires overnight. You can't really run something like that down.

It's quite fascinating how social networking has become such a
massive thing, brought about by internet technology, and how it
has produced some of the largest companies in the world: Google,
Facebook, Twitter, etc. The problem with this is that some of the
young kids these days obviously admire those achievements and
believe that they will be able to replicate them, and despite being
told that there's a one-in-a-million chance of it happening to them,
they still aspire to it and ignore the old-fashioned, traditional ways
of getting into a business or a career. But I've spoken about that in
this book already.

I find Twitter very useful; it's a great tool. To be perfectly frank, it lets me speak directly to the public. True, most newspapers will give me an audience if I offer to give them an interview, but they will not necessarily give me the freedom to say exactly what I want. Twitter does. I can express my views without having to worry about whether a newspaper editor is going to cut out half of what I said, or decide it's not newsworthy enough to print.

Journalists are always starved of stuff to write about and people to have a go at, so they are the biggest followers of celebrities on Twitter. Many a time, you will see articles referring to what somebody has tweeted. With that in mind, and of course I'm very careful about what I say, I will deliberately post something on Twitter, knowing that they will pick it up hook, line and sinker. It works like a dream.

That reminds me of one of the people I admire tremendously, Michael O'Leary from Ryanair. He has a real cavalier approach to things and is a man after my own heart, as he doesn't take any shit from anybody. And he doesn't seem to care what the media prints.

For all people complain about Ryanair, it's thanks to companies like his that air travel, once considered an absolute luxury, can be cheaper than going by train or filling your car with petrol. I know a lot of people will argue that there are many caveats attached to trying to secure an EasyJet or Ryanair flight but, at the end of the day, if you play the game correctly, you can still get a cheap flight that's roughly 10 per cent of what one would have paid a cartel-operated scheduled airline twenty-five years ago. It's quite amazing how people have so quickly forgotten this and, like with all things in life, they've become complacent and started to complain that the service is not good enough or they're not being treated properly.

And, quite rightly, Michael O'Leary's always looking at ways to make extra money. I guess he sees his passengers as bargain hunters, and whilst he doesn't treat them with contempt, he's very focused on making a few quid, and so charges extra for drinks and food, which one would have normally got free of charge on the old scheduled flights. Now that Ryanair is supposedly planning to charge passengers £1 to use the toilet, I often joke that he's going to take it a stage further by having toilet paper printed with 'Please use both sides.' I almost think that Michael O'Leary is a little mischievous and loves the controversy, so I might put my suggestion forward to him.

It's not just that I sometimes like to use Twitter to stir up a bit of controversy myself. Until Twitter existed, you had no real right of reply to the press, so one of the reasons I enjoy using it is that it allows me to hit back – and it works! Whenever I see something negative written about me in a newspaper, I will go on Twitter and slag off the journalist in question. This results in a load of followers agreeing with me and slagging off the journalist even more – which I'd imagine is the first time that one of these pathetic cretins has ever had any criticism voiced against them. And when they see it, they don't like it, so I've found that it does shut them up. There are serial aggressors from certain newspapers who are always niggling away at me, but as soon as I've whacked them back on Twitter, they've gone quiet. Some may argue that this is like throwing down the gauntlet. If my lawyer reads this, he will be licking his lips and clearing his diary.

My biggest run-ins have been with the *Daily Mail*. I think they are the nastiest people on the planet. I've never seen such a negative bunch of people in all my life. To give an example of how they look for the nastiest angle on every story, when poor Amanda Holden tragically had a miscarriage, loads of people, including me, went on Twitter to extend their condolences to her. What did the *Daily Mail* do? They got columnist Jan Moir on the case – she slagged off the people who had expressed their sympathy to Amanda, labelling them show-offs! How cold-hearted can you get?

The *Daily Mail* can make a mountain out of a molehill. They will take an anomaly and make a big story out of it, portraying it as the norm. They'll find the odd case of a patient who's been left in an NHS hospital corridor, then write an article implying that that's how *every* hospital operates; or they'll find the one-in-a-million person who's been badly treated by the police and, again, write an article to convince you that those are normal police procedures.

They are nasty, nasty people, so you can imagine my delight when I went on Twitter and did my own survey. I asked all my Twitter followers in the UK to tell me what their most hated newspaper is. I asked them to choose only one, and I ran the survey for about a month. Thanks to the assistance of Jamie Oliver and Jonathan Ross, who pooled their followers with mine, the survey took in over a million people.

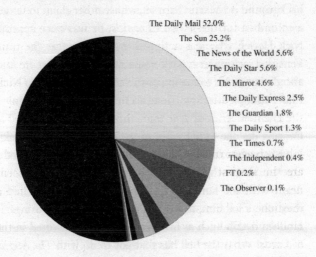

The Daily Mail 52.0%

The Sun 25.2%

The News of the World 5.6%

The Daily Star 5.6%

The Mirror 4.6%

The Daily Express 2.5%

The Guardian 1.8%

The Daily Sport 1.3%

The Times 0.7%

The Independent 0.4%

FT 0.2%

The Observer 0.1%

We received a tremendous number of replies. The result? The *Daily Mail* was by far the most hated newspaper in Britain. In fact, I had many, many tweets cursing the *Mail*, but I'm pretty sure, if memory serves, that no one came to their defence. This is very unusual, as when I debate a topic on Twitter, there are usually some people who have an alternative view. I put the results in the form of a pie chart, showing the votes for each newspaper, and published it on my Facebook page, and I sent it to the editors of every national newspaper. You won't be surprised when I tell you that no one replied. I think I must have touched a nerve there, demonstrating that Twitter is powerful and *does* allow you a right of reply.

It seems I rattled the *Mail*'s cage, as they tried to retaliate, this time in a sneaky sort of way, taking great care not to defame me, in carefully worded snipes. I did a BBC documentary on the state of football, which was shown on Sunday 8 May 2011. The *Mail* dragged out the usual suspects, such as Martin Samuel, the so-called guru of football, who wrote on 9 May that I didn't know what I was talking about in my football documentary. As a bit of background on Martin Samuel, whose other claim to fame is being a columnist for the *Jewish Chronicle*, he was once approached by Nick Hewer, who was acting as my PR man at the time of the Venables sacking era. Nick respectfully asked that he take a balanced view in his following of the affair. He replied to Nick, 'Sorry, I have to look after my friends.' Oh, that's all right then!

The new series of *The Apprentice* was launched on 10 May, and the next day the *Mail* hauled in the jealous, publicity-seeking Luke Johnson, who claimed that *The Apprentice* was a load of rubbish. One could see why the *Mail* had appealed to this idiot, who had a death wish for fame, and I expect the *Mail* team had acted as researchers for him, as his article, amongst other things, included random details such as how many times I had voted in the House of Lords! What the hell has that got to do with *The Apprentice*?

This was followed on 13 May by their 'expert' TV correspondent Paul Revoir. As I've mentioned in chapter 6, he made the claim that the use of the BlackBerry in the second episode of *The Apprentice* was in breach of the BBC guidelines on product placement, and implied, by way of a snipe, that it was being promoted because I had been quoted in the past as an admirer and serial user of the BlackBerry. Then, in the same week, there were a couple of smaller snipes from two other geniuses, Charlie Sale and Richard Littlejohn. So all in all, within the space of six days, an outside observer could see that my Twitter comments about the *Daily Mail* had really touched a nerve.

Being perfectly frank, as well as using Twitter to give me the right of reply to some of the trash in the newspapers, it's been very helpful in promoting things such as my autobiography; no question about it. I used Twitter to let people know the book was coming out; I ran little competitions to see how well people had picked up on the content of the book; I even gave away a few signed copies to the competition winners.

I also use Twitter to let people know when *The Apprentice* is on, and I try to make the viewers' experience more interesting by doing some live tweets while it's being broadcast. And, of course, it goes without saying that I use Twitter to beat up Piers Morgan.

I have known Piers for many years, and I do admire what he has achieved. I first came across him as the editor of the *Daily Mirror*, and I wrote a business column for the *Mirror* for quite a while. It was one of the very few newspapers that was friendly towards me in the football days, which I'm sure was his way of recognising the fact that I gave his chief sports writer at the time some very good stories. But I also believe that he admired, as he would put it, my 'balls in standing up to the football mafia'. Indeed, on one nasty occasion, when I was embroiled in a court case against the *Daily Mail*, he was instrumental in using the database available to his newspaper to bring up some old stuff I needed to use in evidence. So, we go back a long way, and it was a sad moment when he had to leave the *Mirror* in 2004, after the paper was hoaxed into publishing fake photographs of the British army torturing Iraqi prisoners.

However, he didn't let this setback stop him. He found himself a new niche in the television world, with his appearances on programmes such as *Britain's Got Talent*, *America's Got Talent* and his *Piers Morgan's Life Stories*. Now he has his own talk show on CNN, taking over after the legendary Larry King resigned. So, yes, I do admire him, but I also feel that I am performing a service on behalf of the British public by keeping him in check, because his head gets a little bit too big sometimes. Twitter is a great vehicle to slap him down – constantly slap him down, I would say – when he's bragging about all his exploits. What's funny is that here is a man who, when I announced to him that I was going on Twitter, immediately replied with, 'Oh, Twitter is just for twits; for idiots. Why would you want to go on Twitter?'

Now he's become a Twitter addict. In fact, I believe he has an illness, because he's obsessed with the size of his following. He feels that it's a real achievement to overtake someone with his number of followers – as if he has jumped up in some kind of Premier League of Twitter users – whereas most people don't give a shit. And so you can quite understand why, my nature being as it is, I have to take him down a peg or two now and again.

He started bragging about his CNN position – which, of course, was a great coup – telling me and the Twitter world how wonderful he is and how famous he is going to be compared to me. Whereas I am only known in Britain, *he* will now be known by over 300 million people throughout the world. He posted pictures on Twitter of the Times Square posters advertising his show, to which I replied, 'Well, at least the pigeons will have something to shit on now,' which caused a great reaction on Twitter and is the type of put-down that is needed to keep this poor sod in line.

I was fascinated to see Piers referring to famous statements made by Winston Churchill and, in a weak moment, thought that he really must be a historian or exceptionally intelligent to suddenly come up with these quotes and use them in the right context while bantering with me and others who enjoy putting him down. So you can imagine how I laughed out loud when I found myself in a suite in the newly refurbished Savoy Hotel and spotted a book of Winston Churchill quotes in the small library in my room. I had rumbled his little trick and found the same book he must have been using. Instead of declaring this find on Twitter, I decided to wait for the right moment and give him a trouncing by quoting from it in an answer I was giving him. It was hilarious to see the reaction on Twitter from other followers. Finally, I couldn't resist telling everyone (including Piers) that I had sussed out his little scam and that he'd gone back to being a dummkopf in my estimation.

I also communicate on Twitter with people such as Jonathan Ross, Dara O'Briain, Chris Evans and a few of the dragons from *Dragons' Den* but, more to the point, I believe that I'm unusual in that I actually communicate with members of the public. Of course, I can't do it all the time, but I do have sessions where, if sensible questions are asked, I will answer them quickly and efficiently, to keep people informed. I think it's a great medium. It's the type of thing you can dip in and out of when you fancy.

One good thing about it is that it's not a treadmill. It's entirely up to me whether I want to be on it or not, and it's entirely up to me if I wish to start a debate about something. It's very useful – considering that at the time of writing I have around a million followers – to be able to use Twitter to get an opinion from people on certain things. For example, when writing this book, I asked people on Twitter, 'What would you like me to comment on? What would you like me to write about?' I gave them a general outline of what the book was going to be – my view of the world, my view of the UK – and they gave me some very interesting topics. And I'm sure I will use it once again, if I ever need a survey – it's much cheaper than using a market-research company, I can tell you that!

I haven't yet worked out the financial coup as far as Twitter is concerned, or indeed Facebook. This fascinates me, because Facebook is allegedly worth billions and billions of pounds, yet I can't see what the business model is. People continually tell me that the business model is all the advertising on the side of the Facebook pages and all that stuff, but I don't really think so. Personally, I don't get it, but then again, maybe it's just that I'm a sixty-four-year-old fart and am missing the point. And as far as Twitter is concerned, I *really* don't get it. Where's the money? Perhaps they're going to pounce upon all the users in future and ask them to pay a subscription. Perhaps they're going to ban people like me from promoting my new book or television programme unless I pay them. I don't know, but someone, somewhere, is paying for all this. Somebody is running the service, and I suppose the good news is that some idiot in the stock market or some investment banker will float Twitter one day and a load of investors will rush in – for reasons better known to themselves – and give it a massive market capitalisation. So good luck to whoever Mr Twitter is, because I'm sure that that's the way the founders are going to make their money.

By the way, Twitter has other uses. I know this only happened because I am somewhat high profile, but I recall once complaining on Twitter that my BT internet at home was down and joking that I was going to get on to Ian Livingston (the CEO of BT) and make his life hell. Well, talk about reaction! I had what seemed to be the entire cast of *Madam Butterfly* down at my house within hours, and the problem was sorted out the same day.

21

Online Bananas

The decline of the high street, and why I prefer
internet shopping.

The advent of the internet has changed people's lives for sure,
demolishing some of the traditional high-street businesses along
the way. I have to say that I do enjoy shopping online when I know
exactly what I want to buy. I am impressed by how the online vendors have got the process down to a very fine art in respect of
displaying their goods and the execution of delivery. I personally
don't like assistants in shops – they get on my nerves – so to have
what is a virtual walk through a shop, with no salesperson doing
your head in, is a delight. I have used the internet to research, for
example, the best price for a watch or aircraft equipment. What's
fascinating to see is that my wife Ann – who does like a good shop
up, to say the least – has managed, after all these years, to become
computer literate, which in a way goes to show that you can do
anything in life if there's an end goal in it for you. She's forever
having parcels and packets delivered to the house. Also, I guess it
is true to say that there's a certain excitement in ripping open the
package when it turns up.

There is no question about it, online shopping is here to stay,
and I fear for the traditional retailers. As technology gets better,
with wider-band internet services, the ability to see the products
displayed in high definition and three dimensions – so you almost

feel as though you can touch them – will only increase the popularity of this way of shopping.

Take, for example, Amazon. What a phenomenon that is. Even if you consider the advantages of a traditional bookshop – where you can have a browse, see what book takes your fancy, maybe read a few pages – well, Amazon's got that covered too. You can sample books online; you can send them back if you don't like them; you can even buy second-hand copies of the books you want. Plus, it's able to carry a much wider range of stock than any bookshop on the high street.

WHSmith, one of Britain's great traditional retailers, would probably be the first name that would roll off the tongue if you were talking about buying a book. And whilst WHSmith is still doing quite well, I think even *they* would agree that their book sales have dropped tremendously. Fortunately, they have other products for which they're well known, to help them to survive, particularly as many of their stores are located in prime positions at airports and stations, handy for travellers who are a little bored and ready for an impulse purchase.

Getting back to Amazon, it no longer just sells books; it sells a whole array of things, from electrical appliances to clothes. It was founded by an enterprising person who not only exploited the virtues of the internet, but also took advantage of an array of courier services that have grown over the years – DHL, FedEx, UPS – all new names we've seen emerge in Britain. Not so long ago, if you wanted to send something somewhere, you simply took it to the post office. Nowadays, one of these commercial organisations will come to you, collect your package and have it delivered in a day – guaranteed.

Things such as PayPal have also sprouted up. It's effectively a way of paying for stuff without having to give away your bank details to the seller. Here's another area where that great institution, the good old British post office, has allowed itself to fall behind.

PayPal, for example, could have been orchestrated by the post office in Britain. What better organisation could you have chosen to arrange for a payment method that's both safe and controlled, with the security of the royal seal of approval behind it? Instead, other commercial organisations stepped in and exploited it.

The post office has woken up too late in trying to compete with UPS and the like. And while it does offer its own type of fast service, it's not in the same league as some of these other commercial enterprises. So why is that? Is it all about complacency? Is it a case of thinking, 'It'll never happen to us – we are British, we're culturally different. These new upstarts won't work here'? How many times do you think somebody has thought like that and woken up to find that their business is gone?

Look at the music industry too. The traditional way of publishing music – originally on vinyl records, then cassette tapes and latterly CDs – is dying. And we're not just talking about the retailers and the record shops; there is also a big problem for the record producers who used to make a lot of money out of the music industry. The internet has spawned many unofficial websites where consumers can go and illegally *download* music. Music which in the past was the copyright of the original artist or publisher can now be sucked into people's computers for free.

Whilst this is being policed heavily these days and a lot of these rogue sites are being shut down, the reality is that this practice has forced the price of music down. A lot of people want to buy their music on the internet now, hence the massive growth of Apple's iStore, as well as sales of the devices themselves: iPods, iPhones and other MP3 players, on which you can store and play downloaded music.

Why is it that Britain's flagship music store, HMV, is struggling? Why didn't it see this coming? Again, was it complacency? It seems that these American-originated sites such as Amazon and eBay have virtually wiped out an entire industry over the past decade.

Woolworths, another retailer known for selling records, tapes and CDs over the years, also lost business. It's a case of people not moving with the times. Or is it that trade unions won't move with the times in wanting to preserve defunct jobs, as in the days when they took industrial action against redundancies at telephone exchanges, trying to hold on to the days when banks of women would be plugging jack plugs in and out all day, or trying to preserve antiquated mail-sorting systems while rejecting modern-day automation?

It does serve to demonstrate that, love 'em or hate 'em, the Americans are so innovative in what they do. Or could it be that they have such a massive market, hungry for new technology, that the founders of these businesses prosper from their home market alone before they decide to go overseas?

I know a lot of American businesspeople, and they don't see any problems opening businesses overseas. To them, it's no different to opening in a different US state. They have a refreshing approach to what they call 'rollout' in the UK or France, or wherever. British companies, on the other hand, think that exporting is something of a black art.

I have to be honest and say that, in the early days of internet buying, I was a little wary of dishing out my credit card details to so-called vendors, so I started off in a rather moderate way, buying small-value items. I used a credit card I set aside specifically for internet purchasing, on which I told my bank to limit any purchase to £100. You heard so many nightmare stories of people's credit cards being abused, and that's what held me back. The banks, of course, got screwed for a lot of money. Their charter to their customers is that, if you are ever diddled by a trader, the bank will reimburse you, and good on them for that. Since those early days, security has been tightened up but, more to the point, I think that 99 per cent of the people offering goods for sale on the internet are honest traders, so one can relax a little bit when purchasing stuff.

However, although you're unlikely to be ripped off, you have to remember that, with the internet, Big Brother is watching you. Information on us all is stored on massive databases now. Even if you unticked the boxes authorising the use of your personal information, Big Brother is still watching you. The technology available today allows companies such as Google to spy on you and see your trends and tendencies. Recently, it was disclosed that the Apple iPhone has some embedded software that also synchronises with the PC the iPhone is associated with. The software can detect the users' movements wherever they go and whatever they do, as far as usage goes. Not many people realise this but, deep in the bowels of Apple's terms and conditions, they do say, in the small print, that they have the right to do so. What do they use all this stuff for? Well, in marketing terms, it's like gold dust – they can evaluate user profiles, which helps them develop new features and products. All this secret data stored by companies can sometimes backfire, as was the case with Sony, whose PlayStation database was hacked, disclosing its customers' personal information, including credit card details.

And what about Google Earth, Google Maps and Street View – is that an invasion of your privacy? Some say it is. I have to say, they are great tools to play with, but it is frightening to see what can be achieved these days.

The explosion of GPS devices in cars is another example of how you can be watched in the twenty-first century. Again, they *are* brilliant, but they can also gather information which could possibly be used to form another database of your habits and tendencies.

I do worry for the likes of Comet and Currys. I worry for them because I feel a bit of loyalty to them, inasmuch as they were once my customers and helped me make my fortune. Nowadays, to be perfectly blunt about it, they are just massive showrooms for people to walk into, have a look at the equipment, have something explained to them by a salesperson, then simply leave and buy the same item at the cheapest price online.

If you were to put this to the bosses of Comet and Currys, they'd probably say that that's not the case but, deep down, I reckon they know that they're between a rock and a hard place. The dilemma is: do you talk to a customer as if he's a piece of rubbish, knowing that he's just trying to suck information out of you before buying the item somewhere else; or do you do the traditional thing and treat the customer as king, then be disappointed afterwards when he says, 'Thank you, I'll think about it,' and goes off and orders it online. I know for a fact that some of these large retailers now make more money by selling extended warranties. It's an easy sale to a person buying a large LCD TV, for example, especially when the salesperson brings in the fear factor of what will happen if it ever goes wrong. The Sale of Goods Act seems to protect most people if the thing is duff within a few days, but it has its limitations. If a piece of electrical equipment goes wrong, there are so many get-outs through which retailers can escape from their responsibilities, and it won't be long before online retailers can also jump on that bandwagon.

Is the market going to change? Has Apple once again taken the lead in this by opening its own stores? Sony has been doing this for years, of course. Some of these stores are company owned and some of them are franchises, but I think that manufacturers of brown goods – TVs, audio equipment, computers – will all end up selling them directly. We saw this with the motor trade many years ago.

Leading manufacturers, who used to have dealerships, are tending to open their own retail outlets. Is it the case that there is no room for a middleman any more? After all, if Currys set up their own website and online marketing – which they have – how can they be the most competitive for an item on their own website yet charge more for it in their shop? As I said, they are stuck between a rock and a hard place.

I spoke to my friend Sir Philip Green, who runs a lot of retail stores in the UK. He told me that one of his possible strategies going forward might be to maintain some flagship stores, but to concentrate more on online retailing. When you consider the cost of operating a shop, with its staff, high rents and all the utility charges and necessary commitments to long leases, and you compare that to offering your products to the whole nation on the internet, there's clearly no contest.

Now, some may argue, 'How can you sell a dress on the internet? People need to see it, touch it, feel it, try it on.' Well, most people know their size and, as I said earlier, with the high-definition, 3D-type graphics and videos that are available on the internet, you can get a pretty good idea of what something looks like. Let's face it, these days we are all aware of the fact that the consumer has the right to send something back if they don't like it. So if you can buy a dress online knowing that you can return it if you don't like it, why bother going back and forth to a shop? And it is this trend that Sir Philip has noted. Internet shopping is quick and simple – it's right up the alley of today's fast-living society. People these days have no time – the world is in a hurry, as far as they're concerned. When my daughter and son-in-law come over to stay with us at our house in Florida, the doorbell is ringing constantly – packages from UPS, FedEx, DHL – she is buying stuff all the time. I'm fed up signing for them. Oh well, at least I'm not paying for them!

There *are* a few things that are not really suited to internet purchasing. I remember that we used to order stuff online from Waitrose or Sainsbury's when we were abroad, to be delivered when we got home. Things like cans of Coke and baked beans – all fine. Also, boxes of soap powder and bottles of washing-up liquid – again, no problem at all. But when it came to fresh fruit and produce and the like, Ann ended up chucking half of it away. Now, let me make it perfectly clear: it's not because the produce was inferior; it was simply because, as women will tell you, when they go to a shop they like to pick up a melon and give it a little squeeze, they look at the apples to see if they're bruised, they look at the colour of the bananas to see if they're ripe or not before buying. You can't do that when you're asking someone to pack it up and ship it to you.

So we've stopped doing that and, instead, we go and buy our bulk supplies from someone like Costco. As I said, for things like soft drinks and cleaning materials, you can send someone off to buy a carton of a dozen or so and not worry about them getting the wrong thing, because you've specified the brand and type and size. Bottom line – do you really want to buy bananas on the internet?

22

Can Cause Heart Attacks

**What makes a good advert, and why I'm excited
about Amscreen.**

I've told you a couple of times that I'm a bit eccentric – some might
say I'm a bit of a nutter – and whilst I generally skip the TV ads
using Sky+, I do sometimes like to watch them to try to work out
what was in the mind of the creator of the advert and what point
they are putting across. This often results in me turning to my wife
and asking, 'Do you understand what that advert was about?'

'No,' she says, 'I don't.'

'Exactly! Some tosser has just spent half a million quid of his
firm's money producing that advert – and neither you nor I know
what it's about.'

Remember that TV advert that showed a lot of car parts all
touching each other and making one thing fall over and another
spin up in the air and all that stuff? Yes, it was creative genius, no
question about it but, to this day I still cannot tell you which car
company was being advertised. And even if I did remember the
name of the company, it wouldn't make me buy one of their
bloomin' cars, because the advert didn't tell us anything about the
car and its performance and its price.

There are some very talented people working in advertising
agencies and coming up with some great creative ideas, as we've all
seen. The Meerkat adverts are another example. They have been so

successful for the company they are promoting that they've even managed to make a bestselling book out of them. I saw those adverts so many times and they *were* funny, though if it wasn't for me asking a few people, I wouldn't have actually known what they were advertising. That's half the problem with a lot of the adverts that you see on TV these days.

Now, I'm a great believer in the Ronseal concept – in other words: it does exactly what it says on the tin. I thought that was a very good advert, and it's still quoted by most people in the advertising industry as a way of saying that they need adverts that are up front and say it all. The problem is, some of these creative people get carried away and de-focus from the real task, which is to sell stuff for their clients. Instead, they're more interested in winning awards or making people laugh.

That's where I come in. Advertising has played a very big part in the success of my companies. As a marketing man, I understood its importance from the beginning. And, as usual, I was heavily involved in the preparation and approval of the adverts. Over the years, many people have presented adverts for my products to me where they've tried to be a little bit too clever. These people are missing the point – that I want to sell some kit! I don't want to win some bleedin' award at the advertising agencies' bash. Believe it or not, Margaret Thatcher was a great admirer of one of my adverts – the one for our word processor. It was a light-hearted advert, in that it showed us throwing typewriters out of the window into a builder's skip, in order to make the point that they were now redundant and that my new word processor was *the* thing to have. Now, there's a good example of the fine balance between getting the point across and injecting a bit of humour.

Of course, the available budget is a big factor, but that can work against you if you saturate the market. Adverts for companies such as Go Compare or We Buy Any Car are on so often that even if you do want to compare prices or buy a car, you're so irritated by their adverts, they'd be the last people on earth you'd go to. They aren't as bad as the ads at other end of the spectrum, where the budget is clearly very limited. I'm thinking of those ambulance-chaser adverts, with some bloke falling off a ladder, or the companies who buy gold, where it looks as if they've got the kids or the wife to make the ad using a camcorder. I mean, talk about waste of money – they may as well not bother. What image does that type of advert project?

In America, on the other hand, they go to the other extreme. Forget all the arty-farty stuff; their ads are really in your face. You get the owner of the company shouting out at a hundred miles an hour what they're selling and what their offer is, and to get on down to their shop immediately to buy it. The multitude of channels available means that it's relatively cheap to advertise locally in America so, for example, a local car dealer or tennis shop can actually get their ad on TV for a small amount of money. You can see they're not spending much by the quality of the advert!

The advertising agencies used to say that I was a bit of a rare breed – an MD who was checking where his money was being spent. They usually deal with a marketing manager who's responsible for spending the company's marketing budget. Sometimes marketing managers get seduced by the advertising agencies and are sucked into producing an advert that everybody talks about because it's funny or clever, forgetting the fact that it's not actually shifting any stuff for the firm.

I've experienced how these creative geniuses at the agencies like to piss your money up the wall to try to win an award. Once, in a weak moment, I allowed one of my marketing people to deal with an advertising campaign for a new laptop computer we were bringing out in the eighties, when we were very successful.

Now, I'm guessing it was because I was a bit busy, but I was guilty of taking my eye off the ball and I'd become a bit slapdash about overseeing what was going on. The marketing manager in question went out on location with a camera crew, up to Lake Ullswater. There was a team of about seven people who went up there, all to take a *still photo* – it wasn't even a TV advert. They travelled up north and booked themselves into a hotel – heaven forbid they go there and come back in a day! And they had to stay there for two days because they were waiting for the right moment when the moonlight, sunlight or whatever glistened on the water. They planned a picture of a pier going out into the centre of the lake, with a person sitting at the end with the laptop in their hands. God knows what that cost! I can't remember and I don't even want to be reminded of it. I went ballistic when I saw this bloody piece of rubbish presented to me – a full-page colour advert for a glossy magazine, with a picture of some tosser sitting at the end of a wooden pier, with only a microscopic view of my product. Right down in the corner, it kind of said, 'Oh, by the way, this is the Amstrad PPC640.'

'What the bloody hell is this?' I said. 'What the hell are you doing? You're going to flip through the glossy magazine and miss it. You're going to think it's a bleedin' advert for a holiday. What has this got to do with laptop computers?'

Needless to say, I trashed that campaign and told them to take a picture of the bloody product and explain what it does, how much it costs and where you can go and buy it. I couldn't have been that wrong because we won loads of awards for some of our great in-your-face, pile-'em-high advertising – the Marketing Society Award in 1985, 1986 and 1987, the RITA Award in 1986, the Management Today Award in 1986, the British Micro Award in 1985 and 1986, the Golden Chip Award in 1985 and the BEW Toby Award in 1986.

One thing I can tell you – from all the business plans my companies made over the years – is: you start off with the top line (sales), the next line is the costs, and the next line is the gross profit (the difference between the two). Beneath that come the expenses (overheads and staff costs) and *then* the advertising budget. I can reliably inform you that marketing people have never been guilty of spending less than allocated when it comes to the marketing budget. The sales may be missed and the costs may get higher, but one thing's for sure – the marketing budget will be spot on. They will blow the lot.

It's the easiest thing in the world to spend money on advertising and forget the fact that sales of the item you're advertising might not be going that well, or that your advert is not drawing the punters in. A sensible person would say, 'Let's pull the advert and think again.' No such luck! You are told about deals that have been done with the media that can't be cancelled, penalties that would have to be paid, and all that stuff.

One of the biggest complaints I've always had is the amount of your advertising budget that goes to the production people and all the other hangers-on who take a slice of it. In the past, the advertising agency got a 15 per cent kickback from the media companies, which was fair enough. But now it's more complicated, and the agencies tend to rely upon media planners and other specialists, so that by the time you've added up all their cuts, only about 60 per cent of the money is left to actually pay for the media, be it television or newsprint.

What's more, it's a bit of a closed shop. Logically, someone like me would think, 'I can come up with my own advert; certainly for newsprint. My own people can do the layouts and the artwork and all that stuff – so I'll contact the media owners directly and do a deal.' But no. As I say, it's a closed shop. The media owners realise that if they start dealing directly with the end customer, they are going to get the big elbow from the advertising mafia. You might find it difficult to understand the power that the advertising fraternity have – media owners are dead scared of alienating them. If you cut them out of their commission, they will end up recommending that their clients don't advertise in your media.

Many's the time I've spoken directly with the media owners.

Naturally, they want me to spend most of my money with them, rather than with their competitors, but when it gets down to the nitty-gritty, they tell me that I've still got to place the advertising through the normal channels. As hard as I've tried over the years, I have to admit I've failed. And so, regrettably, even adverts created by our own company, with no input from agencies at all, had to be placed through the correct channels, with commissions paid down the line to all the various people I previously referred to.

Be under no illusion, the impact of a good advertising campaign really *does* shift stuff off the shelves, no question about it, but in this day and age it's getting harder and harder to have the impact you used to achieve when there were just a few limited ways in which to advertise. If we go back thirty years, all you had on television was ITV; now you have hundreds of channels, all fighting for your advertising budget. This also weakens the impact of your advert because you have to spread your money around. The advent of the internet has brought about a massive decline in the circulation of newspapers, which has lessened the impact of newspaper advertising over the years.

Instead, the internet itself opens new avenues to get your message across to consumers. It's not an easy thing to do because, as you all know, in order to view a particular advert or website, you need to be coaxed to do so – the chances of you coming across it by accident are millions to one. However, Google have really cleaned up, as far as that is concerned. When Google first came to the market as a glorified search engine, people started to question their business model – where were they going to make money? Well, they're not questioning it now! They've worked out a tremendous scheme whereby advertisers pay Google to be at the top of the pecking order when you type in the sector of business you're interested in. The Google revolution has also spawned companies that specialise in advising other companies how to get their website viewed or higher up the Google pecking order. Google have realised this themselves and are always changing the technical rules for their search criteria. Having a constantly moving target makes it difficult for ordinary punters to get their listings up the Google pecking order by back-door means, without paying Google.

What we need to remember is how much information Google have on us all, and how much power that gives them to influence, if not control, our purchasing decisions. So much so that in May 2011 Facebook attempted to try to stir things up a bit and hired a PR firm to spread stories about Google Social Circle, their networking site, alleging a lack of security as far as privacy is concerned. It was discovered that the culprit behind the alleged smear campaign was none other than Facebook. Imagine the conversation that took place between the head honcho of the PR firm and someone at Facebook. Did the PR guy say, 'I always advise my clients to attack their competition'?

So there you are, two giant companies that have spent billions positioning themselves as nice, cuddly guys, the cool geeks who just want to make the world a better place, when in fact they are ruthless corporate enemies who will cut each other's throats given the chance.

It's not just the internet that has given advertisers new opportunities. They can use Bluetooth technology. You may have seen it yourself, if you have a mobile phone that is Bluetooth enabled – suddenly an advert will appear on its screen. That's because you've walked past a hidden Bluetooth zone that has sent out an advert to your phone, inviting you to click or respond in some way or another. As an example of this, beer companies might have Bluetooth transmitters around a football stadium. They will capture hundreds of people's mobile phones, making offers such as a free beer if you click on this.

Unsolicited text messages are also a pain in the neck and are very misleading. In some cases, they sail very close to the wind as far as the law is concerned. I'm sure most of you will realise that you should never respond to them, because if you do you'll end up on a database somewhere. You'll be hooked for life as a mug punter who is going to be bombarded.

So these days, advertisers really have a dilemma over how to spread their money about, especially when you consider the many and varied forms of media – TV and newsprint, the internet (including advertising on other people's websites), street hoardings, sides of buses, text messaging – to name just some. It really has become a sophisticated arena to play in.

Some time ago, I decided I would try to divest some of my business interests into another kind of industry, one that relies upon advertising, rather than selling a product and trying to make a profit on it. I had to give up making most consumer electronics products because, with the explosion of China into the market, the competition became very cut-throat and margins were eroding all the time – unless, of course, you had that killer product that everyone was looking for. So at Amstrad I decided to produce something called the e-mailer, which was a phone that had a screen on it. And, just as with mobile phones, Amstrad subsidised the cost to make the price very attractive to consumers. They were told that the phone was subsidised because they would be receiving adverts from time to time on the screen. My idea was that if we sold enough phones, it would be like a Trojan horse sitting in people's homes and advertisers could get in to exploit the consumers as they passed by the phone. The theory behind it was that, unlike a television advert, where you can skip past it or go away and make a cup of tea, you couldn't help seeing this advert because it was on your telephone screen, and you're always using the phone for one reason or another.

We sold about 450,000 of these phones and set about trying to sell advertising. It was here that I learned another big lesson – that the advertising mafia are sick and tired of hearing about new ways of advertising. To be blunt about it, they are pretty lazy. They tend to stick to proven solutions – TV, newspapers, street hoardings – and anything new that comes along, they shy away from. This is because they know the conventional form of advertising does bring results and, as I've just mentioned, there are so many places to advertise now that it's already hard enough for them to spread their clients' budgets in order to deliver the necessary impact.

I also learned another lesson: the first wave of what was classed as 'internet advertising' failed miserably. These were the kinds of adverts you'd see on the side of a person's or a company's webpage, which you were supposed to glance at inadvertently. This was hyped up as the next revolution in advertising, but it bombed. It was bad timing as far as we were concerned, because when we brought our e-mailer to the market, with our Trojan horse idea, the media mafia didn't sign on to it at all. They categorised it as internet advertising and lumped it together with the other failed idea. Despite our protestations that it was something new and different, we couldn't crack it.

The technology enabling us to deliver adverts was fantastic. As an example, insurance companies could advertise on the e-mailer, and there was a little red button next to the screen. The advert would say, 'If you are interested in home or car insurance, just press the red button,' and when you pressed it, the e-mailer would dial straight through to the advertiser's call centre. I mean, what more could you ask?

You can imagine how frustrated I was that the thing didn't take off. Our good friends at Sky TV did quite well out of it. We placed a lot of their adverts on it when they were trying to get more and more subscribers – they even confirmed in writing to us that it actually worked. Well, it must have worked because they kept spending more on advertising. But despite us showing these testimonies to other people, we could not tempt the advertising agencies, media buyers or planners to recommend it to their clients. As I've mentioned, we were subsidising these phones to the tune of £50 a pop, the idea being that once you had a mass population of phones in homes, the revenue from advertising would ultimately come in as a kind of cash cow to repay your investment. But due to the advertising mafia's lack of vision, we had to give up on it.

This was around the time that I sold Amstrad to BSkyB, and there was one little consolation: the accountant at BSkyB told me recently that a lot of these e-mailers are still in people's homes, and the revenue coming from them *did* eventually pay off the capital investment, although it took about ten years.

I've learned in business that sometimes you can be *too* early to the market. Knowing this, I decided again to take the technology we used in our e-mailer and apply it in a different way. And if you've been in any garages lately and gone to pay for your petrol, you may have noticed a screen just above the cash till. Well, they are *our* screens, from my company Amscreen. The idea is that while customers are queuing up to pay for their petrol, they can see a series of adverts that rotate through a carousel of approximately ten per day. We have thousands of these screens across the country now and, once again, the business model is that *we* pay for the screens and install them in the garages. This time we are going to persevere, working in co-operation with the media fraternity as a media owner and accepting that we have to play the game with them.

The technology in these screens is quite fascinating – to put things in simple terms, imagine that the giant screen is nothing more than a BlackBerry. Every screen has a SIM card in it, plus, effectively, a mobile phone and a powerful computer. This means we are able to send new adverts to each screen without the need to send a bloke round there to load the screens up. In fact, within seconds, we can change the live news rolling across the ticker tape on all of the many thousands of screens across the country. We can flip one particular advert off and put another one on almost instantly. We can also schedule adverts for certain times of the day. For example, early in the morning we might advertise items that people might buy to eat for breakfast; or later, around six o'clock in the evening, we might advertise something that's going to be on TV that night. One of our advertisers, the GPS SatNav manufacturer TomTom, provides live traffic information which is tailored for the area in which the screen is located.

I can't tell you how much detail we have to go into to convince the media planning people that the product works but, just as an example, thanks to some technology acquired from an Israeli software company that specialises in security, some of our screens include a camera which can view a person and work out their age and gender, as well as whether their eyes are actually focused on the screen. We can run a report each and every time someone looks at the screen. This is gold dust for the advertising fraternity – concrete information on the number and type of consumers they are reaching. It is not achievable in any other form of advertising media. But even with all that information, we are still up against the problem of convincing the media planners to advise their clients to allocate some of their money away from traditional advertising. I've had no end of rows with them, asking them how they gauge responses to the large street hoardings you see when you drive along the road. I never get a straight answer.

Anyway, I am not going to give up, because I believe this is the way things are going to go, and it's the old, old lesson: if you can't beat them, join them! When we first tried to sell advertising on our e-mailer phone, most of the advertising fraternity fobbed us off by saying, 'Give us some proof that it works.' Well, there you are, folks, you can't have a better answer than that – you cannot *prove* that someone watched an advert on ITV in the middle of *Coronation Street* in the same way that you can prove that someone actually looked at the advert in the petrol station.

And, in addition to petrol stations, we are now fitting screens in convenience stores (at the checkouts), as well as places like WHSmith and in doctors' surgeries. Think of the dwell time in the surgery, when you are sitting there waiting to go in and see the doctor. It seems a no-brainer but, once again, it is like climbing up Mount Everest trying to convince them that they've got their captive audiences. You would think that leading chains of chemist shops like Boots would bite our hands off to be able to advertise that they have a shop down the road where you can get your prescription filled. We've been in negotiations with Boots for nearly two years, trying to trial something, and that's because the people there don't want to take a risk; they don't want to try something new. They want to spend their valuable advertising budgets where they know it works. In the end, even the most patient of our staff gave up on Boots, concluding that they just don't get it.

But, as I said earlier, the penny is going to drop, and when it does there's another phenomenon which always fascinates me – when something starts to work and becomes hot, suddenly it's the idea of the advertising fraternity, never mind you've been telling them about it for the past five years. No, it's now their idea; they think it's great because they've heard that one of their competitors has had it off big-time. And there have already been some Amscreen success stories, with companies like American Express, who advertises regularly, and Sky TV, who also gets the plot. They could see how it works, not to mention, of course, that in the WHSmith stores there were adverts for my autobiography, *What You See Is What You Get*, because it made sense. So we're getting there, and all I can say, again, is: watch this space! We've got something, and I'm going to persevere.

You might wonder why we're not targeting pharmaceutical companies to advertise their products in doctors' surgeries. I thought that this was one of the obvious things we should do, only to find out that this is not allowed in Britain for some reason or other. Admittedly, the giant company Pfizer *does* advertise on our screens, but only in a kind of flag-flying way, saying how Pfizer's wonderful research and development is there to help patients. It is non-specific as far as any drug is concerned, which is the complete opposite to adverts you see in America, where prescription drugs are actually advertised. The adverts tell you to ask your doctor to prescribe a particular drug to you. I mean, I don't know if you are like me, but if I ever tell my doctor what I think I'm suffering with, he gets the raving hump and, quite rightly so, because *he's* the doctor! He always says, 'Yes, never mind about that, let me examine you and *I'll* tell you what's wrong.'

Can you imagine not only telling your doctor what's wrong with you, but also telling him what drug you want? It would go down like a lead balloon.

But what's funny about these adverts is that at the tail-end, after they've pushed their drug at you, there's someone talking at a million miles an hour, saying, 'Be aware of the side effects that can be caused by this drug. It can lead to diarrhoea, it can cause kidney failure for those who have poor kidneys, and people who have high blood pressure should not take this drug, or anybody that has any cardiovascular problems, blah, blah, blah.' After watching the advert, you could be forgiven for thinking that, although you may just be suffering from arthritis, if you take the pills you could end up doing your kidneys in or having a heart attack! Funny kind of advertising, as far as I'm concerned. Another waste of money – is it an example of a marketing manager being given millions to fritter away? Let's face it, some of these drug companies make so much money, they sometimes have to find a way to blow it, and there is no easier way than on advertising.

I wish I could get my hands on some of the advertising money that goes into football sponsorship and divert it to Amscreen instead. Can you believe the fortune that some companies pay to put their names on the front of football shirts? I can never work it out. I mean, in the old days at Tottenham, when I was there, we might have got a sponsor to pay something like £2 million to put their name on the shirts. Nowadays, you hear about £20 million deals. I don't get it, to be quite honest with you, and I never have. It's even more frustrating because you can talk to those same companies and tell them that, actually, if you advertise on Amscreen, or on my old e-mailer phones, I can *guarantee* you some response – but they'd rather spend £20 million with some football club to have their name on the shirts, which are seen on TV. It's all a branding exercise, as they're not selling a specific product. The irony of it is that you would imagine, perhaps, that it would be the sports brands that put their names on the shirts – not at all! You see telephone companies, consumer electronics companies, travel companies and financial companies advertising. I say it's a total, absolute waste of money, and I guess you might understand now why it frustrates me. If I could just get these companies to try us, it would certainly wake up the marketing manager, as far as value for money is concerned. And I guess the same could be said about every kind of media in the country – they must be as frustrated about it as I am. Is it once again some marketing manager somewhere on a big ego trip? Can it be as simple as him deciding to divert some of the company's budget to a football team he has supported all of his life? I can't say for a fact that that's what it's all about, but I'm pretty sure – well, I know, in fact – that in *some* cases that's how it's worked out.

As I once famously said in a speech I gave in the eighties, 'Marks & Spencer says the customer is king, British Airways says we love our customer, but at Amstrad . . . we want your money.' I was being honest – we're *all* after your money, we're all after you buying our products and services. That's what makes the commercial world go round. That's why advertising has always fascinated me, and always will. That's why it has become a kind of personal hobby of mine to continually study the trends, as pathetic as that may sound.

And let's not underestimate another powerful force in advertising – PR companies. Some of them are very good at their job, and I've often said that a piece of neutral editorial about your product or service is worth its weight in gold. People aren't daft – they know that adverts are paid for by the product owner, so they expect them to say that their product is the best thing since sliced bread. But when you hear it from a third party, it hits home much more. This is where PR companies come into their own. When the iPod first came out, for example, some PR company did a great job in making sure David Beckham was seen with white headphones in his ears and the iPod dangling. PR companies spend a lot of time, and charge companies a fortune, organising product placement, with celebrities being seen either wearing a certain item of clothing or using a certain product.

The launch of new products is very important and has to be carefully handled. I am a great advocate of hiring a big venue and inviting a select audience of journalists to try out the product or service. This approach has been exceptionally successful for me over the years. My good friend Nick Hewer, who is now my assistant on *The Apprentice* was responsible for organising the launch of many a product. Nowadays, since Nick has retired from PR, we use another young and exciting company – Frank PR – to launch our products for Viglen and promote the Amscreen service. In fact, if you go to www.bit.ly/vid-ad, you will see a great viral advert that was produced by them to promote the Amstrad videophone. Viral ads are clever little things that fly around the internet, on places like YouTube. They catch viewers' attention by being funny or interesting, and at the same time get their point over about the product.

*

Never assume that advertisers or advertising agencies have any social conscience or morals. That's why we need the Advertising Standards Authority, which is supposed to preside over adverts to ensure that the content is not misleading in any way. It's the reason you normally see (at the bottom of some adverts, particularly in newspapers) some very small print. Whilst they do their best to invigilate these things, I think they could do a lot more, particularly in the financial services industry, where the big headlines are very misleading and it's not until you read the small print that you understand, if you're intelligent enough, what you're letting yourself in for.

Advertisers are ruthless in their never-ending quest to get kids as consumers, and I don't just mean by persuading them that they want a new flavour of breakfast cereal or soft drink. The sexualisation of children through inappropriate advertising is finally being recognised, but it isn't the only culprit. Take clothes retailers flogging sexy underwear to children, for example, or magazines targeted at ten- to thirteen-year-old girls with headlines on the front such as 'How to kiss your boyfriend to give him a stiffy.' The law is crazy in this sense because so-called adult magazines are relegated to newsagents' top shelves, out of the sight of youngsters, whereas this stuff is amongst the Janet and John books. You know what it is like – tell a kid that something is taboo, and they will want to do it. If you say they can't have it, they want it. In the music industry, I understand there are sometimes two versions of a popular song: one with the expletives in and the other rewritten to pass the censors (as the market is for youngsters). Supposedly, the version including the expletives is okay if you're above a certain age. Who are they kidding? What a scam! Of course the kids only want the naughty one.

I think it is fair to say that our children are being robbed of their youth by this laissez-faire attitude. You almost feel like a mug if you ask your young niece or grandchild if they want a Barbie doll for their birthday. They look at you as if you're mad. 'Are you kidding or what?' No, they want some iPod vouchers, so they can download songs, most probably gangster rap, the adult version of course.

23

My Little Slice of London

The changes I've seen in the City, and the bureaucratic hurdles that face property developers.

London is constantly changing, and nowhere more visibly right now than Hackney Marshes, which I drive by from time to time on my way into the City or the West End.

At Hackney Marshes, I recall a place called Eton Manor, where schools like mine would go for sports days and events. The area was just acres of open grassland, with loads of football pitches scattered about, as well as some industrial sites and warehouses. Nowadays, this whole area, from the Marshes stretching through to Stratford, has completely changed, mainly due to the fact that the Olympic village has been built there. It's very impressive as one drives by, but I wonder whether this is going to be another white elephant. What's going to happen to it once the Olympics are over and done with?

I don't often have cause to go back to Clapton or Hackney, where I was brought up, but in 2010 I did a documentary on my life, with Piers Morgan, which turned out to be quite good. It required me to go back to my old primary school at Northwold Road, which, of course, brought back quite a lot of memories. In fact, the school hadn't changed much at all, although I'd remembered the assembly hall being some massive place. When I saw it again, it was quite small. It's funny how, as a youngster, things seem so large.

I did notice one major change when I was in that assembly hall. I happened to look out of the window and I saw the skyline of the newly developed Docklands, including Canary Wharf. It suddenly occurred to me that, as a kid, I used to go down to the River Thames and walk around the old docks and warehouses. I loved watching the hive of activity of the boats arriving and being unloaded, the cargo being transferred into warehouses and then being loaded at the roadside on to lorries. What an amazing transformation there has been, when you consider that the River Thames was the receiving point for most of the trade cargo coming into the country. How antiquated it seems now, all those multi-storey warehouses with hand-operated cranes poking out of the top, offloading cargo from boats and then loading it on to flatbed lorries. One often wonders why no one had the logical idea of using containers and finding an area where you could build flat warehouses, so stuff could go in one door and come out the other on loading bays. I guess it's like other things in life – things develop through trial and error. Suddenly the penny dropped and someone realised that all the manhandling was inefficient. On the subject of the changing face of Docklands, one has to be impressed at how it's been transformed since the days of commercial cargo activity by the conversion of many of these riverside warehouses into high-priced apartments, and how a whole wave of restaurants and shops has grown around it, making the area a very fashionable place to live and socialise in.

When I did the documentary and visited Woolmer House, the flats where I was born and grew up, again, I remembered the playground (the area separating the various blocks of flats) as a giant place; however, seeing it so much later in life, it turned out to be very small. So did our flat itself. In fact, I could not believe how small it was. I found myself checking whether there had been some refurbishment carried out by the council that had made it smaller, but of course there are certain things that cannot change – the front-to-back dimensions of the building, for example. The windows looking out over the road were in the same place – therefore, this flat was indeed really tiny. I visited the upstairs part of the flat, where my bedroom was located, and, again, this came across as tiny. I can't quite understand this phenomenon – I put it down to the fact that maybe, as a small kid, things appear to be big, and when you grow up, they look smaller. Or is it that the places I've become accustomed to are on a much grander scale?

Seeing the new Docklands skyline prompted me to tell Piers Morgan that one of the biggest changes I've noticed is the move away from manufacturing, retailing and import/export and the massive growth of financial services. During my lifetime, I grew from a small trader to someone who floated his company on the stock market and had to deal with the people who now occupy those glass towers. They are not my favourite people, and I am not on many of their Christmas card lists either.

I also have cause to drive through the East End of London on the way to the City, through areas such as Petticoat Lane, Brick Lane and Aldgate. There, I have seen one of the biggest transformations. As a young kid, I'd visit these places with my father, and most of the market traders and shop owners were Jewish. These days, it is an Asian community – so much so that the street signs are printed in Bengali. The Asian traders are very similar to the Jewish traders – very industrious, hard-working and enterprising. Meanwhile, the Jewish population migrated to areas such as north-west London and Essex. Some of them grew their businesses from small traders to large organisations; a classic example of hard work and experience resulting in prosperity. Even with this massive generation leap, we have already seen success stories from the Asian community, people who started as simple stallholders and are now running large businesses. It really goes with my ethos of starting small and learning from the bottom. To my mind, there is no finer example of entrepreneurial spirit than some of the Jewish traders who started on market stalls, or indeed some of the Asian traders these days.

I have plenty of time to notice these changes when I'm driving, thanks to London's roadworks! If anything winds me up, it's road-works, particularly when you drive past, having been stuck in the narrowed-down traffic, only to see that no one's actually working on the road. And I often wonder: who initiates the roadworks and what are they actually doing? More importantly, why, on the reg-ular routes that I travel on, do you seem to have times when you think, 'Thank God, it's over at last,' and then, blow me down, nine months later they're digging up the same bit of road again. And the explanation is that the first time the road was dug up, it was the gas company; the second time, it was the water company; and the third time, it was for telecoms or the electric company.

With all of these busybodies we seem to have in government and the local councils, you'd have thought that they'd be able to co-ordinate these things so that all the work can be done at the same time. I mean, who makes the decision to resurface the road? Is it some jobsworth in the council who has got a budget to spend and spend it he will?

Even without roadworks, the traffic congestion in general is a nightmare. There was a time when I could leave my home in Essex and be in the centre of town in twenty-five minutes. Nowadays, depending on the time of day, it can take as long as an hour and a half. What has brought this about? Have people become so affluent that everyone owns a car? Are there more cars on the road? What is it? The congestion charge in central London has failed to deter people from driving there. Perhaps the escalating cost of fuel is just starting to hit home for certain people, who might start to think about using other forms of transport. Dare I say, bicycles?

Getting back to the changing face of London, as a kid, for a special treat in the school holidays, my mum would take me on the bus to Oxford Street, to visit places like Selfridges. Then we'd walk all the way down Oxford Street until we reached Tottenham Court Road. Now I look at Oxford Street and it's a mass of chain-store retailers, all jockeying for position, with glitzy shopfronts and signage.

Nearby, the back streets around Soho used to be full of little workshops and were a centre for the garment industry; now they've been turned into studios for the media business. It seems that Soho's the place for the media yuppies. I often wonder, as I walk down Berwick Street and the other side streets and look at all the signs on the doors of the various media companies, how they all make a living. It's a bit beyond me.

Another fascinating thing is how areas such as Islington and Hackney have become very popular with a new breed of young executives. It makes me laugh to hear that old houses in Hackney, which used to be considered working-class slums, are now selling for hundreds of thousands of pounds, and it's *the* place to be. A similar phenomenon has occurred in Islington, where in some areas we're talking millions of pounds to buy a house. So there is hope yet for area regeneration. If you'd told me as a kid that certain roads in Hackney would be sought after by a new generation of young executives, I would have told you that you were talking a load of rubbish.

What fascinates me even more is that someone must have kick-started this revolution in Hackney and Islington. It didn't happen all of a sudden that a whole row of working-class houses were trans-formed into high-class accommodation. What was it that made them fashionable? Was it the impact of the Docklands regenera-tion? I guess, if one thinks about it logically, the large corporations, banks, media companies and newspapers that occupy some of the giant tower buildings in Docklands needed to employ hundreds of thousands of people. Hackney and Islington are quite close and a nice commute, so maybe this is the knock-on effect of building, effectively, a giant new commercial city. From what I've understood, there has been a similar regeneration in Manchester.

I'm particularly interested in the giant buildings that are going up in the City – the skyscrapers, as they'd have called these massive constructions in the old days. Interestingly enough, many of these projects were started when money was freely available in the banking world, and I wonder whether these buildings, which take years to complete, are going to be viable. Only time will tell.

I don't know anything about how consent was obtained in the past, but it seems to me that today there is a whole host of authorities who each poke their nose into the decision process of whether to allow certain buildings to be erected. Some of these people, who are concerned with our heritage, want to preserve the old-fashioned qualities of England. Whilst I go along with that, as with many other things, it's gone a bit mad, so some of those giant skyscrapers, which may have been thought of eight or nine years ago, have taken *that* amount of time just to get past the bureaucratic hurdles and consultations that have to be undertaken with the various government authorities.

One such project is one of mine. I acquired a lump of real estate on the corner of Bishopsgate and Liverpool Street, opposite the Great Eastern Hotel. You can't imagine a greater landmark than that – even at my ripe old age. In my naïvety, I thought that we would be able to simply put up a scheme for a new retail and office complex. Well, they say you're never too old to learn. Three years later, we are absolutely nowhere. There are so many commentators poking their noses in – all putting in their tuppence-ha'penny-worth. Can you imagine a whole group of civil servants and goody-goodies sitting round a table, all with certain agendas? When you think you've overcome one obstacle, another one pops up. As I've got older, I've learned not to get too frustrated and, more importantly, to keep out of it. I let some of my staff, who have much more patience than me, deal with the bureaucracy. As one of them put it to me, 'If you were at the meeting we were at the other day, you would have leapt across the table and smacked the person right in the face.'

Funnily enough, I recently bumped into my friend Gerald Ronson, a famous property developer, who has developed a massive project very close to mine. I expressed my frustration to him and started telling him a few of the horror stories that had gone on. He simply shook his head and told me that his project has taken *fourteen years* to get to the stage where he can start building it! And he finished off his words of wisdom by saying, 'And as for you – you keep your bleedin' nose out of it. You don't want to go anywhere near these people, otherwise nothing will ever get done. It's not for you, Alan. Let your people deal with it.'

So one day – hopefully not in fourteen years – I'll be driving down Bishopsgate, see another example of London's changing skyline, and know this building belongs to me.

24

Money Isn't Everything

What motivates me, and what I admire in others.

People often ask me about money. In particular, they say, 'Does it make you happy?'

Well, in my case, there was a stage when it did make me happy. I'd seen how my family had struggled in the East End of London, living in their council flat and trying to make ends meet. I decided I wasn't going to live that kind of life; I was never going to be treated by employers in the same way as my father was. And so, yes, when I got to a certain stage – perhaps when I floated my company in 1980 and got two million quid stuck in my hand for selling 25 per cent – yes, I was happy, no problem at all. Happy because I was set for life, my family was set for life, and I didn't have to rely upon anybody. I could provide for myself; I was independent. But, beyond that, money does not bring me any happiness.

I do enjoy being able to carry out what I like to do best in life, and that's business. There's nothing better than doing a good deal and making more money. But I've got more money than I could ever spend in my lifetime, and no doubt my children could ever spend in their lifetimes. I'm not obsessed with accumulating it and hoarding more of it; it just happens to be a by-product of the things I do in life: deal, trade, buy, sell – that's what I do.

There *are* some people who are obsessed with the amount of money they have, and I've met lots of them. Some of them have so much money, but act as if they're still paupers. I ask them, 'Why is it you carry on in this way? What is it about you? You've got plenty of money, yet you don't live your life. What's the point? Move into a better house. Get yourself a better car. Go on holiday!'

I can't understand it. Now, I won't say that I'm extravagant or a spendthrift, but what's the point of having all this money if, for example, I don't have a nice house and a nice car and a few other little toys to play with, such as my aeroplane? I'm not going to go and buy 500 bottles of Crystal champagne and sit on a beach in St Tropez. I don't shake up a bottle and spray it over people to show I'm wealthy, as if to say, 'Hey, look at me. I don't care how I throw my money away.' No, that's not me.

And I don't need six aeroplanes, or four boats, or twenty cars, or five houses in the same place. I spend money – yeah, fair enough, and of course I spend much more than the average person spends, but money is not my god.

Some people reading this will say I'm talking a load of rubbish, that money would solve all the problems in their lives. Of course, money makes things easier for people, but I also think that's a pretty shallow way of looking at it. There are people who are very content with their lives, who are content with their jobs, who are content with their family, and don't desire money. And you know what? I admire those people as much as I'd admire some billionaire, because they're living a life that satisfies them. They don't have a driving desire to do anything other than provide for their family, have a reasonably good standard of living, relax, go on holidays and enjoy themselves. I mean, how bad could that be?

Could I be one of those people? No. I'm up and down like a yo-yo. My wife says to me, 'Why don't you sit down and relax? Why are you always, running into your study to look at emails, looking at your BlackBerry? Why don't you do what people normally do? You know, just take a day off; just lounge around.'

Well, because of something that's in me, I can't do it. And that's why I admire those people who can. In fact, I have this stupid guilt that goes back as far as I can remember. For example, if I'm out somewhere during the working week and find myself passing my home at, say, three thirty in the afternoon, having come from a meeting somewhere, I figure it's pointless to go into the office just for the sake of it, so I end up at home, walking around impatiently in my study, feeling that I am cheating, that I should actually be working. And it's not until around six o'clock that that feeling leaves me.

At the time of writing this book, I am sixty-four years old. Some people would say, 'Why are you still bothering to work? If I had all your money, I would have stopped working ages ago.' But, as I've already explained, it's in me to carry on working, and I don't know when I will stop. I guess it will be when I don't like doing it – if that day ever comes – or when it becomes blatantly obvious that I'm becoming a bit senile.

I have to have something to occupy my mind all day long, to keep me busy. That's never going to change. I remember many years ago – well over forty years ago – one of my friends saying to me, 'If I had £100,000, that would be it. I'd give up work and retire.'

How stupid does that statement sound now? Of course, £100,000 is a lot of money (and it went much further forty years ago), but that person would still have been skint within a few years. Of course, I'm not saying that I think the amount of money I've got won't last me for the rest of my life because of inflation – it's not a case of that, because I don't care. As I've always said, if I lost it all, as long as I had my health and strength, I'd be able to go out on the Monday morning and make some money all over again to provide for myself and my wife.

I don't know when I'm going to stop working, although working, for me, is a little bit different these days, mainly because – thanks to the internet – I can work from home, from America, from Spain, from my office. As I often tell people, most of my staff don't know where I am, but they *do* know that I'm on the case 24/7.

I'm still quite enthusiastic about projects such as *The Apprentice*, which is not my full-time job, but when we do the filming I can slot it into my work pattern.

Things like writing this book are time consuming but, again, I like the challenge and the idea of doing it. I've also enjoyed the experience of discovering how the publishing industry works. To me, life is kept interesting by learning the way that various businesses operate. I've seen the TV industry, and I've now seen the publishing industry. Both of them are expert in what they do and both of them are quite fascinating. So these are the types of things that interest me and, as long as opportunities come along – whether they're new deals, new companies, new TV programmes, new projects, new books to write – I'm pretty sure I will keep myself very busy for the rest of the time I have left on this planet.

In fact, I've even got my exit from this planet worked out too! As you'll have seen from this book, I am a bit of an autocrat or, as my wife might say, a control freak. Over the years, it seems that each and every time I've tried to explain to people how to do something, or have asked others to get something done, I've ended up either interfering or sorting it out myself. And so I've told my kids that on my tombstone they must inscribe: 'He had to do it himself.'

Appendix One

My Speech to the House of Lords, 24 March 2011

I am grateful to the noble Lord [Nigel] Lawson in bringing this debate. He may recall when he was chancellor under Baroness Thatcher that I was one of her blue-eyed boys – the young fellow from Hackney who had done well, a prime example of entrepreneurial spirit. She hauled me all over the place, displaying me as a model of what can be achieved. I was in and out of Downing Street more often than the window cleaners.

The thing is, my Lords, I and people like me are a dying breed. When I went to the bank as young man, with my hand out, they thought I was part of the Morecambe and Wise team. 'Do you have any collateral, a balance sheet, some history of profits?'

'No,' I replied.

'Well then, clear off,' was the response.

I, like many others, realised at an early age that if you want something, you have to get it yourself. My idea of government support was: you supply me hospitals, schools, a police force, roads to drive on and a good environment for me to do business in – that will do me fine – but don't poke your nose into my business.

If we reflect back, say, fifteen years, it was customary for a person – dressed in a pair of designer jeans, a nice blue blazer and a white, open-collar shirt, a bottle of Evian in one hand and wonderful Windows presentation in the other – to walk into a bank, mention the words 'dot com' and walk out with £5 million.

Well, those days are over. We know what went wrong there, and we also know what a mess the banks got into recently.

But the penny has not dropped with some people. We still have, in some cases, an expectancy culture, where people still think there should be money freely available to finance lost causes, or poorly run companies, or the whim of an idea.

When I was employed as an adviser to Her Majesty's government last year, I had occasion to visit many small-to-medium-sized enterprises across the country, and I spoke to several thousand businesspeople. The question most frequently asked of me was, 'What can the government do to help my business?'

And my reply, my Lords, was not one which was perceived as helpful. I told them, 'Do not rely upon any government to assist you in running your business. You are people who have chosen to go into business – which is very enterprising, and I'm pleased about that – but do not expect to get any advice from the government on what new products you should make, what ideas you should pursue, what services your business should provide, or how to market your products and generate income – because that's what *you're* supposed to do.

More recently, I remind people: 'Who is there in government who can dish out such advice? Just step back and look at them.'

Take, with the greatest of respect, the current Business Secretary [Vince Cable]. He's never been in business! He's never run a business! He's been an adviser or a politician all his life. He has never touched the coalface. I mean, frankly, what does he know?

It is this realism that brings me on to my next point.

The current government, in my opinion, is very good at window dressing the demise of the economy by blaming it all on the banks. It is very convenient to repeat continually the same old broken record: 'It's not our fault; it's the banks' fault; it's the previous government's fault.'

Well, let's look at this for a moment. True, the banks were irresponsible and they have been told in no uncertain terms to get their act together.

But having told the banks to get their house in order, the current government is constantly bleating that the banks aren't being helpful in lending money to small businesses – whereas the message to the small business community should be one of realism: understanding that no one is going to lend money to a lost cause. The traditional criteria of showing some assets or having some historic record of profits are things which banks are now looking at before they part with their money. They are definitely open for business; that is how they make some of their money.

In my recent seminars, I've received comments from some people along the lines of, 'The bank has been outrageous; they've actually asked me to put up some collateral – my house, for example!'

Well, I'm very sorry, but why not? Why should they take a risk on you if you're not prepared to take a risk on yourself?

In my capacity as a business adviser to the last government, I visited many Business Link Centres, which I understand are government-funded. The cost of running these organisations was something in the region of £250 million per year. To be perfectly frank, apart from meeting a nice bunch of people, there was no real business advice dished out other than simple stuff you could pick up and learn for yourself by going on the internet.

I would urge the government to redeploy money spent on these types of initiative in other directions. As an example, there are so many empty premises around the country – large factories and warehouses that can be converted and made into 'incubator factories'. These could contain a core factory and silo workshops on the periphery. The core factory would be accessible to the individual businesses, like satellites around a nucleus.

The government should come clean in its message to help small-to-medium-sized enterprises. You cannot, on the one hand, tell the banks, 'You've been naughty for being irresponsible,' and on the other hand say, 'Go and be irresponsible again and help lost-cause businesses with no asset backing.'

Give SMEs the facts of life. By all means be bold, be adventurous, but be realistic. Don't expect anybody in Whitehall to give you any hints and tips on how to do it, because basically that's the blind leading the blind. You are the businesspeople; you are the ones with the ideas, and you are the ones who are going to drive your businesses forward. But, regrettably, like everything else in life, there are no free lunches.

All government can do is provide a good business environment – assistance from HMRC, for example; Export Credit Guarantees if you are successful enough to find export customers; tax breaks for entrepreneurs who sell their businesses; and tax deductions for investment in R&D.

But here's the final point. In taking advantage of all these wonderful tax incentives announced in yesterday's budget, might I just bring everybody down to earth again and say, 'To benefit from them, you have to make a profit.'

And how to do that, my Lords, is something on which this government is not capable of advising.

Appendix Two

My Message to Small Businesses for 2011

An article I wrote for the *Daily Telegraph* in January 2011,
which says it all about the climate at the time.

I am sure that many owners of small businesses (SMEs) are considering what they are about to face in 2011. True, there are doom and gloom messages from the government, not helped by David Cameron, who, in covering his backside, stated that he sees 2011 as very challenging, still singing the same song, 'We are cleaning up the mess we inherited.' A bit of the broken-record syndrome, I think.

My message to those who run a small business is that at this time of year it's good to have a long look in the mirror and rethink your strategy. May I suggest that whatever plans you are thinking of, don't – repeat, don't – rely upon the government or banks or anybody else to give you ideas. Unless you sign on to the fact that it is you alone that runs your business, you will be going down the wrong road. It's all about you.

Consider why you started your business. I assume it was because you have some experience or expertise in your field – and that is the big point: you mustn't rely upon anyone else. It's going to be you who defines the way forward. I am sick and tired of people asking what to do and going to networking meetings and seminars expecting to glean some gems of wisdom. These events are money-making exercises and benefit one party and one party only: the organiser. They have become an escape for people to justify sitting around wasting a day BSing with each other when they should be working. You will learn nothing other than that there are a load of other people in the same boat as you.

Moaning about the banks is another thing that winds me up. Get real! Banks are businesses, just like yours. They are there to make money from their customers and, just like you, the more customers they have, the more they will make for their shareholders. They are not a charity, and they do not have to lend money to any Tom, Dick and Harry. They are not cheap; they'll charge you to breathe, with arrangement fees and other costs. They should only be used to your advantage. Consider the cost of money as if it is another expense you have to bear, no different to any other costs you have. There has to be a reason why you need the money.

So ask yourself why you're going to the bank for money. What do you need it for? I spoke to a person a while ago who ran a dry-cleaning shop. He had obviously bought all his equipment a while back. His day-to-day consumables are just the chemicals he needs to clean the clothes. That, plus his utility bills, rent and salaries are his expenses. He has a cash business, and yet he was moaning about the bank not lending to him. When I asked why he needed the money, he said he was in debt.

'Why are you in debt?' I asked. 'You are not a shop that has to buy stock. Are you opening other branches? Do you need the money to buy new plant and equipment?' No, it was simple – he was running at an accumulative loss. It was so basic – his takings were less than his outgoings, and had been for ages. So he wanted the cash to pay his salary and his staff's salaries, as his business could not generate it. Sorry, mate, you are totally unjustified in complaining about the bank. They don't back losers. You are insolvent – simple as that. What he needed to do was refocus and see how to start to make money and not just cover overheads.

It is incredible that the simple basics of business go out of the window with all of these modern-day so-called theories and principles. You don't need spreadsheets and complex business plans; you need a pencil and a plain sheet of paper. Take my example of the dry-cleaner. On a sheet of paper he should write down his monthly costs of rent, utilities, staff and consumables. From this, he will get a figure and understand that, unless he takes in excess of that figure each month, he will lose money. This is a quick sanity check, a wake-up call that all small businesses should do.

In my autobiography, *What You See Is What You Get*, I explained in detail that when I started my business in 1967, there were no free lunches. No banks lending. You wanted something? You paid for it or got it yourself. And when you could show that you had a good, viable business, then and only then would 'Come and see me' be the words of the bank manager.

I feel sorry for young people who have lived through the madness of the last ten years or so and grown up with an expectancy culture. They witnessed irresponsible lending from banks to people who had a whim of an idea. It's all over, folks! Banks are now back to the old days. Forget them unless you have clear road map of how you will repay them or how you can make money from these expensive loans.

It's hard for me in this article to cater for all aspects of business. I am conscious that there are service businesses, such as recruitment agencies and estate agents, where the only asset is the people. There are people who make things and sell them (not enough, I would say). There are hairdressers, car mechanics and a variety of shopkeepers. The principle is the same whatever business you are in.

As mundane as it might sound, I did a health check every week when I started. I was conscious of my expenses, including my pay, as well as the cost price of the goods I was selling. As mad as it might sound, I wanted to cover my expenses by Wednesday of every week, so that profit made on Thursday and Friday was going to accumulate to net assets – I needed targets. There were weeks when I didn't make it and I had to find the determination to step up a gear the next week, to try to make up the deficit.

You are the only one who knows what to do with your business.

There is no shame in looking at your competitors or reading up on what new trends and ideas are around. By all means spend valuable time at exhibitions. Consider, if you are a shop, for example, that while you have a mass of overheads, any new venture you might wish to diversify into – product- or service-wise – can be done with little or no increment of your existing overhead. Think of expanding your range of products or services. Look at the climate and see what new services are required these days. Just as one example, if you are in the recruitment industry, health and safety is now a big thing with firms. Trust me, you don't have to be a rocket scientist to gen up on it. Instead of wasting your time at networking seminars, you may as well sit in your own premises and research it, and then perhaps add providing H&S people to companies as one of your offerings.

In my early days, I used my suppliers to finance my stock. The bank would not touch me with a bargepole. First of all, you need to build up trust with your suppliers. Treat them as if you have a tax bill or electricity bill. They must be paid on time. There is nothing wrong in establishing extended terms, such as between thirty and sixty, or even ninety, days. The suppliers will go along with it if you build a history of trust with them. But never buy more than you would normally buy just for the sake of it. You have to pay, and you can only pay if you sell it and, by that, I mean make a profit, not just turnover. A retail business sells for cash and, if you have suppliers who offer you terms, you can use this cash flow to stock up with a more diverse range. That's business.

I conclude by saying again that it is you and only you – no one else. You know what to do, otherwise you should not be in business. It's just down to hard work, discipline and determination, combined with your knowledge and experience of your sector. Trust me, you will be satisfied and happy with yourself.